I Am
Worthy

I Am Worthy

Break the Spell of Unworthiness,
Reclaim Your Divinity,
and Unearth Your True Power

Christine Gutierrez

TARCHER
AN IMPRINT OF PENGUIN RANDOM HOUSE
NEW YORK

Tarcher

an imprint of Penguin Random House LLC
1745 Broadway, New York, NY 10019
penguinrandomhouse.com

Most Tarcher books are available at special quantity discounts for bulk purchase for sales promotions, premiums, fund-raising, and educational needs. Special books or book excerpts also can be created to fit specific needs. For details, write: SpecialMarkets@penguinrandomhouse.com. Your local bookstore can also assist with discounted bulk purchases using the Penguin Random House corporate Business-to-Business program. For assistance in locating a participating retailer, e-mail B2B@penguinrandomhouse.com.

Library of Congress Cataloging-in-Publication Data

Names: Gutierrez, Christine (Psychotherapist), author.
Title: I am worthy: break the spell of unworthiness, reclaim your divinity, and unearth your true power / Christine Gutierrez.
Description: [New York]: Tarcher, [2025] |
Identifiers: LCCN 2024044563 (print) | LCCN 2024044564 (ebook) |
ISBN 9780593543399 (hardcover) | ISBN 9780593543412 (epub)
Subjects: LCSH: Self-esteem in women. |
Self-actualization (Psychology) in women. | Spirituality.
Classification: LCC BF697.5.S46 G88 2025 (print) |
LCC BF697.5.S46 (ebook) | DDC 158.1082—dc23/eng/20250209
LC record available at https://lccn.loc.gov/2024044563
LC ebook record available at https://lccn.loc.gov/2024044564

Printed in the United States of America
1st Printing

Book design by Shannon Nicole Plunkett

The authorized representative in the EU for product safety and compliance is Penguin Random House Ireland, Morrison Chambers, 32 Nassau Street, Dublin D02 YH68, Ireland, https://eu-contact.penguin.ie.

* * *

To my perfect daughter, Mar de Luz.
You are worthy of it all.
For you were born worthy.

* * *

✳ Contents ✳

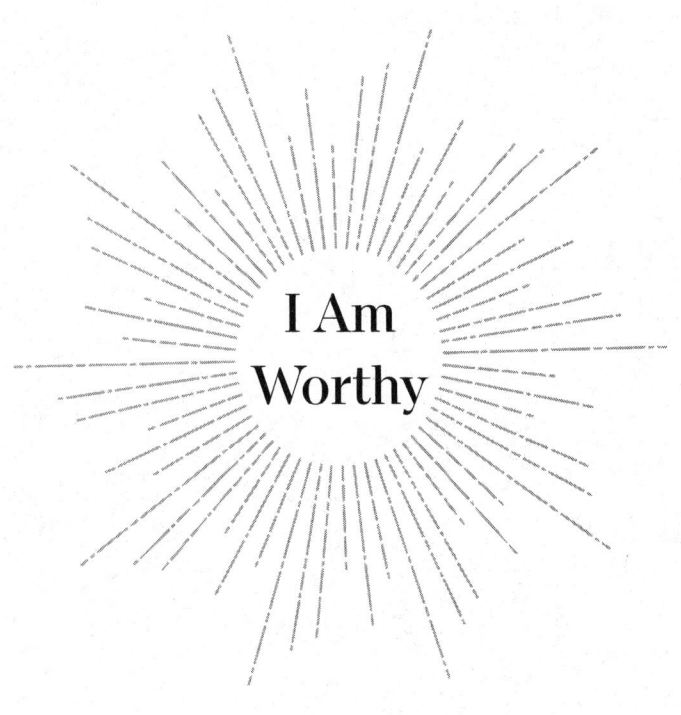

I Am
Worthy

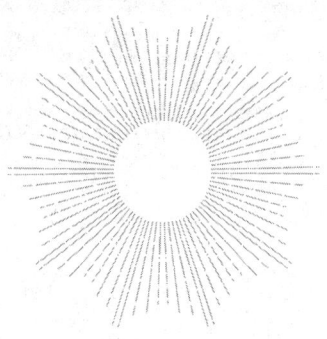

Invocation

Before you dive into the book, let's pause for an activating meditation to help you remember and reconnect with the worthy woman within. Repeat after me:

- *I open the portal to remembering my worth,*

- *The deep-down-in-my-cells worth,*
  the holy inherent divine worth.

- *I reclaim the knowing that I know deep, deep in my bones,*
  that I am the living altar,
  that I am the prayer answered.

- *I reclaim the knowing that I know deep, deep in my bones,*
  that I am part of the most sacred tapestry of all,
  that of the Great Divine Mother,
  who wove the fibers of me, which are indelibly woven,
  from the same stuff as my ancestors, the stars and Earth.

- *I am part of the Great She: La Diosa.*

- *I remember and reclaim my worth.*

◎ *I reject all parts and memories and stories that say anything contrary to this.*

◎ *I am worthy.*

◎ *And so it is.*

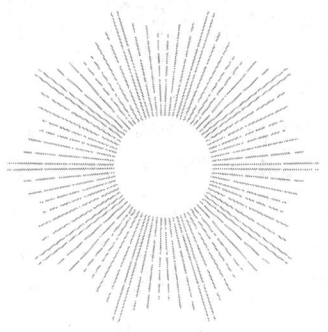

Introduction

You are allowed to have everything you want.

—Brianna Wiest

What if I told you that you are loved and worthy simply because you exist? What if I told you that in reclaiming your worth, you could transform every area of your life? If you have opened this book, it is because you feel a deep knowing that there is more and that reclaiming your worthiness holds the key.

This book is a portal into the unshakable remembering of your divinity, inextricable from your feminine body and spirit. Here, you will bring together all the scattered parts of your being. You will reattune to your inner compass so that you can unearth the buried treasure that lives within you, waiting for your rediscovery. You will learn to listen to the voice of La Diosa, the goddess, the worthy one who lives within you. In the history of your suffering and triumph, you will find the key that opens the door that is yours to unlock. You will weave together the threads of your own tapestry, which will be the map that leads you home.

Working with women for nearly two decades as a therapist and spiritual mentor, I have witnessed time and again a core theme, infused throughout different life phases and circumstances, under many names, intertwined into a variety of stories: "I don't believe I'm worthy." Not worthy of love, of success, of happiness, of abundance, of spiritual connection, of tenderness, of the good things in life. The specifics vary, but when it comes down to it, there is a gnawing sense of unworthiness that plagues women today.

Often, at first glance, the women I interact with have rich, full, beautiful lives, so the message of unworthiness is more subtle. They may feel unworthy of remaining in the mystery of not knowing . . . unworthy of rest . . . unworthy of the medicine of their own tears . . . unworthy of asking for and receiving help . . . unworthy of breaking down and letting the "I've got this" façade crumble apart . . . unworthy of meeting whatever life brings with it, even if it's struggle, with eagerness and a fighting spirit. Some don't identify with feeling unworthy, but they share stories about their inability to set boundaries with their boss, their frustration about not being able to find a partner who honors them, their exasperation about not having it all figured out. These are stories laced with shame, with pressure, with self-attack and self-judgment—all of which dilute these women's fundamental gifts.

Many of these women have dedicated their lives to making sure others are taken care of, to nurturing the flame of worthiness in the people they love. These women range from CEOs to yoga teachers to stay-at-home moms. In every single one of them I have seen the primordial spark of true brilliance—sometimes it shines through bright and clear, and other times it is muted by the belief that they just don't get to have what they want in this lifetime.

Very seldom will these women just come out and say they

don't feel worthy. Sometimes their language is fancy and complex, and I have to be like a spiritual archaeologist who goes excavating beneath layers of ancient stories so I can arrive at that core feeling of unworthiness. Some have gotten so good at masking unworthiness that it can sound like overachievement, confidence, put-togetherness, accolades, and even pride. And yet when you listen to the silence between the words, it speaks volumes. After all the years of emotional and spiritual work, these women are still seeking validation and deliverance from the world around them, not realizing that the antidote can be found only within.

What I want for you, and for women everywhere, is freedom from the spell of unworthiness.

I am deliberately choosing to use the word *spell.* I believe that in many ways, we are under the spell of unworthiness. And in order to break that spell, we must acknowledge there is one. Unfortunately, many women today are under the spell of patriarchy, which is partially responsible for the situation we find ourselves in. To that end, in this book, we're gonna visit some deep and heavy topics. These problems were (and are) worse for poor women and women of color, who have so often been treated as less than human and not deserving of the dignity of white women.

We have *a lot* of deep unlearning to do, yo.

Our sense of unworthiness is not our fault (something I will repeat throughout this book). We live under systems of oppression that include racism, patriarchy, homophobia, and persistent inequality that has come from centuries of capitalism and colonialism. Some of us are born with the message that we are inherently less worthy than others—because of our sex, nationality, economic status, educational status, the color of our skin, and so on. Systemic unworthiness is at play here, and throughout this book, we'll peel back the layers to arrive at a deeper understanding of why women feel unworthy in the first place. I am here to help you reclaim your power from all the spaces and places that have taken it from you.

The Journey to Worthy

If you're new to my work, I am a clinically trained licensed therapist who fuses ancient wisdom and practices with modern Indigenous forms of therapy. As a Latina woman—NYC-born, with Puerto Rican roots—I pull from this well of wisdom and from the medicine that I learned from my abuelita, which was all about recalling our dreams, depending on the power of prayer, lighting candles for those who needed support, and recognizing that faith moves mountains. In addition to the beautiful teachers I have learned from in the fields of depth psychology, shamanism, Tantra, and mindfulness training, I've done a great deal of internal work and have also learned from the reflections I have received from countless clients. Throughout all this, I have come to consider myself more of a mystic, a healer, a mother, a gatherer, a poet, a holder of space, a priestess, a student, a spiritual mentor, and a guide.

For years, people have asked me, "What is the core of the work you do?" My response has always been the same: At the root of it all, I'm here to remind people of their worth—particularly women, and, even more specifically, Latinx women and women of color. The word *worth* always jumped out at me as if it were alive, demanding that I weave it into as many hearts and souls as I can. As I continued to receive this message, I came to realize that the soul of worthiness wished to speak even more fiercely and specifically than ever before in this book.

A dictionary will tell you worthiness is the quality of being "good enough" or "deserving of respect or value." I believe this definition falls short. For me, the definition of worthiness is the understanding that one's true value is inherent and that one need not do anything or be anything to be worthy. You are born worthy. That's it. Pause. Breathe that in. When we think we've got to be good enough to deserve to feel worthy, we stay stuck.

I have made it my life's work to help you unbury the worthy one who lives within you, but I am not here to "rescue" you or anyone else, because one of the great messages of this book is that we are ultimately journeying into the spiral of our own hearts to rescue ourselves. In this process, you will meet the parts of yourself that you've denied, repressed, pushed away, controlled, or silenced. You will be guided to reclaim the lost pieces of your worthy woman soul self, for she holds all the pieces that have been shunned, and all the qualities you feared claiming. The angry parts, the sensitive parts, the parts that speak up, the parts that take up space, the sensual, the wild, the free, the out-of-the-box parts. You'll reclaim them all, to be your worthy woman self, authentically and radically.

I want to be clear that this book is meant to be brutally honest, but the voice of worthiness is the voice of the compassionate Diosa Herself. This is not about "tough love," which can all too often be another excuse to beat ourselves up. As women, we have been taught that we have to fix everything—and that when things don't work, it's our fault. We have been taught to reject ourselves and to treat ourselves punitively, because if we do so, someday in the future we'll be "good enough." But this line of thinking is fixated on a binary of "right" vs. "wrong." It still keeps us stuck in a loop of *doing* rather than *being*. The process needs to change from one of fixing to one of loving, from one of judgment to one of deep compassion and self-acceptance.

We are here to lovingly make a home for our wholeness—which is, by turns, miraculous and confounding—and to let it be. This means unlocking the doors behind which we have shoved the parts of ourselves we may have deemed unacceptable. Because when all these parts come together, our bold, worthy soul self comes forth. We come to acknowledge the gifts inside our wounded, exiled, inherently worthy parts. We are no longer afraid to meet their gaze. Instead, we look upon them and sincerely say: *I see you. I love you. I understand you. I am holding you.*

It's so important to recognize that when we women reclaim our wholly holy selves, we change the world. Because whether we choose to give birth to children or not, we are the harbingers of life. Without us, everything ceases to be. It don't get more motherfuckin' powerful than that, my friends!

Throughout this book, you'll notice sets of Unworthy Lies and Worthy Truths. I encourage you to start to make up your own as you read and incorporate the principles of worthiness into your own life. There is so much deconditioning that we need to do, individually and collectively, and I'm going to do whatever I can to plant those seeds and disperse those reminders so that you can tap into your own learning/unlearning edges. Here's the first one:

UNWORTHY LIE:
We are unworthy.

WORTHY TRUTH:
We are inherently, deeply, and wholly (holy) worthy.

+

The Flow of This Book

Some of you are coming to this book after having read my first book, *I Am Diosa* (*Diosa* is Spanish for "goddess"), which I wrote to help women dive into their childhood trauma and how it affects their lives as adults. After that, I received a download from spirit that my next book would be on worthiness—one that explicitly talked about unpacking the wounds of unworthiness, and how the overculture and systems at play contribute to why we don't feel worthy.

In this book, we are going to untangle the web of unworthiness that keeps us ensnared by exploring ten pivotal areas of our life.

1. Peace

2. Connection to Spirit

3. Rest

4. Abundance

5. Soul Purpose

6. Health

7. Growth and Flowing with the Seasons

8. Community

9. Fun and Pleasure

10. Love

The first and last chapters of this book will constitute a deep dive into worthiness and the radical idea that you don't have to do so much as lift a finger to own and know your worth. The other ten chapters will help you to reclaim your worth in the aforementioned areas. All chapters contain exercises, meditations, and rituals that I've designated as Worthy Work, in addition to Worthy Affirmations and Worthy Truths to keep you focused and inspired.

It is normal to feel that your worthiness is "stronger" in some areas of your life than others. For example, maybe you have a career and a life purpose that you are 100 percent kicking ass at, but your sense of community is in shambles or you're running on fumes and your health is suffering. It is also normal for your general sense of self-worth to ebb and flow, especially when you are starting out on this journey.

The intention of *I Am Worthy* is to bring awareness to your internal worth and to clearly identify the ways you might be blocking your capacity to receive and maintain the flow of goodness in your life. This is not about arriving at a final destination; it's about opening up to this multifaceted exploration of worthiness—from the inside out, one day at a time, one moment at a time. Let this book be your own personal worthy woman manifesto. Write in it, dog-ear the fuck out of it, and pass it around to the women in your life who might need a loving reminder of their own worth.

Many Latina women like me, as well as other BIPOC (Black, Indigenous, and people of color) women in general, have been longing for spaces in which to reclaim our worth. For me, these experiences speak to a greater dissatisfaction as we all navigate a world in which we are diminished if we don't fit into the narrow boxes that society has created to keep us in our place. I speak from my own set of experiences and beliefs, but I have written this book for everyone. While I will use the experiences of women to frame stories of worthiness, I give you full permission to cross out any language in this book that doesn't fit who you are. Whether you're white or BIPOC, male or female or Two-Spirit, I invite you to change any words or ideas that don't vibe with you and replace them with your own. And if God/Goddess/Diosa isn't your flow, use *universe* or *spirit*, or whatever else fits best.

While we all walk with specific wounds that can be fully understood only by others on a similar path, at the end of the day, every single one of us can relate to the feeling of unworthiness in some area of our life. And as you work through the book, you'll be guided to consider the unique path you've walked, and to retrieve wisdom and medicine from your wounds. I recommend keeping a journal dedicated to this process.

One more thing: I ask that you go at your own pace. If you have additional support from a coach or therapist, I invite you to share your insights and work through some of the deeper themes in this book with them in the reclamation of your worthy self. Keep a journal by your side as you read, both to respond to the Worthy Work journal prompts and to write down anything else you feel. Trust your flow, be compassionate with yourself, and give yourself both grace and the discipline/devotion to follow through on what your worthy one tells you to do—because I guarantee that her voice, even if it's just a faint pulse in the background, will grow stronger until it is always there to offer you direction and wisdom you can act on.

In the end, the goal of *I Am Worthy* is to help you transform the way you think and feel about yourself. You will be led to unearth all the things you have lost so you can finally rely on your true self to lead the way. Just imagine what would have happened if all the parts of your worthy, authentic soul self had been honored, held, validated, and accepted. Not just the "easy" parts, but the dark parts, the parts of you that are not polished or buttoned-up. The fierce part, the hood part, the part that is witchy and deep. All of you. You have the opportunity to give that gift to yourself now.

Now is the time to stop shape-shifting and fitting yourself into roles that aren't really you. Each time you do this, your self-worth is diminished. And we ain't come here to play small—we came here to *shine*. The parts of you that have been conditioned by the dominant culture hold the keys to the true unconditioned self that you'll find on the other side. All the Worthy Work you will do here is meant to help you access your answers so that you can fully embody your self-worth.

1

You Are Worthy of Worthiness

*I am learning that this body is not a battlefield but a home to
a heart that is worthy of the tenderness it aches for.*

—Cailin Hargreaves

A few months into my sobriety journey, I walked into a small basement full of strangers for my Alcoholics Anonymous meeting and noticed a sign on the wall that said "Let us love you until you can love yourself." Something immediately lifted for me when I read those words. It was like the sign hanging on the wall knew my secret: I didn't feel worthy of love, and I was terrified of being supported. I tried to mask the feelings of unworthiness with a variety of methods: perfectionism, control, bouncing from one relationship to the next, pretending to have it all together, and addiction, to name a few. I wanted so badly to feel worthy of good things, but I didn't. It was in admitting to myself that I *didn't* feel worthy that I finally went on a journey to reclaim my worth in all the ways.

In that room, I felt that I could take off my armor, that I didn't have to be so strong, and that I didn't have to lie or try to cover up my imperfect human parts. For the first time, it was okay that I didn't love myself, because they would love me until I could.

As someone who had always prided herself on being a type A person, this was a huge lesson for me. We as a society are compensated for thriving. There is little room for breakdowns, for reflection, for healing, for the often long and arduous process it takes to go from Point A to Point B, and the even longer process to get to Point Z. We're obsessed with results, and we go so fast we can barely breathe. We disconnect from our bodies, trying to optimize our performance and hack our efficiency. Even if we have the semblance of being put-together and strong, on the inside, we're crumbling.

We are often taught that when we have x, y, and z (the relationship, the dream job, the perfect house), *then* we'll finally be worthy. The problem is, it doesn't work that way. There is always something we will never have, a next level to reach, another set of Joneses exhorting us to keep up and look good as we do it. As most spiritual traditions have told us for eons, worth isn't something that comes from the outside. It's an inside job. Worth is intrinsic, and it's soul work to dig deep and recognize this. Our sense of worth cannot stop at an intellectual knowing; it is the pearl that has to emerge from the oyster of our core self.

When I stepped into that meeting room, I'd been teaching other women the principles of self-love for years already, and while I believed in my message wholeheartedly, I didn't feel worthy of love. I didn't feel worthy of peace. I didn't feel worthy of happiness. I didn't even feel worthy of feeling worthy, which is the subject of this chapter. It took breaking down in front of people I didn't know to recognize I needed time and space to break down and work on myself.

It was there that I realized that no matter what, I needed to heal and learn to feel worthy—because if I didn't, I would keep replaying negative patterns that pushed me down further, robbed me of my power, and kept me in a cycle of unworthiness. I recognized the ripple effects this would have for me and the people I cared about, as well as the women I dreamed of someday touching with the uplifting message that screamed to me from my soul.

I was here to help other women do their Worthy Work, but first I had to come to terms with just how unworthy I felt. A variety of accolades had come and gone, but they didn't change the despair I woke up to every morning and went to sleep with every night. I had come to the realization that so many spiritual seekers finally do, a swift kick to the gut that moves them into meaningful action: I knew that even if I *did* manage to get the things I wanted, it would be only a fleeting sense of external validation rather than a reflection of my deep self-acceptance and worth.

That's when I went on a quest to heal and reclaim my worth.

This Thing Called Worthiness

The word *worth* has compelled me for so long. Intuitively, I have always known that it's the key to unlocking the doors to a life that truly feels good. But . . . what even is it? What is it not? How can we unpack it so that we see how it's actually operating in our own life—not as a concept, but as a reality? How do we reclaim it?

Worthiness is defined as "being good enough," and we as human beings, especially women, often struggle with feeling good enough. Being a good enough child, a good enough friend, a good enough caregiver, a good enough partner, a good enough worker or business owner, a good enough artist or creator. At its core, a sense of worthiness is the belief that we are valuable and deserving of love and respect. It is the understanding that we are enough, simply because we exist. Worthiness is not something that can be earned or achieved through external accomplishments or validation. It is an inherent aspect of our being that can't be taken away or diminished by external circumstances.

Your sense of self-worth impacts whether you believe you are a good person who deserves good things or a bad person who deserves bad things. Beloved researcher and author Brené Brown has noted that our self-worth isn't some mysterious thing that exists separate from who we are in the world; it can be located inside the stories we've learned to tell ourselves. It also exists in our willingness to be vulnerable and to live in what Brown calls a "wholehearted" way. When we are living wholeheartedly, we have faith in our ability to deal with situations, challenges, and relationships. This doesn't mean we expect that everything will work out; it just means we believe our feelings, goals, and desires have value. We believe we are worthy of showing up as our wholehearted self in every moment.

This means we risk being vulnerable. A feeling of unworthiness is often connected with a fear of being vulnerable, as we believe negative outcomes might mean something negative about our core self. But worthiness is connected with the willingness to live in a full-out way. Even if our heart breaks, it breaks us open to our most authentic self. We may risk embarrassment or judgment (and sometimes, let's be real, worse), but if we don't live wholeheartedly, we risk never having our needs for intimacy and connection—with our true self, and with others' true selves—met.

Self-worth is key for so many reasons. For starters, if we don't feel worthy, we will constantly attempt to validate our worth in external things—other people, opportunities, accomplishments, possessions, substances. We won't feel worthy of good things, because deep inside, we don't value ourselves. If we don't value ourselves, either we won't be able to cultivate a life that we love, or we'll live feeling like an imposter for receiving our desires and having our needs met. It is imperative to build this relationship to our worthiness so that we can live a life grounded in an internal relationship to self that is solid and feels deserving of a beautiful life.

Ultimately, worthiness is important because it shapes our beliefs about ourselves and our place in the world. By cultivating a sense of worthiness, we can live more fulfilling and meaningful lives, and contribute positively to the world around us.

Worthiness isn't optional. When we believe that we are worthy, we are more likely to take risks, pursue our goals, and assert our boundaries. We are less likely to be swayed by validation or criticism, and more likely to trust our own intuition and inner wisdom. Conversely, when we struggle with unworthiness, we are more prone to self-doubt, anxiety, and depression. We struggle to assert our boundaries or pursue our goals, fearing that we're not good enough or deserving of success. We seek validation or approval from others to feel worthy, rather than trusting our own inner worthiness. We may even tolerate unhealthy or abusive relationships, or struggle to form connections with others.

It's important to remember that you don't have to be "perfect" in order to be worthy. In fact, displaying enough vulnerability to reveal the tender, even flawed, parts of oneself *is* a strong display of self-worth. You're owning that you're human, that you might have fears and insecurities, but that you still believe in your inherent goodness. When you do this, you can stop resorting to coping mechanisms like constantly having to prove yourself, perform, or please. Instead, you can be real with others and yourself. You can say, "I am good enough, just as I am."

Let's take a moment to get crystal clear about what your self-worth is *not*!

Your self-worth is *not* based on:

* External validation
* Your job or career
* Your body or physical appearance
* Your social media following or engagement
* Your finances or money
* Your grades, external awards, or recognition
* Whether or not people like or approve of you

It's tempting to view any or all of these as a reflection of your worth. The thing about worth, though, is that if we're not deeply connected to our own inherent worth, we block the good stuff, no matter how much we want it. As a result, it doesn't happen, or we feel unsatisfied when it *does* happen, or we sabotage it when it arrives and then end up losing it again.

You may have seen this play out in your own life or the life of someone you love. Someone attracts a good relationship, or more money, or a unique opportunity for exposure and recognition, but they don't feel worthy of it, or they fear losing it . . . so they attract drama or a crisis that takes it away or prevents them from enjoying it. Then they decide this is proof that they weren't deserving to begin with. In this self-fulfilling prophecy, they create what they *don't* want rather than creating what they both want *and* deserve.

As spiritual beings on this human journey, I believe we

are here to learn and grow, and to become even more of who we are. We get to look at the areas of our lives that have blocks and love those parts up until they feel whole and healthy. I believe it's our spiritual mission to heal the areas of our lives that we struggle in and, in turn, access the love and blessings on the other side of that challenge. It's time to break the blocks and reclaim your worth.

But the question still remains: How do we go about building our self-worth?

To get started, let's move into some Worthy Work; the following assessment will help you identify where you stand right now in your sense of worthiness. Remember, there is no "good" or "bad." I still have moments when I vacillate on any given day, which is when I call on La Diosa and allow myself to be bathed in her love. The information that follows isn't meant to make you judge yourself; it's here to expand your awareness and help you grow!

Worthy Work: Self-Worth Assessment

Below is a list of statements dealing with your general feelings about yourself. Please indicate how strongly you agree or disagree with each statement.

1. On the whole, I believe I am worthy of love.

   Strongly Agree   Agree   Disagree   **Strongly Disagree**

2. At times, I think nothing good will ever come to me.

   Strongly Agree   Agree   Disagree   **Strongly Disagree**

3. I am deserving of good things.

   Strongly Agree   Agree   Disagree   **Strongly Disagree**

4. I believe I can easily attract good situations into my life.

   Strongly Agree   **Agree**   **Disagree**   **Strongly Disagree**

5. I can be proud of who I am.

   Strongly Agree   **Agree**   **Disagree**   **Strongly Disagree**

6. I feel that other people get good things and I don't.

   Strongly Agree   **Agree**   **Disagree**   **Strongly Disagree**

7. I'm a person of worth.

   Strongly Agree   **Agree**   **Disagree**   **Strongly Disagree**

8. I wish I could love and respect myself more.

   Strongly Agree   **Agree**   **Disagree**   **Strongly Disagree**

9. I often feel something about me is inherently wrong or not "good enough."

   Strongly Agree   **Agree**   **Disagree**   **Strongly Disagree**

10. I am loving and kind to myself.

   Strongly Agree   **Agree**   **Disagree**   **Strongly Disagree**

*Scoring: For items 1, 3, 4, 5, 7, and 10, give "Strongly Disagree"
1 point, "Disagree" 2 points, "Agree" 3 points, and "Strongly Agree"
4 points. Items 2, 6, 8, and 9 are reverse-scored; give "Strongly
Disagree" 4 points, "Disagree" 3 points, "Agree" 2 points, and
"Strongly Agree" 1 point. Add up the scores for all ten items. Higher
scores indicate higher self-worth.*

Remember that doing this work might bring up a mixture
of feelings and maybe even some old stories you didn't know
were buried deep inside, so allow yourself to feel them and

write down whatever comes up. Worthy Work encourages us to become emotional archaeologists, digging up information about our feelings and giving ourselves the space to consciously choose what works for us and what no longer aligns.

Another thing to keep in mind is that this book explores a variety of different areas of your life. You may feel more worthy of good things in some areas than you do in others. If you'd like, you can complete the Self-Worth Assessment for each area we will cover, or you can take a moment to use your intuition and gauge where you might fall in each area.

I ask you to bring loving awareness, mindfulness, and consciousness to your thoughts. Explore what they say. Jot them down if you'd like, but remember to never trust the lies that unworthiness speaks to you.

The Conditioned Self vs. the Worthy Self

In order to step into our worthy woman self, we need to recognize the ways in which our conditioned self has hijacked our consciousness.

The conditioned self is the part of you that was influenced by external factors. These influences do not belong to our authentic self, but come from learned behaviors and beliefs we have internalized for the sake of survival. For example, if we were conditioned to believe that our most important quality is our physical beauty, our conditioned self will rely heavily on this external quality, perhaps at the expense of inner qualities like kindness or curiosity. The conditioned self is characterized by fear, competition, individualism, a feeling of victimhood or helplessness, and an overall sense of low self-worth, whereas the authentic self is characterized by love, collaboration, community, a feeling that problems can be solved creatively, and an overall sense of confidence in your self-worth.

I also think of this part of the self as the inner colonized or wounded woman who has been subjected to social and cultural values and judgments at the cost of her own connection to herself. When we are wounded, we harden our hearts and create fortresses that others cannot scale—but neither can we. Because the conditioned self has been colonized by the falsehood that the external world—with all its assumptions, projections, and superficial assessments of success and worth—supersedes our soul self, we can't actually let in any of the goodness that might come our way. Instead, our wound keeps replaying the same message: "I'm not good enough. I'm not smart enough. I'm not pretty enough. I'll never get what I want. My life is a mess." And so on and so forth.

The wounded self arises as a defense that can keep us from increasing our expectations, and it's also a conditioned response to different forms of abuse and neglect. The truth is, as the rest of this chapter will delineate, very few of us got the love and acknowledgment of our soul self that we yearned for in our developmental years. This can lead to the internalization of feelings of shame, self-doubt, and even self-hatred. The more the wounded self takes over our life, the less agency we feel we have. Sometimes the sense of internal sovereignty that comes from a strong sense of connection to the worthy self is lost altogether. We might feel alienated from who we truly are.

The following table offers some distinctions between the conditioned/colonized self and the worthy/soul self. It's important to read it with an open heart and mind. The ways our conditioned self can show up aren't always obvious to us. Even if you didn't previously see yourself as someone with a worthiness wound, or you saw it in one area but not in others, let yourself be compassionate in your honesty.

Conditioned/Colonized/ Wounded Woman Self	Worthy Woman/Soul Self
Believes we must earn money, rest, love, pleasure, abundance, and even the right to exist	Knows we are worthy of all the good things life has to offer simply because we exist
Bases self-worth on external yardsticks (money, material possessions, patriarchal beauty standards, other people's opinions)	Bases self-worth on an intrinsic experience of wholeness and wholeheartedness
Hides parts of the self that may be deemed unacceptable, imperfect, or less than by social/cultural standards, in order to be liked or deemed worthy	Leans into vulnerability and the spectrum of one's full humanity, knowing this is what leads to authentic connection with self and other
Is overly boastful and/or puts other people down in order to feel better (superiority complex)	Recognizes everyone has their own unique mixture of strengths and weaknesses, and doesn't derive pleasure from knocking others down
Can engage in self-erasure and self-deprecation around those who are perceived to be "better than me" (inferiority complex)	Engages only in healthy, self-loving inner and outer dialogue, placing self on the same level as others
Name-drops and seeks connections with those who have status, wealth, power, fame, etc., in order to convey significance	Treats people as individuals worthy of dignity and respect, rather than as status boosters
Focuses on self-enrichment and individual fulfillment at the expense of caring for and serving others	Recognizes that worthiness doesn't occur in a vacuum; focused on developing one's inner resources both to meet individual needs and to be a force for community and social change

Conditioned/Colonized/ Wounded Woman Self	Worthy Woman/Soul Self
Nurses chronic regret for the past and unhealthy ruminations about the future	Is firmly rooted in the present moment, with all its blessings and complexities
Tends to compare self to others, and to continuously feel "less than" or "better than"	Recognizes that the only real person to compare ourselves to is our past self, in that it's always possible to become a better and more whole version of who we already are
Harshly judges other people (especially women) for their "deficits" (e.g., slut-shaming, unfair comparisons, projections)	Treats others with empathy and respect, recognizing that patriarchy and other divisive forces would sooner see us fight one another than collaborate as sisters
Feels that overgiving, overworking, and not being resourced are all normal and acceptable	Knows we must give only what we can to others and honor our own needs first and foremost
Suffers from imposter syndrome, self-doubt, and persistent insecurities, which impact both internal and external relationships	Recognizes that while there's always room for growth, one has unique gifts, traits, qualities, and life experiences that make one deserving
Thinks we must fit social norms to be safe and ensure our place in society	Trusts in the true, authentic soul self, even if it goes against the grain, because that's where happiness can be found
Procrastinates on the experience of feeling good (e.g., "As soon as I get that job, lose weight, etc., I'll be happy")	Welcomes amazing experiences and opportunities in the here and now, with the knowing that "I deserve it!"

Conditioned/Colonized/ Wounded Woman Self	Worthy Woman/Soul Self
Sabotages relationships and opportunities out of fear that things won't work out, "They'll find out who I really am," or other fears that get in the way of accepting goodness	Nurtures relationships and opportunities, trusting that things will work out for the highest good and that even if something doesn't work out, it was an important learning experience
Has overly rigid or overly porous boundaries that are not always explicitly communicated to others	Keeps and maintains healthy, self-honoring boundaries
Stifles true voice, thoughts, and feelings out of fear that what one has to say isn't worthy of being heard	Shares authentic voice in the moment and is receptive and appreciative of others' authentic voices
Pretends "everything is okay" and puts on a mask that doesn't match internal feelings and thought processes	Demonstrates genuine feelings with care and compassion toward the self, especially when those emotions might include rage, fear, sorrow, or other activating emotions

I can attest that I've been influenced by the voice of the conditioned/colonized/wounded woman self—we all have. It can insidiously sneak into our inner and outer dialogue when we least expect it. I have trained myself and my clients to start examining our comparisons, judgments, knee-jerk reactions, and anything else that severs us from the whole-hearted voice of our soul—and to get really fuckin' curious when this happens. It's a beautiful process.

Often, we aren't necessarily 100 percent in either the wounded woman self or the worthy woman self; we're some-where along a spectrum. Where do you think you stand on this spectrum? Honestly evaluating where we may feel more or less wounded or worthy can lead us down some important roads, with our own unexamined stories serving as unexpected detours. This can take the sting out of our judgments and open us up to more compassion, care, and curiosity.

*Where are my thoughts and
actions leading me?*

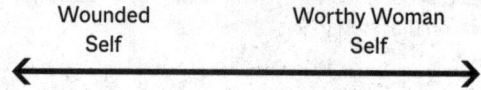

Wounded Self — Worthy Woman Self

This spectrum can be used as a guide to ask yourself if a thought, action, or behavior you're displaying is bringing you closer to your worthy woman self or taking you further away from it. Use it as a tool to bring awareness to your decisions and to help you make worthy choices more often than not.

Worthy Work:
Where Are You Wounded? Where Are You Worthy?

On one side of a piece of paper in your journal, write "wounded woman self," and on the other side, write "worthy woman self."

Referring to the table in the previous section, think about each of the ten major areas of your life: peace/mental wellness, spirituality, rest/relaxation, abundance/money, career/soul purpose, health/physical vitality, personal development/growth, community, fun/pleasure, and love (romantic relationships and sexuality). Give yourself permission to be radically honest about the downloaded beliefs you have perhaps taken on from the overculture. Take a look at the beliefs and stories you carry about each of these areas. Don't be surprised if there are both wounded woman beliefs and worthy woman beliefs in the same category.

This will offer you important information as you move through the rest of this journey. When you're finished writing, notice the area(s) of your life where you struggle the most in terms of worthiness. Why do you imagine these areas are challenging for you? Feel free to write about this. Also, gently observe how you feel in your body as you reflect on all of this. Make note of those feelings and observations.

Here's an example of what this might look like:

Area of Your Life	Wounded Woman Self	Worthy Woman Self
Peace/Mental Wellness	I always feel depressed and anxious, and like I can't set healthy boundaries.	I protect my peace of mind and set boundaries that are self-honoring and keep my nervous system settled.
Spirituality	I give value only to what I can see, and I fear my spiritual gifts.	I give myself permission to create ritual and magic in my everyday life.
Rest/ Relaxation	I must work hard and lose sleep in order to take care of everything that needs to be taken care of.	I know that tending to my rest is key to living a well life.
Abundance/ Money	There is never enough. I am not able to be well paid for doing what I love.	There is more than enough to go around, and the universe is a place of abundance and possibility that will always support me, especially when I am on the path of my soul.

Area of Your Life	Wounded Woman Self	Worthy Woman Self
Career/Soul Purpose	I am of no value. Others are already doing enough without me. I am blocked and don't feel my voice or gifts deserve to be seen.	My medicine is of deep service to the world. My gifts are uniquely given to me by the divine, and there is space for all of us doing good work in the world.
Health/ Physical Vitality	It's easier to zone out and just do what's easiest (eating fast food, not getting enough sleep).	My body, mind, and spirit are incredible sources of information. When I attune to them, they tell me what I need, and I joyfully give it to them.
Personal Development/ Growth	I fear getting older and will do what I can to stay and act young.	I honor the process of getting older and stepping into more and more of my true self at every age.
Community	I am alone, and I can get through life only by trusting and depending on myself.	I am community-made. In community and village, we heal, grow, learn, and thrive.
Fun/Pleasure (Hobbies and Extracurricular Activities)	I am serious and must be bogged down by stress and responsibilities.	I get to have fun and live a fun life. I prioritize joy, no matter my age.
Love (Romance and Sexuality)	Relationships inevitably end. Being vulnerable means giving away your power.	True love is possible.

Cycles of Worthiness and Unworthiness

As we ask ourselves about the self we are operating from, it can also be useful to familiarize ourselves with worthiness and unworthiness cycles.

A worthiness cycle occurs when we are led by a belief in our own deep worthiness. When this belief is strong in our consciousness, it is affirmed by worthy thoughts, which lead to worthiness in our actions. This feeds a cycle of worthiness, in which we act in ways that are wholehearted and that celebrate our authentic self.

A woman in a worthy cycle doesn't expect everything to be rainbows and roses 24/7. She is perfectly capable of responding to difficulty and challenges. For example, a woman in a worthy cycle might experience friction in her relationship with her partner. Perhaps she feels she is being taken for granted, or that her partner is not contributing to household labor. Instead of allowing the resentment to simmer until she implodes or explodes, she recognizes there's a problem. She might take time to sit with herself or talk to a trusted friend who reminds her of the importance of establishing loving boundaries. Her sense of worth will dictate the way she communicates with her partner, as well as what she chooses to communicate, and how she shows up after the discussion has occurred. This is important, because based on how we choose to respond, it's possible to either stay in a worthiness cycle or be pulled into an unworthiness cycle.

An unworthiness cycle occurs when we're caught in a belief of our unworthiness. We internalize these feelings, which are then translated into behaviors and actions that demean and disrespect ourselves and others. This feeds a cycle of unworthiness and toxic behaviors. Again, an unworthiness cycle can impact the way we respond to conflict; for example, a woman in an unworthiness cycle reacting to the same conflict in the previous paragraph might blow up at her partner and end up feeling guilty and ashamed, which causes her to sublimate her own needs and to continue to simmer in resentment.

An unworthiness cycle can also impact the way we respond to great things happening in our life. Maybe a woman in an unworthiness cycle meets someone who thinks the world of her and who expresses how much they love her and want to be with her. She might end up feeling smothered by this expression of genuine love. She might say, "How could they possibly be sincere? Why would they want to be with *me*?" This self-sabotaging attitude can lead to a premature breakup; all the while, the person caught in the unworthiness cycle might not even know it! She might think she dodged a bullet by leaving someone who was too "needy," never considering that she had been keeping the other person at an arm's length because she was afraid of being vulnerable.

It's important to note that worthiness cycles can be instigated by beliefs that are fed either internally (by our own inner personal and spiritual work, self-affirmation and self-compassion, purpose-driven activities, and so on) or externally (by praise, the presence of supportive friends, a powerful experience, and so on). A feeling of worthiness begets more of the same—when we feel good about ourselves and are surrounded by people and opportunities that mirror our goodness back to us, we are more likely to remain in worthiness cycles for longer periods.

Unfortunately, this is also true for unworthiness cycles, which can be generated from within (a feeling of inadequacy, making mountains out of molehills, a general sense of being "not good enough" or "less than") or without (a death or personal loss, an illness, someone in your life treating you in abusive or neglectful ways). When we find ourselves caught in this spiral of defeat, it can be difficult to get out of it. In fact, some part of us may grow comfortable with the situation, no matter how painful it is, because it seems preferable to the unknown.

Remember, when we feel worthy, we're excited about stretching our wings and moving into new experiences, even if they're unfamiliar or incite feelings of anxiety. Remaining in an unworthiness cycle can create a sense of inertia and a complacency that keep us from changing less-than-ideal conditions in our life. We may ask, "Why bother?" Even worse, we may be completely oblivious to the fact that we are in an unworthiness cycle, because we start to see the sad state of things as "just the way it is."

I know I've gone through periods of my life when things just seemed so fucking hard, I couldn't imagine myself being able to expend the kind of energy it would take to shift my situation. Some part of me remained unconvinced that I deserved good things—and the longer I remained inside my unworthiness cycle, the more entrenched that belief became.

Thankfully, the shift doesn't require you to turn your life upside down all at once. Some of the most powerful transformations I've ever made have come from building tiny habits over time. We can actually turn our worthiness into a habit that we make stronger and stronger poco a poco, little by little. In fact, this book contains rituals and activities we can use repeatedly to feed our worthiness over time. Even if we don't feel 100 percent in our worth, these tiny mind shifts can help us start thinking and acting from a place of worthiness.

It's important to note here where the energy is coming from within you as you go on your healing journey. Is it from self-respect and compassion or shame and not-enoughness? If it's the latter, take a moment to breathe deeply. Inhale and exhale until you feel yourself come back into your body. Then repeat to yourself, "I allow myself to love all parts of myself, not because I am inherently bad or unworthy, but because I am deserving of healing in my human journey."

The Lost Pieces of Soul

In my previous book, *I Am Diosa*, I wrote about the shadow self, a concept pioneered by Carl Jung that describes the parts of our personalities we push down and keep hidden, even from ourselves, because we don't like them and don't want to acknowledge them. These parts don't match the ideal attributes we've been taught to value by our family, society, or other external factors. The thing is, these parts of our true self that hide in the shadows don't just idly sit there. They regress and become wild. If left unexamined and buried, they end up coming out in destructive ways.

I grew up with parents who were loving, but who also had extreme anger problems and were abusive. I learned that in order to avoid punishment, I had to avoid being who I really was—not because I was doing anything wrong, but because my parents were emotionally unequipped to tend to me and the emotions that come with healthy child development. I kept certain parts of myself, like my desire for safety and peace, in the shadows, because I knew it wasn't safe to show them. As an adult, I have often stayed in situations that were unhealthy for longer than normal because I had been repressing the desire for safety and security for so long. It took years of therapy, spiritual work, and self-compassion to bring this part of my shadow self to the surface and believe I was worthy of safety.

In overt or covert ways, we have all learned that if we were less this or more that, we could more easily get our needs met, be loved, and survive. But this isn't always aligned with the true self, the worthy self, so we must unpack our reasons for seeking self-preservation at the expense of expanding into our authenticity. No matter what kind of childhood you had, if you're here reading this, you have the capacity to unpack these stories and reclaim your true self that lives in the shadows. It's time to not just survive but thrive. No more following unwritten rules that don't serve you! It's time to write your own worthy woman rules!

The Impact of Patriarchal Systems

One of the reasons many women struggle with feelings of unworthiness is the impact of patriarchal systems that valorize male power and dominance at the expense of women's rights and autonomy. These systems perpetuate the belief that women are inferior or less valuable than men.

Gender inequality can range from economic injustice (according to a recent study from the Pew Research Center, women earn only 82 percent of what men earn in the United States—and those numbers become even more dismal when we look only at the earning power of women of color) to being excluded from positions of social and political power (women hold only 35 percent of senior leadership positions). Overall, women are more likely than men to experience poverty, lack of access to resources, and gender-based violence. Today, women around the world face challenges to their reproductive rights and agency over their own bodies.

In subtler ways, patriarchy diminishes values and roles that are associated with women and the feminine, like caring, nurturing, compassion, collaboration, and gentleness.

Stereotypical definitions of masculinity (which I want to emphasize are *not* the traits of divine masculinity) are positioned as socially dominant. In such a paradigm, it becomes second nature to exploit and marginalize women.

I also believe there is an often unexamined aspect of patriarchy that has an enormous impact on women's sense of worth, and that in order to genuinely come into our worth, we must confront it—and that is the way religion and spirituality have been commandeered by a male-centric paradigm that places women at the bottom of the hierarchy. The image of God that most of us have inherited is a distant male Father God. There is no mother who gave birth to this father or who occupies the throne next to him as his partner. This is true in Judeo-Christianity, but many other cultures harbor a similar prejudice. Unfortunately, when Christian European cultures colonized much of the world, the feminine was often removed from Indigenous spirituality and religion. Consequently, the message we receive is that male authority is the natural order of things—not just in the human realm, but in the realm of the divine. In the absence of stories about the feminine face of God, La Diosa, we lose touch with our wholeness.

Patriarchy manifests in unique ways, depending on where you are in the world, but the underlying message of patriarchy is the same: Women are little more than objects to be controlled by men, who are superior to and have natural authority over women. Even among supposedly empowered women, internalized patriarchy can create a knee-jerk aversion to other women and to the domain of the feminine, hijacking our capacity for solidarity and self-compassion. If we're taught from birth that women are "less than," untrustworthy, weak, unintelligent, overly emotional, and a host of other stereotypes associated with femininity, how do you think we'll respond? It can become a coping mechanism to side with patriarchy; if you can't beat 'em, join 'em.

This can look all kinds of ways. Some women might strengthen their masculine traits or simply not identify with their feminine traits because they've been taught that men are superior. (Of course, we all have both feminine and masculine aspects, and while it's healthy to balance them, we have to be cautious about the ways we may be more identified with the masculine because of internalized patriarchy.) Other times, women might feel they have no choice but to take on their mandated role as the "nurturer," prioritizing the needs of others over their own, which can lead to a sense of guilt or shame when they do put themselves first. Women are also subject to unrealistic beauty standards and the rampant objectification of female bodies in media and advertising, which can lead to further feelings of inadequacy and unworthiness—and the desire to fit in, even if those standards don't ultimately serve us.

Overall, our sense of worthiness is impacted by externalized and internalized patriarchy in ways we may not realize or see. This isn't because we are ignorant or clueless; in fact, patriarchy is something all of us have learned to live with, to a certain extent. For many women, it can be key to our survival to downplay the impact of patriarchy on our lives. A lot of women might fear the feelings of of rage, betrayal, and helplessness that often accompany a recognition of patriarchy and its toxic effects on people of all genders.

Despite the impact of patriarchal systems on women's worthiness, it is possible to reclaim our self-worth. Worthiness gives us courage to challenge patriarchal systems and advocate for gender equality and women's rights. It involves building communities of support and uplifting other women, rather than competing with or tearing one another down. Throughout this book, I'll provide practical strategies for cultivating self-love and self-compassion, explore the role of community and support in building worthiness, and offer guidance for challenging patriarchal systems. I call this the Worthy Revolution, because a huge part of this journey involves challenging the status quo and advocating for change in a system that has historically devalued and repressed women. It also involves recognizing and celebrating the unique gifts and strengths that women bring to the world, and advocating for a more inclusive and equitable society.

Worthy Work:
How Patriarchy Has Touched Your Life

It's traumatic for us to grow up in a patriarchal culture, and we internalize this trauma in various ways. Give yourself lots of grace and compassion as you explore some of the ways we have internalized this patriarchal culture. Here are some examples:

* **Comparison:** In the patriarchy, there is a hierarchy. In the matriarchy, which we will discuss on the next page, there is a circle of all wisdom keepers helping one another. In what way does the patriarchal lie of comparison show up in your life?

* **Believing we need to do it on our own:** Patriarchy sells the lie that we should do things alone. The concept of the village is removed, and we are taught that rugged individualism makes you stronger and better. But we are all connected, not just with others, but also with nature and spirit. In what ways have you internalized this patriarchal lie?

* **Being the best:** In patriarchal traditions, the focus
  tends to be on conquering others and being the winner
  in a zero-sum game, whereas traditions that value
  collaboration believe that trying to be better than
  someone removes the focus on communal well-being
  and that we can view an exceptionally skilled person
  as a role model rather than as a source of competition.
  How does the patriarchal lie of wanting to be better
  than others show up in your life?

Think of any other patriarchal ways that might have influenced you and journal about them. We will continue to
unpack this theme in the rest of the book, to really make sure
that any attachments to beliefs that are in direct opposition
to our worth are seen and explored.

Honoring the Matriarchy

Matriarchy refers to a social structure in which power is
shared between men and women, but women hold a central role (spiritually, socially, and politically) and the feminine principle is honored and revered as that which brings
forth life. Eminent twentieth-century archaeologist Marija
Gimbutas was one of the people who brought the concept of
matriarchy into the mainstream. She argued that during the
Stone Age, goddesses were widely worshipped and societies
were organized around the needs and values of women. Collaboration reigned supreme, and men and women coexisted
harmoniously.

According to Gimbutas and other scholars, matriarchy
was shattered in Europe when patriarchal societies invaded
and replaced the fertile, curvaceous mother goddesses—
represented in a range of prehistoric statues and sculptures—

with warring male sky gods. Conquest became a way of life—conquest of land, material goods, and women. In this way, women were reduced to second-class citizens, seen as little more than chattel for most of recorded history. During this time, in Europe and around the world, symbols and religions associated with the life-giving goddess were forced underground or channeled into fairy tales, folklore, and gentle "maternal" figures like the Virgin Mary, who was depicted as being subordinate to God the Father *and* God the Son.

Gimbutas and others believe that this exacted a heavy toll on modern civilization. Matriarchal cultures were rooted in a sense of collaboration and connection not just to other people, but to nature as a whole. The loss of matriarchy also accompanied the loss of inherent self-worth. Patriarchal cultures are, by definition, highly stratified—value is assigned to people on the basis of things like status and social standing rather than on their innate qualities. Usually, at least in ancient times, a Father God (which can be replaced by any of the modern deities we've come to worship, from science to capitalism) demands unquestioning loyalty and obedience, and any deviation from this comes at a severe cost. Self-trust is sacrificed for trust in the people, institutions, and deities that "know better."

In contrast, matriarchies revere the goddess as a symbol of the divine feminine, representing the inherent value and dignity of all life. In these traditions, the concept of inherent worth is often linked to the idea of interconnectedness—and all beings are seen as essential aspects of one large web. Thus, in matriarchal cultures, maintaining balance within this intricate web is crucial. By recognizing the value and dignity of all life, these traditions encourage us to cultivate compassion, empathy, and respect for ourselves and others.

I want to be very clear that matriarchy is not about canceling men or dishonoring the divine masculine. Once upon a time, the divine masculine shared his throne with the divine feminine. However, our patriarchal systems are out of balance and for too long have amplified the traits of the toxic masculine: entitlement, domination, valuing intellect and physical brawn over heart. We must be honest and recognize that patriarchy has harmed men, possibly almost as much as it has harmed women, and all of us deserve better.

Of course, turning the dial on our social structures takes time, and more recent generations of women, men, and nonbinary folks are doing important work that is moving us in the direction of equality. One of the most powerful things we can do is acknowledge our own internalized patriarchy and take steps toward dismantling it.

One of my teachers, Sarah Durham Wilson, notes that one of the major aspects of orienting toward matriarchy, even though we live in a patriarchal culture, is to move from the "immature maiden" to the "mature mother." The immature maiden is the one who is upheld as a paragon of femininity within patriarchal cultures; she is docile, pretty, appeasing, and "nice." Remaining in the bounds of what is considered socially acceptable keeps her dependent and disconnected from who she really is. In contrast, the mature mother is the one who has located her genuine power.

It's important to note that the word *mother* refers to the energy we carry, not necessarily whether we have given birth or choose to mother a child. The energy of the womb, which we will explore further in Chapter 7, equips us with the wisdom to birth a new model—through our nurturance, deep care, devotion, creativity, and desire to better the world within us and around us. For me, the work of stepping into the mature mother is all about integrating the divine feminine that lives within all women: La Diosa, the Divine Mother herself.

This mother within helps us to question our beliefs and be curious about where they came from. She helps us to explore our rich inner world, and she brings to our awareness the possibility of a new way of being. She also engenders self-compassion and permission to be kind and soft with ourselves, valuing understanding over judgment.

I believe that, together, uniting the threads of a more compassionate, life-affirming Earth community, we can bring back the most supportive aspects of matriarchy and use them to build a whole new world in which future generations can flourish as their wholehearted selves. The soul's essence, the blueprint that each of us was born to birth, can rise to the surface and radiate from deep within us, like a vibrant sun, when we do our Worthy Work. By being the midwife to our own soul self, we will live each day with a deep sense of worthiness—and when we lose track of it, we can always come back to center and steady ourselves. But to establish the true self, we must learn to honor it, no matter what our family, society, patriarchy, and the overculture have told us.

UNWORTHY LIE:
Things have always been this way, and patriarchy is the normal and natural order of things.

WORTHY TRUTH:
Our ancient feminine roots know there is a better, more nurturing, more powerful, more equitable way to live—and as diosas, it is our power and responsibility to birth that way into the world!

Worthy Work:
Dig Deep into Your Roots of Worthiness

"What we resist persists" is a popular saying for a reason. The universe has a way of bringing us new experiences that trigger our wounds so we can examine and heal them. We can choose to voluntarily dig into the source of our wound, or we can attract people and situations that force us to. When we don't look at the wound—the thing that hurts or makes us feel not good enough—life will bring about feelings and experiences that are similar enough to that original injury or pain that we can actively begin to *feel* and *heal* our hurt. Unfinished business needs to be attended to, for in it lies the soul medicine for our evolution.

Unfortunately, we live in a society that glorifies numbness and running from our pain—that gives excessive merit to positivity and not enough value to the holy medicine that comes from looking at your shadows, wounds, and fears head-on. Even if you are someone who feels confident and intrepid about most things in your life, I encourage you to go deeper and to look within yourself to see which lies of unworthiness you may have attached to, consciously or unconsciously.

Let yourself freewrite in your journal with the prompts below. Awareness of our wounds and our worthy woman desires requires radical honesty, vulnerability, and permission. I want you to give yourself permission to truly go there. This is your sacred space for *you*.

1. How are the seeds of unworthiness scattered within you? Were they planted in your relationship to your body, your creativity, your sexuality, your romantic connections?

2. Who has planted the seeds of unworthiness in you? Family, society, patriarchy, friends, religion, your former self?

3. Where are the habits, beliefs, and lies of unworthiness wreaking havoc in your life?

4. What are the dreams and parts of yourself that are yearning for reclamation? For example, maybe you've always wanted to write a book, do volunteer work in another country, or reconnect with your love of salsa dancing.

5. What qualities would you need to build that would help you acknowledge your true, inherent worth and to reclaim the parts of yourself that want your attention? What are some helpful activities or areas of exploration that could allow you to do that?

6. Can you commit to taking three small actions this week that would move you in the direction of reclaiming one big dream you identified in question 4?

✳ Worthy Affirmations ✳

◎ *I was born worthy.*

◎ *I don't need to do or accomplish anything to be worthy. Worthiness is in every cell of my body.*

◎ *I radiate and reclaim my inherent worth.*

◎ *My worth stems from a deep connection to myself and to the feminine face of the divine.*

◎ *The holy truth of the matriarchy is a seed within me that I am bringing to life.*

◎ *All the domains of my life are now becoming an extension of the core worthiness I radiate from deep within.*

You Are Worthy
of Peace

Peace in your home. Peace in your mind.
Peace in your heart. Peace in your soul.

—Lalah Delia

We cannot have a Worthy Revolution without it being a revolution that allows us to experience peace. In all cultures of the world, myths abound about the peace that is possible when we are no longer at literal or metaphorical war with ourselves. In such myths, the land flows with milk and honey, the lion lies down with the lamb, and the presence of La Diosa is palpable in everything, from a child's laughter to the blades of grass that dance in the wind, from the depths of the sea to the secret chambers of the heart that long for so much more.

For me, peace is the sensation of being in right relationship with self, others, Earth, and a greater sense of purpose. It is the joy that we get to drink when we are in true alignment with our soul self, who is able to integrate both her humanity and her divinity, and to relax into her wholeness. Because life is not meant to be a struggle. It is meant to be a bold adventure with so many treasures and gifts along the way. We get to mine the gold of our soul's desires, to live inside the peace of being entirely comfortable inside our skin, to be deeply in love with our lives.

Peace looks different to every single person, but it has some characteristics that are common across the spectrum of our lived experiences. In my lived experience, peace is connected to a nervous system that is at ease and well-functioning, such that my amygdala has not hijacked the greater wisdom and intelligence of my body and spirit, which are working in harmony. Peace is the ultimate harmony—the symphony that comes from all aspects of life dancing and making music together. Peace contains all polarities and paradoxes, because it is the still point that we get to experience in the middle of the storm.

Peace is the knowing of our true nature, which is infinite. It is not the absence of challenges. In fact, one way we are able to step into our true worth is to learn to face the challenges that threaten to tear us apart. It is to weather the storms with calm and equanimity—a steady attendance to our life and needs. The opposite of this is being easily ripped out of alignment by distractions and turmoil that seem beyond our control—trauma (both intergenerational and individual), family and societal expectations, oppressive systems, and so on.

When we reclaim our peace, we reclaim an integral aspect of our soul's worth—the one that says, "I will not go against my own North Star by allowing myself to be infected by false thoughts, behaviors, habits, and beliefs." This is especially powerful for BIPOC women (and women in general), whose lives and fates have historically not been in our own hands. The cries of our grandmothers are calling for a greater reckoning—the kind of justice that will set right a world plagued by violence, conflict, and the annihilation of our agency as women.

When we become purposeful rebels in the Worthy Revolution, we move in the direction of peace—not just for ourselves, but for all the women who came before us, and all who are here and will come after us. To do this, we have to acknowledge that safety and peace can feel like far-fetched dreams in a world where there are so many systemic obstacles—patriarchy, racism, classism, ableism, inequitable distribution of resources—at play. In addition, we may be facing personal obstacles, including illness, grief, and loss. All of us are impacted by these intersecting factors in unique ways, so I want you to be gentle with yourself as you move through this chapter. But for now, we will focus on the controllable factors involved in finding our peace, even as we recognize that there are many other things beyond our control.

Reparenting the Soul and Breaking Generational Chains

We're in the kitchen, and I hear my mother say, "Que desastre. Yo soy una boba. Que estúpida soy." *What a disaster. I'm so dumb. I'm so stupid.* She had accidentally let some of the avena, or oatmeal, boil over, and she was involuntarily revealing her inner dialogue. She had grown up with abusive caretakers who were highly critical and unforgiving. They didn't normalize mistakes and certainly didn't love her for making them. Without her full awareness, much less her own volition, she took on that critical self-punishing voice as her own. Then, years later, her daughter—me—hears it from the living room. And without meaning to, I inherited this inner voice as my own. If I was working on a school project and accidentally dropped some glue on the paper, I'd say to my-self, "I'm so dumb. I'm so clumsy." The cycle of self-criticism and self-abuse, and the lack of space to grow and learn is continued through a lineage of toxic patterns.

Dear one, I want you to know that if you have a similar self-punishing voice that blames and shames you for not be-ing smart enough, pretty enough, or worthy enough, this is very likely something you inherited not just from your par-ents and caregivers, but from an entire toxic system that is in the water we drink and the air we breathe. Women in partic-ular have learned to internalize this voice, perhaps because we think if we can keep ourselves "in check," maybe we'll escape external judgment, or, even worse, persecution. After all, how many of us had foremothers who were persecuted— not just for their errors, but for their magic, their genius, their unique beauty?

Something I've learned from witnessing the women in my family, as well as the thousands of women I've worked with over the years, is that if you rob someone of their self-worth, you rob them of their agency. The abuse that a woman might have dealt with in her formative years is perpetuated through the words she tells herself daily, which translate into the actions she allows herself to take and the joy she lets herself feel. This is not just an individual virus; it is commu-nicable, and she is sure to pass it on to her daughters. And it doesn't matter if she's a loving mother. My mother loved me, but I didn't soak up only her love; I also internalized the way she spoke to herself and others. She modeled the standard for what it meant to be a woman in the world.

Growing up, I witnessed a lot of stress. As a sensitive child, I suffered from a constant sense of anxiety and abuse that came from the outside as well as from within me. My ner-vous system had downloaded the pain of my family members, especially female family members. There was far more drama and discontent than there were healthy demonstrations of holding space for joy, pleasure, and fun. Of course, those things existed, but they were far more infrequent. The stress of mundane matters had caused the adults around me to bottle up their emotions. Thus, they didn't know how to tend to their own feelings, or to mine.

Truly, despite the wounds, my family members, especially the women, are resilient as fuck. Yet beneath the surface of their vibrant personas, many carry the weight of generational toxic patterns. It is within the depths of their struggle that I found the power to unlock a brighter future, one where peace reigns supreme and the chains of the past are broken. This required going on a radically honest journey of self-discovery, empowerment, and an unwavering belief in my worthiness.

If you aren't familiar with the idea of generational trauma, it constitutes the harmful effects of mistreatment or abuse that pass down from generation to generation—among families, communities, and even entire nations. The impacts of misogyny, racism, addiction, abuse, natural disasters, and poverty can lead to a slew of physical and mental health problems, as well as emotional challenges that are not always easy to articulate, much less recognize.

I know that I, like so many other women, come from a family of survivors. In my family, talking about our trauma or our pain was viewed as weak, pathetic, hardly the best use of our already scarce resources of time and energy. This is especially true in BIPOC communities. We are told to value what we already have instead of complaining, being greedy and ungrateful, or demanding more. In my family, we were taught to bury the mountain of rage and anger. Many of us turned to substances, workaholism, men, and other distractions to numb our pain, failing to recognize that peace begins with rooting out the poisonous lies that end up finding a home in our bodies and minds.

Over the years, I have done an enormous amount of soul retrieval work, emotional repatterning, and communing with my healed ancestors so I could fully get, on a cellular level, that the burdens of the past are not mine to carry. My ancestors want more for me, and yours want more for you.

From a tender age, I knew that part of the work I wanted to do in my life was to break toxic patterns and maintain healthy ones to the best of my ability. In order to do this, I had to cultivate compassion for the reasons my foremothers had carried so many burdens they ended up passing down to me. They had carried a heavy load, and they were badasses for giving their all for me. Many of them were also living with the unhealed wounds of a history of violence and colonialism. In many ways, their focus had to be on physical security: enough food to eat, shelter, and schooling and clothing for their children. Emotional security had been left on the shelf, because basic needs had to take precedence and there was no capacity to care for the needs of the heart. In many families, such patterns are so normalized that it's difficult to recognize healthy alternatives.

When I make a mistake or experience something challenging in front of my daughter, I try not to do what my mother did around me. I simply say, "Oops, it's okay, mistakes happen. I'll figure it out." And when my daughter, Mar de Luz, drops a cup of water on her play mat, tears of joy and pride come to my eyes when I hear her say to herself, "It's okay, I'll get a little paño [rag] and clean it up." I think to myself: *We did it*. My daughter's father and I have modeled self-love and self-compassion for our daughter. Love breeds love, and a deep sense of inner peace has the potential to prevail across the generations, even in the midst of turmoil. That kind of peace is unshakable as the foundation of our worth.

This small example demonstrates the power of breaking generational patterns in the simplest of ways, especially through our daily treatment of ourselves. When we make a mistake, do we offer ourselves compassion and care or judgment and harsh words? Do we incessantly obsess over the past and ruminate over the future, or do we give ourselves gentle reminders to stay within the present moment? Do we embrace both our strengths and our flaws or do we hold ourselves in positive self-regard only if we have achieved something that other people find impressive? Do we practice self-care on a daily basis or do we run ourselves ragged and forget to nourish our bodies, minds, and spirits with the essential nutrients that will keep our own personal temple to La Diosa clear and clean?

The mothers I witnessed in my life were hard because they weren't safe enough to be soft. When I realized this, I broke down. I could suddenly see the ways I held internalized pain and unworthiness, having been a deeply sensitive child and soul who required the kind of warmth that met and held all of me. But how can someone hold all of you if they cannot hold all of themselves?

The central pain of my life, of not being met by the softness that a deep part of me knew was my birthright, was alchemized and transmuted when I learned about La Diosa, the all-encompassing archetype of the divine feminine who was soft and strong and large and warm enough to hold all of me. As I learned to settle into her and to let her support me, I understood who I was, and what I actually deserved. I understood and mourned that my mother, father, grandparents, and many of those who came before them had perhaps never received this divine reassurance of what they also deserved. I knew this mother without knowing her, because she lived in my veins. Her blood was my blood, as well as the blood of my ancestors, who longed for my peace and restitution.

What would happen if we took the time to look at the generational patterns that don't serve us, along with the ones that do? After all, I'm not suggesting that we throw out the baby with the bathwater. My family also taught me the power of hard work, devotion to one's principles, and so much more. When we bring an unclouded awareness to our history, we can determine the gifts and traditions we want to move forward, as well as what we want to do differently.

I believe that inside each of us lives our own personal code of knowing: knowing what will fulfill our soul's desires, what will bring genuine happiness, and what will lay our careworn minds and bodies to rest so we can finally experience peace. I can't say what your code of knowing is, because it's unique to every single one of us. However, I can say that it is deeply connected to your intuition. It allows you to determine when something is "off," when you're being disrespected, or when social and familial norms violate your sacred knowing. I believe that the things we view as "off" are the things we are meant to do differently, the maps of peace we are meant to give birth to.

The Wounds of Colonialism and the Battle Scars of Our Ancestors

My family came from Puerto Rico, a beautiful region with a complex history, colonized first by Spain, then by the United States. From a young age, I knew there was something wrong about celebrating Christopher Columbus, who had raped and killed women and children in Borinquén—the land of my Taíno ancestors. In addition, I knew there was something wrong about the addiction in my home. Alcohol was my family's way of coping with unresolved childhood trauma and systemic racism and poverty, and although I had no idea what the link was, some part of my unconscious mind understood that the suffering that played out in excessive drinking and violent behavior in my home had something to do with the shame we carried—a vestige of the times when the rivers ran red with our blood.

Prior to the arrival of European settler colonizers, alcohol was not the norm in most Indigenous societies. Scholars have argued that the origins of alcoholism among the Indigenous peoples of North America lie in a constellation of cultural, social, and economic forces that have everything to do with factors like genocide, land theft, and attempts to demolish Indigenous cultures. They've also argued that Puerto Rico's continued colonization may explain why depression is the most significant mental health concern among Puerto Ricans in the U.S. mainland. Just as patriarchy can be internalized, so can colonialism, as the cultural ideas imposed by the colonizers emphasize their own superiority—and the inferiority of those who are colonized.

How does this impact many people of color who have both Indigenous and European origins, like so many Latinx folks? Well, the National Institutes of Health has conducted studies into health outcomes among mestizo people (people with both European and Indigenous ancestry—they might identify as white or nonwhite, but their origins are mixed). One study that delved into historical trauma in this group, as well as resilience and healing, suggests that there is what I would call a soul wound correlated with losses of language, society, culture, and land—often manifesting in physical and mental disorders, economic struggle, violence, fear, discrimination, shame, loss, and despair. The researchers who carried out the study found that the ways to address this wound included a deep, restorative connection to land and home, as well as an awareness of the historical dimensions of this trauma—which goes well beyond personal behavior.

By shining a light on the patterns that have haunted our families for generations, we reclaim our agency and challenge the status quo. We also build resilience—not just for ourselves, but also for our communities. For me, resilience means being able to talk about our trauma in a productive way that opens up a space for upliftment: laughter, connection, and celebration of our shared bonds and the strengths of our culture. Unfortunately, this isn't always possible among communities of color—or any communities that have experienced displacement or outright genocide—where "pride" is often accompanied by a searing shame it can be hard to talk about.

I have heard of "listening circles" within Indigenous communities, where young people and elders alike come together to hear one another's stories and share vulnerable sentiments. This is an important step toward healing that I hope will someday infuse all communities that have suffered violence that gets propagated through our genes. There is also a therapeutic modality called Family Constellations that uses a "field" of collective healing and the group energy of assembled individuals to address intergenerational healing and the breaking of unhealthy family patterns and norms. This method can help if you're interested in breaking generational patterns that arise from systemic patterns.

Ancestral healing is also gaining in popularity; this is the practice of connecting to what I call our "kind ancestors" and having them guide us from the spiritual realm in which they exist. There are times when I know that the work I'm doing is not just my work, but also the work of my late grandmother, Maria Luisa. In these moments, I might light a candle or say a simple prayer: "Grandma Luisa, help me to break the ancestral wound here that has lived in our maternal lineage for centuries. Guide me to the tools of our ancestral gift on the other end." There is power here, especially for those of us connecting to our Indigenous roots. It's important to remember that the purpose of working with these wise and benevolent protective guides is to ensure that we are holding sufficient boundaries in our own healing process while sending love and good energy to our lineage—and knowing we have the power to break toxic generational norms that re-create and perpetuate the wounds of colonialism.

Even if we don't belong to a family or community where we can openly talk about such matters, we can individually continue to hold on to our awareness and use it as a guide when we notice an old pattern that is no longer in alignment with the woman/soul we desire to be. Through introspection and honest reflection, we can become conscious of the patterns we unconsciously perpetuate, allowing us to take necessary steps toward healing and growth. We can say, "Suffering has harmed my people for generations. I am ready to transmute this poison into medicine that will impact all future generations, as well as aid in the healing of my ancestors."

UNWORTHY LIE:
I am destined to perpetuate cycles of generational trauma and to carry my family's unhealed burdens with me throughout my life.

WORTHY TRUTH:
I am capable of reweaving a new lineage with peace as the golden thread that holds it together. Just as my ancestors were worthy of peace, I am worthy of peace—and that's what they want for me!

Worthy Work:
Undoing Generational Patterns of Unworthiness

Undoing patterns of generational trauma can be a lifelong journey, but it begins with awareness. Take time to journal on the following questions, which will help you bring to light the ways you may have downloaded generational toxic patterns. These questions can guide introspection, but if any specific memories or stories rise to the surface as you think about your own lineage, follow the code of your knowing and consider your role in carrying forward or transmuting those stories.

1. What recurring patterns or behaviors have you noticed in your family that are also present in your life (e.g., a harsh inner critic, patterns of addiction, passive-aggressive tendencies, the need to be busy all the time, a martyr complex)?

2. How do these patterns impact your well-being, relationships, and overall happiness?

3. In what ways have these patterns limited your sense of self-worth or belief in your abilities?

4. Can you identify events or experiences from your family history that may have contributed to the development of these toxic patterns?

5. How do these patterns align or conflict with your personal values and aspirations?

6. Have you ever caught yourself engaging in behaviors or adopting beliefs from your family that you swore you would never repeat? (Please be kind to yourself here. None of us consciously adopt toxic behaviors or limiting

beliefs. Generational trauma is unconsciously inherited, and it is only when we start to consciously exercise awareness that we discover our agency to change those patterns.)

7. Are there certain triggers or situations that tend to bring out these toxic patterns in you? If they seem hard to identify, pay attention to physiological reactions in your body that are similar to the ones you had as a child when you were enacting these patterns or watching others enact them—for example, a racing heart, a dry throat, tightness in the jaw, etc.

8. How do these patterns manifest in your relationships with others, whether romantic, familial, or professional?

9. How do these patterns intersect with your cultural and gender identities?

10. Are there specific cultural expectations or societal pressures that contribute to these patterns?

11. What patterns of strength did you learn from your family? These might be traits like hard work, generosity, a deep reverence for family ties, etc. These generational gifts will come in handy as you unpack the negative patterns.

Our ancestors passed down traditions, beliefs, and behaviors, creating a blueprint for our lives. Yet some of these patterns are rooted in trauma, oppression, and limited opportunities, and have perpetuated cycles of pain. We can acknowledge that certain aspects of how we were raised and the beliefs that were instilled in us were unhealthy and even harmful, while also recognizing that most people are doing the best they can, given the resources in their possession. By doing our Worthy Work, we acknowledge the toxic threads that bind us, and in doing so, we begin to loosen their hold. You'll use your responses to the questions above to reclaim the pieces you wish to get back in your journey of undoing generational wounds and reclaiming generational peace.

We all have these coping habits from the past that we created, often unconsciously, to protect ourselves. If a pattern that once saved us is no longer useful, it needs to be honored for its years of protection and service, not shamed. This does not mean we should make excuses for bad or toxic behavior; it simply means we use the wisdom of curiosity to explore where it came from, recognize that it is no longer useful, and set healthy boundaries—without judgment, but with deep clarity. If we are still connected to the people who handed these patterns down to us or who continue to perpetuate them, we may wish to invite them into a similar contemplation of the impacts of generational toxic patterns on their own lives. If these loved ones aren't available to shift, that's okay. You can undo the patterns in your own life by setting boundaries and making new choices, so that you are no longer caught in the whirlwind of a toxic dance that destroys your peace.

Undoing Toxic Webs of Drama

One of the things I've noticed throughout my work as a therapist and through my own experience is that the generational patterns that get passed down to us can contribute to the conflicts we experience in our lives. I've found myself working with clients who initially come to me to talk about everything from abusive intimate relationships, to feeling caught up in power struggles at work, to struggling with setting boundaries with intrusive family members. Although the "problem" may seem to be with the other person or situation, the *content* of the issue is often not as important as the *context.* We can often trace certain patterns that tend to get perpetuated in all our relationships: self-silencing, people-pleasing, martyrdom, or even sabotaging perfectly healthy relationships to support an old story that we don't deserve support and kindness.

I often talk to clients about a common pattern that can contribute to toxic cycles of unnecessary drama and hijack our peace of mind: the Karpman triangle, also known as the drama triangle. Developed by Dr. Stephen Karpman, this model identifies three different roles that feed into one another in any given "dramatic" situation: victim, rescuer, and persecutor.

* **Victim:** People who take on the role of the victim feel oppressed, powerless, hopeless, and saturated with shame. They may be hypersensitive and fail to take responsibility for their actions, instead projecting blame onto a (perceived or actual) persecutor. They do not usually display qualities of resilience or self-awareness, and they may have difficulty making healthy choices. They are often riddled with feelings of unworthiness and a lack of strength to change their internal dialogue.

* **Rescuer:** The rescuer is the one who immediately shows up as the knight in shining armor. Often women may take on the role of rescuer, as they have been conditioned to caretake and put others' needs before their own. Although a rescuer may seem like a benevolent archetype with good intentions, they often display qualities of codependency and may enable a victim's sense of powerlessness. The message they consciously or unconsciously transmit is that the victim isn't capable of getting better without them. Moreover,

the rescuer might end up collapsing beneath the weight
of their self-imposed responsibility and start to feel
resentful toward others.

* **Persecutor:** Finally, the persecutor, which can often be
   the most difficult of the archetypes to recognize in
   ourselves, is the one who is perceived as the oppressor of
   the victim. It's important to note that the persecutor
   may not actually display oppressive behaviors, but,
   depending on the situation, even something like setting
   boundaries or assuming an authoritative role can cause
   them to step into this part of the triangle. In extreme
   cases, persecutors can be critical, angry, and controlling,
   and might even bully or threaten the victim.

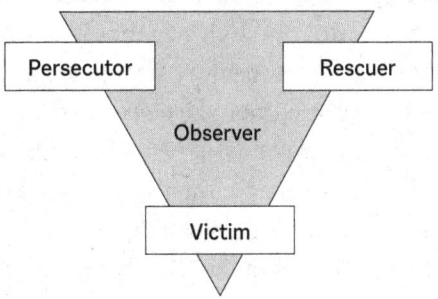

People can play these roles either consciously or unconsciously, and much of the time, we cycle among all three
roles in our relationships, especially within family systems.
We may even unconsciously assume a particular role because
the others have already been taken. Many times, people don't
necessarily even want to be in the role they've assumed, but
generational patterns can end up hijacking what we want for
ourselves.

I once had a client who was caught in a drama triangle with two close friends. Friend A (the persecutor) had a strong personality and often acted in harsh and controlling ways toward Friend B. Friend B (the victim) was hesitant to express her true feelings to Friend A, but would often complain to my client about how toxic and mean she was. My client, who had historically been in the rescuer position between her parents, didn't realize she was taking the same role here and enabling the toxic triangle by patiently listening to and putting up with her friends' drama. In fact, until we began unpacking the situation, she didn't realize that she often found herself caught in the middle, doing what she could to attend to other people's needs (especially those of the victim) while putting her own needs on the back burner.

Looking at where we tend to get stuck can help us to establish any obstacles to peace. In family dynamics in particular, we must be mindful of the things that take us out of our regulated spaces. Often, unhealthy people intentionally (or unintentionally) poke at vulnerable places within us to get us to "fall off the healthy wagon." So, when in doubt, it's always best to stop what you're doing, drop the fight, and breathe.

Choosing peace is one of the most important ways you can protect your worth, because it helps you maintain boundaries that keep you safe and healthy, and that increases your sense of self-trust—which goes hand in hand with building self-worth. When we get better at choosing peace, we automatically remove ourselves from toxic drama triangles and refrain from acting like we're the general manager of the universe. Instead of remaining stuck in the struggle for power, we reconnect with our inner source of power.

Consider any of the situations you might be in that zap your energy and peace. Do you notice any particular patterns? Who are the people who most trigger you, and why?

Do these people tend to be victims, persecutors, or rescuers? What role do you typically take in the drama triangle? What is one reminder you want to set for yourself now so that when a future triggering event occurs and you sense that you are being entrapped in a toxic web of drama, you can make a different choice? Make it your metaphorical sticky Post-it note to yourself, professing that you are worthy of peace.

Taking Off the Masks We Wear

We all wear a variety of "masks" throughout our lives. What is a mask? It's a role or identity we take on in order to hide our authentic self and present a self that is more acceptable to the people or society around us. You're wearing a mask whenever you pretend to feel something you don't really feel or to be someone who isn't truly you. We often start wearing masks at a young age, especially in situations where we feel physically or emotionally threatened. Examples of masking include:

* Acting like everything is fine when it isn't
* Saying you don't care about something when you really do
* Pretending to be super-nice when you're angry inside
* Acting angry when what you really feel is hurt
* Saying you can take on more when what you really want and need is to be held and supported

On the following page is a chart of common masks we wear to hide who we are from others and to keep the peace in our family, peer group, and other situations. (We'll learn about positive masks or archetypes, which we can call on to catalyze our own sense of inner worthiness, in the next chapter.)

Mask	Traits of Mask
People Pleaser	Depends on praise and approval from others; often exceeds own personal boundaries to caretake; has difficulty saying no; puts up the front of always being available and agreeable
Bully	Struggles with a deeply rooted sense of shame that is off-loaded by putting others down and attacking others before they can attack
Social Butterfly	Relies on being outgoing, charming, and charismatic, which can sometimes come across as superficial or lacking authenticity; often needs to be busy and has difficulty being with self
Controller	Is often rigid with ideas about what is and isn't acceptable; finds it difficult to let go; this can manifest in control over personal habits or control over other people's behavior
Avoider	Unwilling to commit; pushes intimacy away overtly or covertly; can come across as aloof or alternate between being distant and being approachable; emotionally unavailable
Self-Deprecator	Constantly disparages, undervalues, or puts self down; tends toward being excessively modest
Clown	Makes jokes and pokes fun at people or situations, not necessarily out of malice, but sometimes as a way to avoid emotional vulnerability
Superwoman	Seeks to be everything to everyone; wants to prove it's possible to "have it all," even if the consequence is being tired and burnt out
Good Girl	Wants to be seen as "good" and acceptable; often takes on other people's goals and desires for herself without stopping to consider if they are her own; is trained to put up an agreeable, compliant front; can be naive about the nature of the world, including not recognizing that not everyone has good intentions

Mask	Traits of Mask
Overachiever	Is allergic to "failure"; strives to be perfect and to win at all costs; is constantly setting goals but finds it difficult to stay present in the journey rather than jumping to the destination; secretly believes the only way to get love is to achieve
Conformist	Tends toward obedience and courtesy; is easily swayed and influenced by the opinions and behaviors of the crowd and finds it difficult to connect with one's own beliefs, values, and desires
Puritan	Tends toward rigidity with respect to self-expression and connection to one's body and sexuality; has internalized many retrograde attitudes about female sexuality in particular
Individualist	Independent, rebellious, creative; at times reactive and dramatic; holds to personal ideals, which can result in feeling disappointed when others cannot meet those ideals; feels isolated and separate from the crowd, which may result in feelings of deep loneliness
Seductress	Depends on sexuality to keep others' attention; comes across as confident, but often wields sexuality and attractiveness to get what she wants; may place a disproportionate emphasis on sensual allure to the exclusion of other values

Please know that many of these archetypes have both exalted and challenging qualities, and they aren't necessarily "good" or "bad." However, they can serve to keep us separated from our authentic self, which is not dependent on a role we are playing. Remember that the overculture and degradation of the divine feminine is often the reason we don't give ourselves permission to be our real selves. But when we activate the worthy woman within, she is so aligned with her truth that she's unstoppable.

I've worked with many clients who were afraid to align with their truth because they believed that being emotionally honest would lead to them being rejected or even abandoned. The masks allow them to hide the elements of their true self—which is vulnerable, tender, and multifaceted—in favor of the role they've chosen. However, I argue that it's impossible to be in genuine and fulfilling relationships with anyone, including ourselves, unless we have the freedom to be 100 percent real. An important aspect of Worthy Work is truly giving ourselves permission to drop outdated labels and explore who we really are.

We have to also remember the underlying reasons for our reluctance to be who we are. Patriarchy doesn't want us to be in our feminine power. If we are continuously people-pleasing, avoiding conflict, or ensuring that other people are comfortable even if we aren't, we stay blocked from our power. It might not be comfortable to step into our power, but we must go there if we want any kind of lasting peace.

And, yes, we may disappoint people who are attached to our inauthenticity. Let's say you are doing this deep personal development work and your romantic partner isn't. You notice that you are embodying your peace. You communicate your needs in crystal clear and kind yet honest ways. You are taking care of yourself and your passions. You are making your joy and purpose and values a priority—but your partner isn't. You aren't their parent, but you notice yourself shouldering the burdens in the relationship. At first you're okay with this, but eventually, you are exhausted. You use the archetype of the people pleaser or the good girl to mask your pain, your rage, your truth, because you're scared of being rejected or unloved. You're not being your true self—and you're not giving your partner permission to feel their growing edges.

But when you choose your personal peace by putting down the masks, you have the power to create new dynamics that lead to soul growth and healthier relationships. Every time I have spoken up from my truth, I have brought life back in. I have breathed worthiness back into my temple. But when I degrade this truth, I deny myself the opportunity to live in and as my worthy woman.

Worthy Work:
Your Masks

Take some time to journal on the following questions:

1. Who are the people you tend to hide parts of yourself from?

2. What are the masks you use to face these people and to protect parts of yourself?

3. What parts of yourself do you feel you are protecting?

4. Consider how each of the following people in your life want you to be in order for you to be loved, accepted, wanted, or valued:

   * *Your partner or spouse*
   * *Your mother/father and/or primary caregivers*
   * *Your child(ren)*
   * *Your employer*
   * *Your colleagues*
   * *Your friends*
   * *Your society*
   * *Your culture*

5. Looking at all your answers, what do you see? What are the identities you wish to break free from? Where are you being called to be more of yourself?

Tools for Increasing Your Capacity for Peace

A lot of what we've discussed so far in this chapter has to do with finding ways to deal with emotional dysregulation, a process that includes three main steps:

1. An internal or external event triggers an emotion or feeling (e.g., thinking about your judgmental mother, which makes you feel sad).

2. You have a thought response, followed by a physiological response associated with your thought (e.g., "She's never going to change," which causes a sinking feeling in the pit of your stomach).

3. A behavior arises from this constellation of thoughts and emotions (e.g., avoiding your mother's calls and stewing in a resentment that you refuse to talk about).

Emotional dysregulation can range from mild to severe, and when we are in its throes, we might "act out" (by crying, screaming, blaming people around us, blaming ourselves, and so on). In other words, we find it hard to regulate our emotional responses and to find a pause between being flooded by our emotions and reacting.

When we're connected to our emotions in a healthier way, this is known as emotional regulation. It basically means that we have the tools to manage and respond to experiences that might bring up a wave of emotion. However, it takes a lot of intentional practice and time.

Research shows that people who grew up in challenging family environments where the nervous systems of the entire group were often dysregulated will be more prone to experiencing dysregulation later in life. I know this is true for me and for many of my clients, so if this is the case for you, please be gentle with yourself and know that there is always a path back to peace.

As we close out this chapter, let's explore some tools that help regulate our nervous systems so that we can truly have peace in our bodies and spirits. Please feel free to add your own preferred methods of emotional self-regulation. May you always be confident that you have the tools and resources to come back to your authentic self—the beautiful spirit who is infinitely peaceful and always worthy.

1. Giving yourself a butterfly hug. Place your hands over your chest with your palms down and thumbs crossed, making the shape of a butterfly. With your hands in this position, gently tap your collarbone/shoulders with one hand at a time, alternating between right and left. As you tap, take deep breaths in and out. Repeat as many times as needed to feel calm (usually at least ten times is good).

2. Getting a hug from someone you love and trust.

3. Practicing meditation and breathwork (although I recommend doing these only when your level of dysregulation still feels manageable, not necessarily when you are severely triggered).

4. Grounding yourself by putting your bare feet on the earth.

5. Working with the elements (e.g., taking an Epsom salt bath, opening the windows in your home to get fresh air circulating, taking time to cook a wholesome meal over a hot stove).

6. Going on nature hikes and forest bathing.

7. Getting enough sleep (at least eight hours—which isn't always possible for many people, so I recommend naps!).

8. Staying hydrated.

9. Exercising.

10. Having a good, long cry.

11. Journaling or collaging your feelings.

12. Using proper nutrition to care for your physical/emotional/spiritual temple.

13. Working with a therapist or mental health professional to hone your self-regulation skills.

14. Having a strong and supportive group of friends and peers who do soul-nourishing activities together (e.g., a regular women's circle, a book club).

15. Doing bodywork (e.g., massage, craniosacral therapy, reflexology).

16. Doing energy work and mind/body medicine (e.g., Reiki, sound healing, acupuncture).

☀ **Worthy Affirmations** ☀

◎ I am worthy of peace and freedom from generational toxicity and unnecessary drama.

◎ I embrace my power and allow it to guide me toward a life filled with peace and joy.

◎ I vow to walk on my soul path instead of on the path that the overculture or my family and society insist that I take.

◎ I vow to honor my true self and to lay down the masks and identities that I have taken on as ways to hide, people-please, and self-protect.

◎ I vow to be authentically me, no matter the reactions I might be faced with (such as anger, disappointment, and rejection).

◎ I continuously come back to myself and my inner peace with gentle practices of self-regulation and self-love.

3

You Are Worthy of Connection to Spirit

*It wasn't that I wanted to replace a male god with a female god;
it wasn't that I wanted to find a religion at all. I was simply
looking for some sense that women might have worth.*

—Sharon Blackie

What we are is a beautiful paradox: flesh wedded to spirit, human vulnerability encased in the omnipresent energy of all that is. We are the microcosm of the macrocosm, but the great irony is, we're too close to see just how magnificent we are. And I'm not talking about our ability to build civilizations, send humans to outer space, and create technology that makes our lives easier. I'm talking about the spark of the divine that is nestled into the heart of every sentient being, which connects us to this incredible universe.

In many spiritual traditions, not just Judeo-Christianity, we are taught that humans were made in the gods' image. We ourselves are reflections of the endless creativity, compassion, and love of the divine. So how did we get things so backward in our world? There are many possible answers, but one part of it is that although we made enormous strides in fields like medicine and philosophy during the Enlightenment, or the Age of Reason, we lost our connection to the divine spark by dismissing religion and spirituality as artifacts of an obsolete and "primitive" era.

Today, many scholars have spoken of how the anti-mystical lens of the Enlightenment seems to have coincided with the rise of capitalism, colonialism, and the transatlantic slave trade—all of which worked to dehumanize and objectify our bodies as units of production, while demonizing the mystical, which was considered to be "irrational" and even dangerous. A spiritual lens disappeared from the great disciplines of the world—whereas centuries before this, fields like science and philosophy were inextricably linked to an understanding of the sacred. The mystical went underground. And while religion continued to be a tool that exercised control over the bodies and minds of entire populations, Earth-based, Indigenous practices of honoring the divine in nature and in ourselves were decimated.

Today, we still experience the erasure and marginalization of spirituality. From birth to death, we are taught to be docile consumers who fall in line with capitalism and fixate on the most mundane and visible matters. We fixate on what we can see, touch, and measure. I'm not knocking the world of the mundane, which I believe is very much connected to the world of spirit, but this one-sidedness makes us forget the existence of the unseen world—the world of miracles, of ancestors, of dreams, of prophecies, of divine intervention.

Many of us in modern culture are bereft of the rituals and ceremonies of our ancestors, many of whom were in constant unbroken relationship with the greater field of consciousness. Instead, we became indoctrinated into the blatant lie that we need to focus on "being somebody," on achieving, on maximizing our body's potential at the expense of our spirit. We are not taught that an integrated life is a life that attends to all aspects of who we are . . . because many of us don't even fully know who we are, especially in the absence of daily sacred technologies that help us restore our bodies, activate our wisdom, hear the voice of our intuition, and fill up with the energy of the divine.

There are so many messages we've swallowed that make it hard to recognize that attuning to the sacred is our birthright. After all, if our overculture has created this idea that worthiness is hierarchical—with the people on top "deserving" more than the people on the bottom—it makes sense that so many traditions have been hijacked by messages about human sin and imperfection. If we're so focused on our inherent unworthiness, how can we possibly connect with the truth of spirit, which lives within us?

Aside from some of the intergenerational and social conditioning that blasts the message of unworthiness at us all the time, I surmise that this core feeling of unworthiness is present because divinity is *so fucking perfect.* How can *I* possibly compare to the magic that underlies that process of turning something from formlessness into form? I'm messy, flawed, wounded, thorny, and, to be perfectly honest with you, a goddamn wreck at times. And of course, that's the paradox—because I also understand that I'm kind, caring, curious, motivated, soulful, and capable. But when you compare your own complex humanity to the brilliant life force that literally makes manifest the unmanifest, it's hard to see an immediate connection. When I gave birth to my daughter,

Mar de Luz, it was by far one of the most otherworldly, divine experiences I have ever been through. I got to meet a new version of me, and I got to see the magic of us as humans, our divine inherent worth and perfection.

This is why giving ourselves motivational talks about our divine worth can sometimes feel at odds with the message ingrained in us that humans are sinful and imperfect. We think we need to be like Jesus or Mother Teresa in order to be worthy. We need to sand down the rough edges of our humanity and be good and pure and sinless all the time. And since most of us can't, fuck it! Why not just join the rat race and focus on the more tangible stuff? This is an aspect of my own religious conditioning that has taken me years to confront, and I'm still releasing a lot of the toxicity that has made me feel less than simply for being alive and human.

When I look into my daughter's eyes, I understand that every single one of us is worthy by virtue of being born. But I often tend to forget this when I look at myself. However, in the ancient chambers of the soul, whispers of forgotten wisdom are constantly calling out to us, urging us to reclaim our worth as women and to ignite a spiritual revolution that transcends time, culture, and religion within the tapestry of our beautiful bodies. In our eternal spirits are woven the threads of divine feminine worthiness.

That term, *divine feminine*, is one that has only recently begun to be embraced by generations of women who are hungry for a connection to something that helps them not only transcend their limitations but also embrace the parts of themselves that are human. My hope is that this chapter will be the beacon of light along the dark path of stepping into our own personal connection with spirituality and the divine.

Decolonizing Spirituality

Before we get too far ahead of ourselves, it's important to ask the question: What is spirituality? I see spirituality as seeking meaningful connection with something that is much bigger than us and that lets us feel awe, wonder, and peace. Spirituality isn't about putting some distant deity far above ourselves so that we feel crushingly worthless and small, even though there may be traditions that encourage this kind of perspective. For me, spirituality is recognizing that there is something much bigger than my human self, a force that holds me deeply in its embrace. It loves all the parts of me that are human. It also reminds me there's something way more to being human than what I might be able to perceive through my experiences and my senses.

Spirituality is what connects us to our cosmic and divine nature, and reminds us that we are not separate from that which we seek and that which we worship—we are integral to it. We are woven into it. Spirituality helps us remember our interconnectedness and our inherent perfection, even though this particular perfection I'm talking about has nothing to do with the way we look, the amount of money we make, or even positive accomplishments in our lives. Again, this sense of spirituality connects us to a core truth: that we are part of the deep mystery that infuses our world with goodness.

Of course, there is a ton of unpacking that needs to be done if we are ever to reclaim our connection to spirit in a way that feels right for us. A lot of my own process has been about decolonizing what I was taught about God, religion, and the nature of existence. The process of decolonizing spirituality begins with an awareness that the society we currently live in was created for the most part by white Christian men. For many people of color, it is the opposite of the worldviews that infused how our people interacted with the natural world and the realm of spirit. Because of Christianity and colonization, so many of those original teachings have been distorted or completely destroyed.

So, especially if we grew up in a more or less Christian tradition, it's important to consider that while there are many beautiful Christian teachings, this is a religion that was forced upon a lot of us and that also created a great deal of damage, especially in terms of incorporating a more Eurocentric worldview and physically and psychologically fleecing us of our original cultures. This is not only true for people of color; plenty of pagan European cultures were forcibly replaced by a patriarchal Christian doctrine with a binary way of looking at the world that separates us into categories of dark and light, good and bad, socially acceptable and socially unacceptable.

While I've always loved the ritual of going to church to connect with something greater than myself, I also always harbored a deep visceral reaction against the dogma I learned there. As a child, I knew there was something wrong in hearing only about God the father, with stories about women reducing them to either the virgin (Mother Mary) or the whore (Mary Magdalene). And don't even get me started on the vicious untruth that humanity was ushered into "original sin" by the mother of us all, Eve. The Book of Genesis treats women's subordination as a natural, God-given truth.

Even if we don't even subscribe to Christianity, there is great power in the stories that get handed down to us. All of us know that on a primal level we learn through stories. This is why I believe the omission of the divine feminine in most Judeo-Christian traditions is harmful to the psyches of women—and also of men, who are enjoined to reject their own feminine aspects. I believe that the removal of the divine feminine was purposefully enacted as a form of brainwashing that keeps us disconnected from our inner worthy woman. We are instead taught, implicitly or explicitly, that access to the divine can occur only through a (usually male) priest or pastor. This takes away our connection to our own divine power, our own divine voice, our own divine role as priestess, the one who is the bridge between human and spirit.

Of course, it's also true that the honor many traditions give to the divine feminine in their stories and myths does not necessarily translate to the treatment of women within their societies. Sadly, all cultures have been subjected to the influence of colonization, and even Indigenous cultures that honor the divine feminine have fallen prey to stories about her sinfulness, deficiency, or nonexistence.

In the past fifty years or so, scholars have worked to bring back the stories of the Great Mother Goddess, La Diosa—like one of my teachers, Dr. Clarissa Pinkola Estés, did with her beautiful book *Women Who Run with the Wolves*. With such books and teachings, we are experiencing a resurgence of the Divine Mother, who never left our side. We are recognizing the many ways she can show up, so that we can embrace all aspects of who we are, including our power. When we remember the magic that lives in our bones and when we join together with other diosas to recollect our power, we change the world. It radically shifts everything when we remember who the fuck we are and come into a greater discernment of the big fat lies that have been used for millennia to control us, manipulate us, and stomp out our fire, our wisdom, our power, and our essential worth.

Take a moment to consider how the patriarchy, the over-culture, and perhaps even your own family may have influenced your relationship to spirituality in a way that has dampened your access to your true thoughts, feelings, and essential worth. In what ways have you dimmed your power and connection to spirit due to fear, puritanical belief systems, or religious doctrine that has enforced shame, dogma, and disconnection from your nature as a divine human?

As a Puerto Rican, I began to decolonize my Catholic roots and to integrate La Diosa by connecting to my Indigenous Taíno roots. Taíno culture is ancient and existed in the Caribbean region, including parts of present-day Puerto Rico, Cuba, and the Dominican Republic. The Taíno people had a rich spiritual and cultural tradition, which emphasized the interconnectedness of all life and the importance of living in harmony with nature. In Taíno culture, worthiness and empowerment were closely linked to areíto, a form of communal dance and song (a quintessentially feminine way of doing ritual). Areíto was seen as a way to connect with the divine and to celebrate the inherent dignity of all life.

Through areíto, Taíno people were able to express their creativity, connect with their community, and celebrate their cultural heritage. This sense of empowerment and worthiness was essential to the Taíno way of life and helped to foster a deep experience of connection and belonging within the community. Today, many people of Taíno descent, including myself, continue to celebrate their cultural heritage and to honor the traditions of their ancestors. This includes practicing areíto, as well as other forms of Taíno spirituality, and passing these values to future generations.

Can you consider the ways your own lineage suffered from colonization? How were their spiritual traditions stripped from them? In what ways can you reconnect with some of the beautiful aspects of your traditions that help you connect in a pure and authentic way to both your humanity and your divinity, to your divine masculinity and your divine femininity?

I realize that you may not feel a close sense of connection to the spiritual traditions of your culture. For many of us whose families have lived in the United States for generations, the process of assimilation may have wiped away any sense of connection to our lineage. This is also something that is worthy of grieving.

I believe that there are seeds of wisdom that exist throughout all cultures on this planet. While I think it's extremely powerful to reconnect with your own roots, it's also true that we all have much to learn from one another. Personally, I love to honor and learn from other cultures. An aspect of spiritual worthiness is recognizing that one culture is not better than another. When we enter into our dance with spirit with a perspective of humble curiosity and respect, we may discover a deep affinity to traditions that are not part of our lineage. I urge you to remain curious and open, but to also exercise discernment. There's a deep difference between cultural appreciation and cultural appropriation. Be discerning and mindful when it comes to honoring the medicine you choose to work with, and be sure to give reverence and gratitude to its land and people.

Worthy Work:
Spirit Release Ritual

Before you dive into this sacred ritual, take time to sit in a quiet place where you will not be disturbed. Journal on the following questions:

1. When do you feel closest to spirit?

2. How have internalized patriarchy and colonization colored your experience of spirituality? (Be tender with yourself here.)

3. Where are you shutting down your connection to spirit?

4. What do you know about the spiritual traditions of your own lineage? How were your people persecuted? Do research, if needed.

5. How did the people of your biological lineage honor spirit? How did they honor the Earth? How did they honor the elements, the moon cycles, and the divine feminine?

6. What does your soul currently need as it relates to your spirituality and connection to spirit?

7. What would most make your worthy woman come alive in your spiritual practice right now?

8. If you truly allowed yourself to feel deserving and worthy of your dream spiritual connection, what would that look like?

After journaling, do the following ritual. Take a moment to gather your items: a pot, matches, candle, salt, paper, pen, sacred herbs (you can use anything you have in your kitchen, such as rosemary or bay leaves), and water in a bowl.

1. Create a sacred space by lighting a candle. Cleanse your space by sprinkling salt water around the space, singing, or burning dried herbs. Feel free to tap into and flow with your creative spiritual self here.

2. Sit in a comfortable position on the floor and come back to your breath. Breathe deeply through your nose, and exhale through your mouth. Repeat until you feel relaxed and open to spirit.

3. On a loose sheet of paper, write a list of the toxic lies you have internalized. They might range from "My nature is sinful because I was born into a female body" to "I will always feel separate from my source." Let yourself purge onto the paper.

4. Now say a prayer: "Divine Diosa, Great Mother, I ask that you help me to gently release the patriarchal and colonized patterns that I inherited from my system. Help me to clear them in my mind, body, spirit, and bones. I ask you to clear all cords, expectations, trauma, and contracts that keep me in these patterns."

5. Light the piece of paper on fire and put it in the pot; you can also choose to do this over a toilet and flush it down the toilet!

6. Feel the patterns leaving your body and your system. Allow yourself to feel the release. Imagine it all leaving through the soles of your feet and being fertilized and alchemized by Mother Earth.

7. To close the ritual, repeat to yourself, "Diosa, Goddess, I ask you to plant the seeds of this ritual into the earth and to water them with love and nurturance, and to shine light on the seeds so that they may grow to help me and help all. And so it is."

8. I invite you to repeat this practice as many times as needed when old ways that aren't truly your way of thinking and feeling about spirituality come up. Most of these patterns are deeply ingrained, so it takes lots of love, compassion, and ritual to shed the distorted lies and reclaim your worthy spiritual truth.

In the days to come, take note of any signs that reveal to you your true spiritual vision of your life. You may come across signs and synchronicities that help you make new connections. You will start to see more easily where you are hiding your witchiness, spiritual gifts, and connection to magic because you've come to believe some antiquated, patriarchal, colonized version of connecting to God/spirit. Bring your new vision into reality by feeling yourself draw it into your holy vessel right here, right now. I believe this to be true so much that I tattooed "Los sueños son las semillas de nuestras realidades" on my left rib. That translates to *Dreams are the seeds of our realities.* You get to birth your dreams into reality. Be committed to embodying this today, as your Worthy Work. Embody La Diosa and walk as the vision that you want for your life, for your children, for your family, for the Earth.

UNWORTHY LIE:

*Humanity and divinity will always be separate,
and I will never be pure or good enough to
connect with the divine.*

WORTHY TRUTH:

*Humanity is an essential aspect of divinity,
and the divine lives within my body,
breath, and heartbeat.*

+

The Many Faces of
the Divine Feminine

An important aspect of the path of the feminine is that it's meant to be an ecstatic path, a path of pleasure even in the contractions of life, a path of bliss even in the breakdowns. It's a path of the full spectrum of humanity and divinity.

The dance between worlds is an orgasmic explosion of bliss. When we embody the divine feminine, we recognize that we can have all of this right now, not in the afterlife or when we achieve some kind of status that readies us for the experience. Spirit finds all kinds of ways to initiate us into an understanding of our own worthiness, but the divine feminine is nothing more than the embodiment of this worthiness. And even when we might not feel it within us, like a loving and gracious mother, La Diosa asks that we invite her into our bones, into our precious bodies, and that we let her fill us with love so we can feel like the queens we truly are.

If you feel disconnected from yourself, from your source, let La Diosa crown you so that you can receive the gift of your worthiness and walk in her footsteps. Let yourself feel her presence in these words. Let her usher you back into your true worth.

I am such a strong advocate of infusing the culture with more stories about the divine feminine—from the myths of goddess traditions around the world to the recognition of archetypes of the feminine that we can turn to when we wish to fill our cup with the truth of who we are. Stories and examples of the divine feminine are needed in order for us to reclaim our sacred essence and power—to remember that, as the womb carriers and life-giving nurturers, we are the very source of life. This helps us own our worth in the deepest ways.

To that end, I want to introduce some archetypes associated with the divine feminine. As we learn about these sacred roles and feminine powers that every woman intrinsically has, we activate the magic within and remember our divine feminine power. What I love about these archetypes is that they give each woman access to her own inner fire, so that she can serve the world in her own chosen way. When women awaken to this deep power, we awaken La Diosa and come back to our inherent worthiness and multidimensional nature.

Like the divine feminine, we hold all of creation in our hands, our hearts, our wombs. Not only do we connect with the great mystery at the heart of everything, we also step into our capacity to tend the Earth and one another. We make ceremony and ritual an intrinsic aspect of who we are.

Archetype	Characteristics
Great Mother	A tender of the sacred heart and the hearts and souls of others; loves caring for and midwifing the true creative gifts of her loved ones; holds great wisdom in her capacity to nurture others and steward them along their individual paths
Compassionate Healer	Counsels and tends to others in their times of deep need; tends to offer a healing balm to those with broken hearts and dreams; is also adept at any of the healing arts, whether physical or spiritual; is an exemplar of the power of forgiveness, especially self-forgiveness
Priestess	Opens her body and soul to channel the rites, ceremonies, and actions that ensure harmony with the forces of creation; honors her humanity but knows she is the embodiment of the forces of creation and will cast away vestiges of her identity that hold her back from acting in honor of the whole; attuned to service
Dark Goddess	Also known as the Destroyer of Illusions; embodies the aspects of the divine feminine that are "darker" but nonetheless sacred: death rites, cutting away toxic illusions, setting boundaries, navigating transformation and chaos, and blooming into regeneration; not always comfortable to meet or embody, but can teach us the most about ourselves

Archetype	Characteristics
Muse	Tends to be artistic and engaged with aspects of music, poetry, dance, and self-expression; may be a muse for herself and others; embodies the divine light of creation and inspiration
Wise Woman	Tends to be quiet, perceptive, and capable of keen insight; often keeps to herself (like witches in fairy tales), but is willing to share her wisdom with those who will truly value and act on it; keeps her own counsel, but also listens keenly to the forces of nature to receive information
Oracle	Similar to the Wise Woman, but most deeply connected to the art of intuitive sight and prophecy; pierces the veils of illusion and communicates with the other worlds and possibilities beyond to bring forward powerful visions for the future
Explorer	Is a master of bringing together the details of a situation and executing marvelous adventures for herself and others; is connected to a range of networks; walks in the liminal space between various realms; has a spirit of adventure and curiosity that makes her a social butterfly hungry for new experiences she can add to the tapestry of her wisdom
Dreamer	Has a childlike, wonder-filled way of looking at the universe; believes in magic and stokes enthusiasm and hope in others; tends to live in a "world of her own" and to love romantic films and fantasy novels; knows that "fantasy" holds a blueprint for a better world; tends to have visionary ideas that she rallies others to get behind so they can be dreamt into being
Empress	Exudes sensuality and beauty; knows that sensual self-expression is one of the keys to a woman's true power; is comfortable with love, affection, and flirtation and is well attuned to the sensual arts

Archetype	Characteristics
Warrior Woman	The archetypal rebel who bucks the system and fights for those who cannot fight for themselves; is always willing to move into conflict for the sake of peace and justice; uses her powerful voice for those who do not have a voice; proves her tenacity physically, mentally, and spiritually

There are so many different archetypes in the world, represented by different goddesses and qualities—from the primal goddess of death and destruction, Kali; to the goddess of compassion, Quan Yin; to the primal creatrix Spider Woman, who generated all of creation. All of these archetypes play an important and fascinating role in helping us understand the myriad faces of La Diosa, but the ones I've described here are very special to me. That's because they represent the gifts our world most needs—those gifts that connect us to our essential life force, our human potential, and our ability to nourish and honor that which deserves to be held up for all of humanity in this time.

These eleven archetypes reawaken us to our capacity for magic and wholeness in today's hectic, disconnected world. They are the ancient keys to planting the seeds of love, harmony, and attunement to the universal mystery—right here on this planet, with the minds, bodies, and souls that incarnated for one powerful reason: to remember our true worth, and to help others to do the same.

Worthy Work: Activate Your Divine Feminine Archetype

For the purpose of this book and your daily life, I want you to create a sacred space where you will connect with your

divine essence through meditation, prayer, or contemplation. This will be your worthy woman altar. I suggest placing
whatever sacred symbols or objects you have on your altar,
which can be as simple as a shelf, a table, or just a corner of
your bedroom. These symbols can be anything you are called
to for a specific reason. One symbol that is calling me currently is the dandelion; for me, it represents dreams travel-
ing from the spirit world to manifest in the material world.
When I see a dandelion, it's like a wink from the spirit world
indicating I'm on the right track. Right now, I have a drawing of a dandelion I've placed on my worthy woman altar to
remind me of this universal support.

I also like to have all four elements—water, earth, fire, and
air—represented on my altar, usually through things like a
bowl of water, fresh flowers, candles, and so on. I usually include photographs of beloved ancestors and loved ones, as
well as symbols of the qualities I'd like to bring more deeply
into my life, like love, purpose, and abundance. Feel into
what colors make you embrace your worthy woman, what
animals, what symbols, what stones. Make your worthy
woman altar feel like the most confident and empowered
version of you.

Once you've created your altar, take a seat. Light a candle
and read over the descriptions of each of the archetypes in
this chapter. Sit silently, perhaps with soft meditative music
playing in the background. As you read over the archetypes,
which one calls most strongly to you? This may be an archetype you're already familiar with or one that longs for you to
embody her at this time. Don't think—allow your heart to
feel it.

For the next twenty-eight days (from the new moon to the
full moon, or the full moon to the new moon, depending on
when you're reading this book), commit yourself to embody-

ing this archetype. Dress like she would, carry yourself as she would, interact with the world as she would, speak in her words. You may wish to place a symbol you associate with your chosen archetype on your altar and go to it every morning to ask for guidance on how you can bring more of her into your life. For example, if you're interested in embodying the Empress, you might place a rose or a picture of a rose on your altar. You might go to your altar every morning and say, "Great Goddess, please lead me to the people, places, and situations that will help to bring forth the Empress within me, so that I may offer love, beauty, and the gift of my sensual feminine nature in ways that bring me pleasure and abundance. Thank you."

Be sure to track any interesting epiphanies or discoveries that you make, especially around your own sense of connection to the divine feminine, as you draw your chosen archetype more intentionally into your life.

Ecstatic Experiences and Weaving the Sacred Back Into Your Life

One of the incredible aspects of having a connection to spirit is that it helps us recognize that we're so much more than we believe we are. The "materialist" view of reality is that only matter is real, that there is no other reality in a universe governed by the laws of physics and science. This can be a soul-crushing perspective, especially for those of us who have had the experience of dancing with spirit through myths, dreams, synchronicities, ecstatic dance, journeywork, and other ways of communing with the aliveness in all of existence. The nonmaterialist view of the universe is that everything is infused with the spirit of La Diosa, and that there is intelligence and consciousness in even the most mundane objects. I find that this mystical way of looking at our lives can provide us with a powerful sense of meaning, purpose, and guidance that helps us navigate the rough rapids and the calm tidepools with greater ease and an awareness of the bigger picture.

While many of us already have some kind of core belief in something that's bigger than us—whether we call it God, Goddess, universe, spirit, or something else—it is the deep mystical experiences of our lives that bring us into a tangible relationship with forces beyond our comprehension. A mystical experience gives us a powerful understanding of the meaning of existence, and it's usually connected to states of consciousness that help us to "see" ultimate truths that are otherwise not accessible in our daily lives.

In 2011, I had what's known as a kundalini awakening, a powerful and deeply visceral experience of the seven chakras (energy centers in the physical and subtle body) opening. It was a spontaneous eruption of sensation that included many physical and emotional transformations, as well as a deepened sense of purpose and destiny. Magical visions and experiences unfolded from this encounter with the great *shakti*—a Sanskrit word that means both "power" and "divine feminine"—that was moving through me. I could feel La Diosa in every cell of my being, and it was intense.

In truth, I don't share this with a lot of people. I have learned not to place too much meaning on this inexplicable experience, which was a gift from the universe that I still don't fully understand. As the Zen proverb goes, "After enlightenment, the laundry." I am less concerned with how to get to an ecstatic experience than I am with how we show up in our everyday lives. After all, I've met powerful spiritual teachers who were also addicts who had terrible relationships with their family members. This is why so many therapists and teachers talk about the importance of integration—which means to fold a mystical experience into the practical aspects of one's life.

Sometimes I meet people who are doing all kinds of things to "come face-to-face with God." I find myself asking: "Okay, but how do you show up in your life? How do you talk to yourself when no one's listening? How do you speak to others? Have you paid your bills? Have you had your annual checkup and gone to the dentist? How do you do the things that are seen as mundane but are actually the things that we're here to learn in this human experience?"

Many people are interested in using psychedelics and plant medicine to get a glimpse of a more expanded consciousness, without fully understanding the intensity of these experiences. I am not against this, although I don't do it myself, but I often find myself speaking to people who are lost, unhappy, and turning to psychedelics for the purpose of escape rather than connection to their daily lives.

For me, any intense mystical experience must be approached with a disclaimer. It can actually be quite dangerous to have a kundalini awakening if you're not integrating that experience with the help of a trained person to help you make sense of it (which I was grateful to have). In addition, the mystical path should be a lifelong one, in which we are not attempting to control what we do or don't encounter, or to place labels on our experiences as if one is better than another. When we're on a genuine spiritual path, we don't try to force anything; we allow the divine to take the wheel and show us what we are ready to see.

I was humbled by the experience of having the unseen literally move through my body, and to hear myself speaking in the language of light; all of it gave me more faith in the unseen. At the same time, the integration was intense. It took a great deal of time to recalibrate my nervous system to this new information. I was very lucky to have trained people around me to help me on this journey of using what I'd been given to heal my heart and mind, and to set me on the path of helping others.

Ultimately, our purpose as human beings is to connect to the web of life, not to use spirituality as an excuse to escape or to set ourselves apart from other beings. We are here to weave the sacred back into our lives on a daily basis—and exalted states of being can flow just as easily from singing to your baby, or making love, or cooking a beautiful meal, or spending time with your friends, or writing a poem. In fact, any one of these can lead to a state of feeling like you are in union with all of creation.

We connect with our true worthiness when we are willing to set up an ongoing dialogue with the divine right in the messiness of our life. Remember, she is not separate from us, and we don't have to reach outside ourselves by diving into some esoteric path or spending lots of money on something that will give us our next spiritual fix. Spirituality is meant to nourish us, not capture us in a spiral of compulsions that take us further from ourselves.

Trust yourself in terms of figuring out exactly what you need. But whatever you do, engage in practices that ground you in your life, bring you down to Earth, and allow you to feel your kinship with all beings.

Here are some of my favorite ways to weave the mundane into the sacred:

1. Work with a spiritual mentor or a spiritually trained counselor.

2. Develop a regular practice of prayer and meditation. This can be a beautiful way of connecting to the divinity

of your own understanding, whether it's your highest self, the voice of your soul, your guides, La Diosa, or anything else. This is about expressing connection to something beyond the limitations of personality and fear, so you can access another dimension of knowing and guidance.

3. At the end of the day, call back your energy from all space, time, and dimensions, so that you feel connected to your body and spirit. (A simple affirmation is enough: "I call my energy and power back from every person, place, thing, or situation where I may have left it or where it was taken. I call my power back now.")

4. Make a habit of writing down your dreams and acting on the wisdom they reveal.

5. Ask the universe for signs to lead you onto your path and purpose.

6. Call in La Diosa and any feminine archetypes that speak to you by embodying them in your daily life, knowing they are a part of you.

7. Spend as much time in nature as you possibly can.

8. Express gratitude for being alive, in this body, on this beautiful planet. As medieval theologian Meister Eckhart beautifully expressed it, "If the only prayer you ever say in your entire life is thank you, it will be enough."

9. Create daily, weekly, and monthly rituals for yourself—especially ones that include the four elements.

10. Connect to your creativity as a gateway to spirit—through singing, dancing, playing an instrument, writing poetry, etc.

✳ Worthy Affirmations ✳

◎ *I am worthy of divine connection, because the divine lives in me.*

◎ *I am always directly connected to spirit and to La Diosa.*

◎ *My body is a temple and a conduit for the great mysteries of the universe.*

◎ *The feminine face of the divine is in me, and I am in her.*

◎ *The universe supports me, and I am divinely guided.*

◎ *I surrender to divine flow, understanding that it reveals itself in my daily life.*

◎ *I am attuned to the whispers of my soul, and I understand that following them creates miracles.*

◎ *I find solace, strength, and peace in my personal spiritual practice—which comes from my intrinsic connection to my worth.*

You Are Worthy of Rest

*Rest, in its simplest form, becomes an act
of resistance and a reclaiming of power
because it asserts our most basic humanity.
We are enough.*

—Tricia Hersey

I ronically, I realized rest was a worthy and necessary priority only when it became harder to come by. As my responsibilities grew as a mother to a little one and as a matriarch of my family, I realized that no matter what was happening and what fires I was being asked to put out, I needed to rest—period. It was sustenance that my body and soul absolutely required.

Through some of my work with my spiritual teachers, I recognized that as much as we live in an overculture that defines "women's work" as mothering children and providing nurturance to their families, this is not work that is truly valued. I believe that mothering should be centered in our

culture, but it cannot come from the patriarchal, capitalist, colonizing mentality of constantly extracting labor from
women. The Goddess did not birth all of creation in order for
us to be incessant production machines.

In order to root into the feminine face of the divine, who
is responsible for connecting us to our essential worthiness,
we women must be cycle breakers and changemakers, not
just the selfless mamas who withstand backbreaking, soul-
depleting work in order to demonstrate our love. This is not
love; it is martyrdom. My teacher Aimee talks a lot about the
false conflation of *mother* with *martyr.* Too many mothers
are shouldering a disproportionate burden of unpaid work
as caretakers. Sadly, caretaking is not seen as the holy, sacred work of the future, which all genders should be joyfully
partaking in.

A culture of genuine care is a culture that honors the
power and importance of rest. If we deny our need for rest
and replenishment, what are we teaching our daughters and
the next generation of women? Beautiful diosa, you are not
a machine. You are Earth. You are nature. In the immortal
words of the Taoist sage Lao Tzu, "Nature does not hurry,
yet everything is accomplished." When we are running on
fumes, we create cycles of dysfunction and martyrdom. Of
course, although I've always known this to be true in my
heart of hearts, it hasn't always been easy for me to live accordingly. Mom guilt is a real thing—and loving my daughter
so fiercely means it's often hard for me to separate from her
for any period of time. This makes it even harder to rest. I
adore being with her, nursing her, mothering her, and holding all of her big emotions with such devotion and compassion. I *live* to mother her. But I came to see that, in order to be
my best self for her, I must also nurture me.

The task of filling up with our own innate worthiness

is all about mothering ourselves. Mothering myself meant creating space to rest, to intentionally regulate my nervous system. And so I learned to weave rest into my life—because everything in my world, including the well-being of my loved ones, relies on it.

I encourage you to read this chapter with a candle by your side and your favorite cozy blanket, or take it to the park or your favorite café. Allow yourself to nurture *you* as you reclaim one of the most important birthrights we have: rest. So often, we are accustomed to absorbing information as we are multitasking, but the invitation here is to make this a sacred practice that allows you to soak up the energy of rest. Because you, my love, are worthy of rest.

You Are Not Your Job

With the start of the industrial revolution in the eighteenth century, we've become a culture that's obsessed with work and turning a profit. We live in a society that glorifies and emphasizes the importance of the hustle, of constant productivity, of giving our energy to our employer (or our own business, if we're self-employed), without rest. The American Dream instills aspirations of material wealth and abundance in us, which we are taught to strive for unless we want to be relegated to the bottom of the barrel. If we have children, we're often enjoined to hustle even harder, so we can give them all the things we never had.

But what do we lose in the process? A 2022 survey from Mental Health America and FlexJobs found that 76 percent of their respondents agreed that workplace stress impacts their mental health; 75 percent reported burnout, a state of being that involves exhaustion, feeling as though your accomplishments don't matter, and feeling disconnected from yourself. Another study reports that burnout is on the rise among everyone, with two demographics at an even higher risk: women and Gen Z.

As in most cases, women of color are impacted disproportionately by the dire state of things. Women of color face multiple barriers in the workplace—including lower wages, workplace microaggressions, and barriers to wealth accumulation and career advancement. Moreover, women represent about two-thirds of the workforce in the lowest-paid jobs—and in that group, Latinas, Black women, and Indigenous women are overrepresented. Income inequality due to factors like systemic racism, high inflation, and stagnant wages has made people feel like they need to be running just to keep up.

We know that sleep deprivation is one of the impacts of burnout; at least a third of adults aren't getting the sleep they need, and women often struggle with sleep more than men do. This is associated with a series of chronic illnesses and disorders, including type 2 diabetes, depression, and heart disease. We are slowly killing ourselves in our attempts to keep up with the Joneses, or simply to keep our heads above water.

Americans in particular are plagued by a centuries-old Puritan work ethic that tells us we need to embrace struggle and toil in order to prove our devotion and steadfastness. Loyalty to one's livelihood has replaced a sense of loyalty to the inner compass connecting us to the divine. We see this when people humblebrag about just how goddamn "busy" they are, or when they flex over getting only a couple hours of sleep. "I'll sleep when I'm dead" is a convenient way to make light of the basic physiological and psychoemotional need for rest. We are a culture whose basic sense of worth is rooted in productivity; even if these ideas aren't part of our own value system, it's impossible not to feel just a little guilty if we decide to take a sick day just because we're tired and could use a few "idle" hours to ourselves.

What's more, all that hard work rarely brings us the promised rewards of wealth and ease, because we don't live in a meritocracy and 1 percent of the U.S. population hoards about a third of the nation's wealth. Yet we keep striving, inundated by ads that tell us we'd be sexier, happier, smarter, more carefree, if we only bought this gadget, that luxury good, or that item of clothing (usually from an ecologically ruinous fast-fashion chain that exploits its workers). We become indentured servants to jobs we might hate just to pay off the debt we accrued to buy a bunch of stuff we most likely don't need. On top of that, our broken healthcare system chains us to jobs that don't meet our deep need for purpose; we can't quit, or we wouldn't be able to afford insurance—and if we're not healthy, we can't keep being "productive"!

It's a vicious cycle, and there are so many factors to blame for why we overwork ourselves, many of them systemic in nature. I also know that the specter of intergenerational poverty hangs over many of us. I have a number of first-generation clients who were often the "first" to do things like go to college, start a business, get a mortgage—and there's so much pressure (some of it self-imposed) to "perform" success. A lot of times, this comes from a scarcity mentality that's been around for decades.

One of my clients told me, "I'm afraid that if I slow down, the paychecks will stop coming and I'll be out on the street. I know it's irrational, but I grew up in a financially unstable household, where my parents were often unemployed and we were periodically on welfare and food stamps. Even though I'm really stable now, I learned from a young age that the hustle had to be constant if you wanted to make something of yourself. And no matter how good things are now, you have to prepare for a downturn, which means you can't just take a break and rest."

The level of hypervigilance she described to me is something I'm absolutely familiar with. Often, it comes from a lack of trust that things will be okay if we rest. Who'll get everything done? Who's gonna put out the fires? We're so unused to the idea that the universe has our back that we don't fill our own cups with the elixir of rest and self-care before we try to help others. Often, we just don't think we're worthy of rest because the world hasn't shown us that it'll take care of our needs. But as a lot of people find when they end up with chronic illness as a result of stress and overwork, our bodies are not machines—they will break down if we keep doing, doing, doing, without rest or rejuvenation.

The overculture doesn't want us to rest, of course. It doesn't want us to redirect our energy to self-care, leisure, or connection with ourselves and our families. It wants us to serve the nameless master of capitalism and to give up our autonomy, our time, our energy, for the hollow promise of success. However, the Worthy Revolution is asking more of us. We must embrace rest as an integral aspect of our journey toward wholeness and worthiness. It's in our power to undo toxic patterns around work, overwork, and productivity at the expense of our humanity.

Rest as a Feminine Birthright

Tricia Hersey, author of the incredible book *Rest Is Resistance: A Manifesto*, says, "When you slowly begin to believe and understand your inherent worth, rest becomes possible in many ways." She also says, "Productivity should not look like exhaustion. The concept of laziness is a tool of the oppressor. A large part of your unraveling from capitalism will include becoming less attached to the idea of productivity and more committed to the idea of rest as a portal to just be."

Hersey is the founder of the radical Nap Ministry, an organization that arose from her experiments with rest as a tool for liberation and healing. As a Black woman in America suffering from intergenerational exhaustion and racial trauma, Hersey discovered that naps and rest were not only rejuvenating—they were lifesaving. Today, she upholds rest as a way of bringing us into a deeper mind/body/spirit connection, as many of us are disconnected from ourselves because of the grind culture espoused by capitalism. Importantly, she and other BIPOC women are spreading the message that so many of us have known deep in our bones but are only now beginning to say out loud: As women and femmes, we don't need to *earn* rest—we must reclaim it as our birthright.

We are taught that we must go, go, go, at any cost. This is clearly reflected in the ways that the United States treats women and families postpartum. They are typically expected to go back to work ten to twelve weeks after giving birth, and sometimes even sooner. As advanced as the United States is, it's one of few countries with no national paid parental leave. This failure in federal policy means that 100 million people, or 80 percent of workers, have no paid time off after the birth or adoption of a child. In March 2023, the Bureau of Labor Statistics reported that about 27 percent of civilian workers had access to paid family leave, and 90 percent had access to unpaid family leave.

How absurd is it that after the remarkable initiation of giving life, women are not held and tended to in the ways they deserve? It infuriates me, as it should all of us if we're paying attention. I believe any system that doesn't provide resources, including financial ones, to women and families postpartum should be charged with reckless endangerment.

The political conversation is often embroiled in the debate around abortion, but the "pro-life" contingent has little to say about the egregious ways that families (especially mothers and small children) are treated. They have little to say about the ways that women's bodies are conveniently exploited to create yet another worker and "productive citizen." They have little to say about how women's bodies need to be honored through the sacred rite of passage that is birth—and how every soul birthed into the world should not have to "earn" their right to proper care and equitably distributed resources. The lack of meaningful discourse about this makes my mama heart weep and scream, especially as I hear the cries of all the women who never got to rest, to be held, or to nurture their infant in the way they needed to.

For when a child is born, a mother is born. Both are learning together and must be held in the sacred embrace of a culture that cares about this elemental bond. Instead, we are inundated with stories of miraculous "bounce backs"—actresses, models, and social media influencers often share their unattainable stories about working out, regaining their prepregnancy body, and getting back to work. It's mind-boggling to see women bragging about their capacity to move past what is inarguably one of the most exhausting and powerful initiations imaginable: the passage from maiden to mother.

Of course, this isn't to malign women who deeply desire to return to the workforce after their children's birth—not at all. However, I believe that we all have the right to that choice—and that periods of intentional rest can help us to better make that decision. We must also be encouraged to lean in to the decisions that are the most life-giving, mother-centered, and family-centered, for they will determine our future. There is nothing wrong with valuing our work, but if it is the sole determinant of our worth, it brings us to a death that is equal parts physical, emotional, and spiritual.

I have noticed that even in so-called progressive workplaces, employers who might appear understanding on the surface are ultimately committed to the bottom line. Many of us fall for the idea that our work colleagues and managers are our "family," which is how so many women are guilted and shamed into giving their all, even though they are essentially disposable—replaceable workers in an economy that values productivity, not souls.

Dear one, I want you to know that you must resist the urge to buy into the belief that the system is here to support you. In truth, it is here to obey the imperatives of capitalism—to use you and suck you dry. But that doesn't mean rest is an impossibility. We must claim our right to it with greater rigor, power, and fire—especially when it comes to fighting for BIPOC women and women whose socioeconomic circumstances have them working around the clock. Trauma, racism, and misogyny intersect in ways that stunt our connection to our true power. But to connect to true power, we need to be resourced enough that it feels safe to go inward. For many of us, it isn't.

My grandmother (whom I call my Gega) worked in a factory, where she made very little money, but she worked her ass off in order to ensure that her children, my father and uncle, had food on the table and clothes on their back. In addition to her factory job, she took care of an elderly woman and cleaned her home, doing what little she could to earn money. I remember how impactful it was for me when I got a chance to see her rest. She loved her plants and still does (in the moment of writing this book, my Gega is ninety-four years old). She would often take time to sing to her plants. Her entire apartment in Bushwick, Brooklyn, was filled with plants and flowers. It was an urban jungle.

The owner of the house, Carl, had a backyard with a fig tree, so my Gega would go pick the figs and we would eat them together. Plant medicine flourished around us. I loved hearing her sing, as we dug our fingers into the earthy figs and she drank her morning cafecito, frothy with warm milk. Her nervous system rested, and so did mine. Though she didn't get to rest often in her life, having left Puerto Rico at a young age to live in New York City, where the hustle was constant, I am grateful that she got a chance to soak up all of her favorite things when she was older. Those moments were sacred for me, and they gave me a strong sense of what is truly valuable: joyful leisure time spent with family members. It helps me to remember that every single one of us is worthy of rest, and we are so much more than our productivity.

UNWORTHY LIE:
My value lies in my ability to work, be productive, earn money, and "contribute" to society through these efforts.

WORTHY TRUTH:
My contribution to society far exceeds my perceived value in the eyes of capitalism. My body is a divine vessel that deserves the rejuvenating power of rest—which helps me establish a deeper connection to myself, my family, and the world.

Overgiving and Boundaries

Women often shoulder the burden of housework and "mental" tasks, like setting up doctor's appointments for their partner, creating grocery lists, reading the kids a bedtime story, managing a family's social life, and acting as the go-to counselor for family members and other loved ones. This domestic/emotional labor, at its core, is about putting other people's feelings and needs ahead of our own—and women are conditioned to be masters of this.

Unfortunately, because this labor is unpaid, it is devalued by our profit-focused capitalist society, even though it is fundamental to the sense of connection, belonging, community, and nurturing we get. In fact, in order for anyone to truly be successful at work, they need to be receiving a fair share of someone else's labor at home. Their domestic and emotional needs must be met in order for them to "get it done."

I am not suggesting that there's anything wrong with domestic labor, but the fact that it is disproportionately placed on women's shoulders and not in the least valued in our society points to a big problem.

I recall talking to a client who was telling me that although she and her husband both work full-time, and she is the breadwinner in the family, she does all the household chores and the work of caring for their five-year-old son. She came to me, sleep-deprived and depressed, and when I asked her what her husband was doing to support her, she gave me a blank stare.

"Support me? He doesn't. The way things are—it's just not something we've even questioned or talked about."

I gently pressed her to tell me why she'd never thought about it before. She paused for a moment before answering,

"I just always saw the women in my family taking care of business without complaining or expecting gratitude. It just seemed like the thing we did to show our family we care about them."

"I get it, but why are you the one who's expected to put your family first without any reciprocity?"

Her brow furrowed as she thought about it. "I've always been a feminist and believed in women's rights, but somehow I don't have a good answer for that," she sheepishly admitted.

We're just modeling what we learned. How many of us women are doing exactly the same thing: going along with inequitable standards without feeling we have the right to demand more? I see this showing up a lot in the way that women tend to overgive in their relationships, sometimes without being explicitly asked to. Men who grow up under patriarchy, even if they call themselves feminists or say they see women as equals, often unconsciously depend on women to meet the role of "helpmate," resorting to weak excuses like "Well, she's better at all that stuff than I am." Often, women do these thankless tasks, even if they don't really want to, because we have a martyr culture that teaches us that overgiving means we're nice and setting boundaries means we're mean.

In order to rest, we must learn to set healthy boundaries that honor our emotional capacity. For many of us, we don't even know what our capacity is, because we don't pause to ask ourselves or feel worthy of checking in with our mind, our body, our spirit.

When I suggested to the aforementioned client that perhaps it was time to set boundaries with her husband around what she was no longer willing to do in their relationship, she was reluctant at first. "I don't want to be overly rigid, because marriage is supposed to be a compromise. I grew up feeling that setting boundaries was selfish because it was all about putting yourself first and not giving the other person a say," she said.

"What if you changed your definition of boundaries?" I asked. "Boundaries are about defining what you will and won't accept. They're not meant to control or change anyone else, but to care for yourself. What if you framed your boundaries to your husband that way?"

Although it took several months of close and honest communication, she was able to set boundaries with her husband that changed the basis of their relationship. As a result, he also started to look at some of the ways in which he'd internalized patriarchal "rules" about the division of labor at home. But this meant they both had to be willing to have the hard conversations—and for her in particular, it meant she had to be willing to prioritize self-care and moments of pause. Talking through all of this created a more solid and supportive foundation for her marriage, even though it was scary at first.

Many women resign themselves to just giving everything they can in a relationship, sacrificing their voice, their self-respect, and their worth in the process. It's time to begin embracing the discomfort of a new way forward so that we can create a new status quo that truly values our time, energy, and labor—and that lets us see rest as a necessity rather than an optional reward.

Worthy Work: Setting Appropriate Boundaries

I want us each right here and now to give ourselves permission to check in with our own needs and desires—with our mind, body, and spirit—so that we know our true capacity before saying yes to anything. Setting boundaries requires that we get really clear about our yes and our no, which means taking a pause to attune to ourselves. You can do the following ritual to help you set healthy boundaries for yourself in all your relationships.

1. Remember the worthy woman altar you built in Chapter 3? Take some time to sit before it and breathe deeply for about five minutes, allowing the mind and body to quiet down.

2. Place your hand on any part of your body that allows you to feel connected to your truth. For me, it varies by day. Sometimes I place one hand on my throat and one hand on my heart; other days, it's one hand on my womb and one hand on my heart. Feel into where you are called to land in your body today. Then take a deep and nourishing breath. Allow the shoulders to gently rest; sit up straight, spine elongated, but with a sense of easeful flow in your body. Give yourself the space to ground your feet into the floor and inhale deeply for three counts; then exhale through your mouth with a sigh. Repeat until you feel yourself soften.

3. Imagine that there's a beautiful cloak of light around you. It automatically opens when you are safe and tightens around you when you aren't. Spend some time imagining scenarios where the cloak is open and where it's closed. You'll get a very strong sense in your body for when the cloak is open and closed, and you'll want to pay attention when you feel those sensations in the future. Jot down some notes in your journal that will help you remember.

4. Now think of a situation in your life—at work, in a relationship, etc. Notice where the cloak of light is when you consider this situation. Is it closed or open?

5. If it's closed around you, consider that this is your body's way of telling you that you are at a no. Write down five specific ways you can set a loving boundary in this situation (e.g., by shutting down your computer after five p.m. every day). Now put those things in your calendar and commit to doing them. You got this, diosa!

Increasing Your Capacity to Rest

A lot of the women I work with are Latina powerhouses. They are *strong*. They have gone through the unthinkable and have still chosen to rise above it all. To most outside observers, they have all their shit together. But I often find myself asking, "What if this keeps you from getting your needs met?" Sometimes they're confused about what I'm saying, so I clarify that "having it together" is a kind of mask.

"Lots of us keep that mask on so tight, it becomes like a second skin," I say. "But what if we need to unravel, to remove the mask, in order to heal? Look, I get it—I was taught that unraveling makes me weak, and it took me years to let myself go there. But I learned that when I let myself unravel, I could finally arrive in the lap of the Great Mother, who's always there to give me comfort and hold me deep as the roots of the trees."

Many of them have never stopped to consider that it's okay to put down their responsibilities—that the world won't stop if they take time to rest. In fact, rest is how we remember we are both divine and human. Our bodies need rest to dream, to restore, to heal, and to reconnect with the parts of our life that mean the most to us (including work!). Rest is needed to recalibrate, to dream, to reimagine what we want our lives to be and look like. Rest is needed to relax our nervous system—which is too often accustomed to being on high alert, making our efforts less effective than they could otherwise be. I say this with the utmost love: We need to slow the fuck down, otherwise we won't be able to fully integrate the realizations we're making. We need more time for music, for nature, for naps, for digesting our food, for spending leisure time with loved ones.

Unfortunately, a lot of us define ourselves on the basis of our busyness, on what we're doing, working on, and producing. We tend to worry that having some downtime means we're lazy. But in truth, as scientists have found, chilling out on the constant activity can activate parts of the brain that are important in our everyday functions.

For example, several parts of the brain work together in what is called the default mode network (DMN), which is linked to memories, daydreaming, creativity, and our overall sense of self—and it gets activated when we're awake but at rest, not paying attention to external tasks. In other words, there's a benefit to simply being with ourselves instead of focusing on problem-solving and engaging in a swarm of activities. When we slow down, the DMN is activated—and so is our ability to heal, to be creative, to understand ourselves, and to reconnect to who we are. Incredibly, the DMN is also connected to intuition and the ability to accurately read situations and predict outcomes. Researchers have suggested three powerful ways to strengthen the DMN: naps (ideally ninety minutes long, but even fifteen minutes is beneficial), positive constructive daydreaming (*not* ruminating on trauma or fantasizing about changing the past), and exercise (particularly "aimless" free-walking).

Overall, engaging in activities that aren't connected to productivity can be a wonderful way for spirit to come forth. Rest offers us a sacred space for feeling divine guidance, a place to daydream and to incubate nighttime dreams that heal our subconscious and transmit powerful messages. Rest allows spiritual downloads to flow, for when we allow ourselves to pause, we can distinctly hear the messages our soul is always sending our way. It is in moments of rest that clarity and guidance have the space to pour in. When we are still, we can receive.

Worthy Work:
Your Rest Plan

Take some time to journal on the following questions:

1. What are the stories in your family that were filled with overwork and burnout? What messages did you receive about overwork?

2. What are the stories in your own life that are filled with overwork and burnout? What messages are you acting out in your life about overwork?

3. What are the stories in your family that were filled with rest and relaxation? What messages did you receive about rest?

4. What are the stories in your own life that are filled with rest and relaxation? In what ways are you willing to welcome and reclaim rest and relaxation?

Next I want to encourage you to take a moment to dream of what it would feel like to make rest a part of your life. Perhaps it's going to sleep earlier, taking a daily nap, listening to a relaxing song during lunch, singing to plants in your home, dancing, meditating, daydreaming, self-massage, or easy-to-watch TV (like reality TV or *Sex and the City*, which can be therapeutic in small doses!).

Now write out at least five actionable ways you'll integrate rest, and then schedule time in your calendar (through the next month, six months, and year) to ensure that you carry out this plan. I usually say that if it's not in your calendar, it's less likely to happen. I also highly recommend carving out at least a day each month to rest, daydream, and give yourself the gift of deep nourishment. I will often do this around my menstrual cycle, so that I can give my body an opportunity to sync up with this powerful time of energetic release. Rest can truly become a way of life, but first you have to welcome it!

☀ Worthy Affirmations ☀

◎ *My body is a divine vessel that I pause to fill with self-care and rejuvenation.*

◎ *I am worthy of rest.*

◎ *Resting is resetting—it helps me tap into healing and joy.*

◎ *Rest restores me to my highest soul self.*

◎ *I take the time to attend to all dimensions of myself.*

◎ *I am so much more than what I can do and produce.*

◎ *I set self-loving boundaries that honor the temple of my body, mind, and spirit.*

5

You Are Worthy of Abundance

Some of the things we have received don't belong to us and some of the things we want to give to the future—to leave as legacy—have never been experienced yet . . . We get to be the ones to choose. To look at what is happening, to get in there, to feel into our bodies and create something new.

—Bliss Mother

What is abundance? Abundance is fullness, it's overflow, it's joy. Abundance is the Earth and all the seeds being planted around the world, the water and sun that nourish our planet and the fruits that fall and the flowers that blossom. It's family, health, prosperity. It is the very nature of our infinitely creative cosmos.

Somewhere along the way of receiving the bounty of our planet, of existence itself, we humans came to develop a scarcity mentality that still fills us with feelings of anxiety, of "not-enoughness," of believing that we need to prove our worth in order to receive the plentiful gifts of our Great

Mother. This is nonsense—a skewed way of viewing our place within a universe that is constantly transmitting signals to us that we get to have exactly what we need, when we need it. It is a perspective that has also been hastened by the rise of wealth inequality, as well as excessive overconsumption that comes from a place of fear that we won't get "ours." But abundance is not about buying things we don't need and filling our homes with items that will help us keep up with the Joneses. It's about tapping into a frequency of energy that is connected to love, trust, generosity—and, yes, to our very sense of worthiness.

So many diosas I work with have made great strides when it comes to upping their abundance game, coming to terms with their scarcity mentality, and recognizing that all of us deserve to be prosperous and to live our lives with all the inner and outer resources that will sustain and nourish us. However, many of us continue to have issues with money—feeling we don't have enough, or feeling ambivalent about whether we deserve it, or worrying about whether it's even "moral" to want it.

When I first started out as an entrepreneur, I didn't have a lot of support as far as money went. Although my family helped me with financial aid through my undergraduate years, I had to be creative when it came to figuring out how to make an income as I built my business. I learned from an early age that I had to be the one to invest in me.

I did my best to make my dream come true of serving a larger number of women through the community I was building, which would offer sisterhood and actionable tools for helping others step into and claim their true worth. I knew that spirit had placed this dream inside my heart so I could bring it to life. I knew I'd eventually make money, but I wasn't under the impression that it would happen right away. Some things that are meant to be take time, just as a seed takes time to grow and requires care and nourishment along the way.

I was patient with my process, but I was also working on healing my mindset around money and breaking out of the old paradigm that said I had to struggle. I created a series of vision boards of what I wanted, which included images and pictures of the things I wanted to bring forth. I also kept a notebook that I called my "magic pill book." I would write down affirmations connected to what I desired, such as: "I am a six-figure Latina business owner making massive impact and ripples of change in the world."

I was so clear that none of this was just about making money—it was about making an impact. It was about breaking free from the cycles of not having a lot and acquiescing to the untruth that Latina women can't be wealthy. There was something inside me that knew I had to be an example of breaking free from this kind of poverty and wealth block, which I was so accustomed to, growing up in a family where we struggled with money. I knew it was possible to center my values and still make money.

Aside from my magic pill book, I routinely made lists of all the things I could do to make money so that my consciousness wouldn't freak out in the absence of a steady paycheck. As human beings, we must be grounded; we have to pay bills and put food on the table, so it's important to put our minds to rest with reminders that we have what it takes to care for ourselves! In fact, I made a list of a hundred different ways to make money, which ranged from walking dogs, to working at a coffee shop, to coaching clients on how to bust through their own mental blocks. This opened up my creative capacity in my subconscious mind, which meant I could chill and accept the flow of abundance in my life, since I'd already identified so many pathways for it!

I did the practical work, and I also did the spiritual work. I would set up altars dedicated to abundance, do my archetypal work, and invite pure source energy into my energetic and physical field, so that I could embody my new mindset. Of course, along with mind shifting and action steps, I also realized that so much of what it's possible to experience is dependent on being born in the right place at the right time. We are powerful beings, and we are also subject to the systems in which we live. I take advantage of the fact that I was born in the United States. Not everyone has this privilege, which I do not take for granted for a second. Those of us who do have this privilege can access abundance not for the purpose of feeding our egos (something the wounded, colonized self wants us to do, because it's under the mistaken belief that it's the only way we can feel worthy), but for giving back to the world around us.

Throughout this chapter, we'll explore many of our deeply ingrained ideas about money, which are cultural, social, familial, and based on our own personal experiences. I believe that this work of opening up to true abundance is for anyone, no matter where they are, no matter their circumstances. The more we lean in to abundance, the more we can generate creative solutions for working with its flow. But of course, while money is one form of abundance, it is not the only one. To that end, we'll explore the many faces of abundance, and how we can tap into the wellspring of abundance that exists at the heart of nature. Remember, we are all manifestations of nature, and when we approach life from an unshakable center that knows its true worth, we tap into our own generative manifesting powers.

Distinguishing Between Capitalism and Abundance

One of the major things I notice in my clients and community members is that, beyond the fearful beliefs many of them have about money and abundance—which range from "I have to work so hard for so little" to "Money is something that needs to be saved, not something I can use to enjoy my life"—is one nagging idea that I think needs to be teased out, for the sake of further understanding. That idea is that money is the root of all evil.

It's an especially difficult one to contend with because it creates cognitive dissonance for us. Most of us understand that we need money in order to care for ourselves and our loved ones, and to experience comfort and a sense that we are taken care of. However, it's hard to square this with the belief that mo' money leads to mo' problems. My clients are savvy and conscientious, so I'm used to hearing them express guilt over "wanting more money, because I know other people have so little, and the world is so unfair." And certainly there's something to be said for the fact that wealth inequality has only increased— and with the extraction of the planet's resources and the greedy and callous behavior of the über-rich, the idea that money breeds power and power breeds corruption seems pretty spot-on when we look at the world around us. Sometimes it seems like we're under a spell of overconsumption that makes us feel even more separate from our foundational worth.

But here's the thing: Money itself isn't bad. It's simply a system of exchange that defines the perceived value of goods and services. In spiritual terms, it's just energy that symbolizes the flow of material and other resources. It requires consensus and cooperation, which are really awesome things! In other words, money isn't the enemy in and of itself.

The thing that a lot of people have understandable beef with is our current system of capitalism, which has contributed to so much rampant wealth hoarding and concentration of resources in the hands of a few. A general mindset behind this economic system is that greed is a good thing because it drives profits and innovation. While this may be true, it's also true that those profits and innovation don't benefit everyone equally, because capitalism depends on worker exploitation to fatten the wallets of the extremely wealthy 1 percent at the expense of the 99 percent. Many Americans are essentially wage slaves who are forced to sell their labor without being able to negotiate a livable wage. The laboring classes comprise predominantly BIPOC and women, who remain in a vicious cycle of poverty through the generations. Today, about 11.5 percent of all Americans live in poverty, despite our country's vast wealth.

All of us have seen the human cost of capitalism's thirst for profit. It depletes people of a sense of power, agency, and joy. It has led to a healthcare and environmental crisis, and it's thrown millions of people into debt.

What does this state of affairs have to do with abundance? Everything! Capitalism has often been mixed up with abundance, because it provides plentiful cheap goods and consumer choices. But that's not the same as true abundance, which, in spiritual traditions around the world, is about community, mutual care, generosity, and sufficiency. Abundance is about having and being enough, not about being able to buy whatever you want whenever you want it. It's about the harmonious flow of resources in and out of our lives. Abundance is about a deeper internal security that gives us the confidence to both give and receive, and to recognize that we ourselves are like a flow-through, a conduit of nature's goodness.

A lot of discourse about abundance is still overly focused

on the "bottom line." Even in spaces that are supposedly spiritual, there might be a focus on making money at the expense of cultivating relationships. Even the ways that people sell their services or goods are focused on reminding people of their "pain points," insecurities, or even just fear of missing out on a good deal. Capitalism preys on a fear of scarcity that probably lives in our genes: that we are not enough, so we will not have enough. Some of the most successful advertising campaigns target this primal human fear, which is intimately connected to our feelings of worthiness.

As I encourage so many of my clients and community members, we have to be careful about the way corporations and industries count on our fear of scarcity in order to exploit us, convincing us that everything we want is running out: our time, our health, our vitality, our intelligence, our opportunities. But, hey, here's a product or gadget that'll temporarily help you feel you've got everything under control . . . that is, until the next time you find yourself nursing feelings of unworthiness that might cause you to splurge on something you don't need. Author and activist Alexis Pauline Gumbs has quipped, "You could say that's like one tagline for capitalism. 'Capitalism: Because your life is scarce.'"

Again, we are all subject to the systems in which we live, which is why such a big part of the Worthy Revolution is all about reclaiming abundance. We might be living under capitalism, but we don't have to buy into its lies. We can—at least to some extent—resist its exploitation and make ethical decisions around the kinds of companies we do business with as well as what we are doing for a living. Does it contribute to the greater good? Does it rely on the exploitation of the planet or other human beings?

Abundance is all about realizing that we live on a planet that continues to generously care for all our needs, even though industries and governments might fool many of us into believing that we have to "earn" the right to meet those needs. I know a lot of people who are translating abundance into a strong relationship with the land. They're taking time to build community gardens, grow their own food, and share it with others—to demonstrate that we don't need to remain dependent on systems that don't ultimately care about our well-being. Although so much more work needs to be done to address the inequitable distribution of resources, we have to begin seeing that our anxiety about scarcity is something that's used to prey upon us . . . to keep us small and lost in fabricated stories of our own unworthiness.

Instead of being consumers inside a system that is perfectly okay with chewing us up and spitting us out, we can connect with the abundance inside and outside of us to become greater creators and collaborators with nature.

UNWORTHY LIE:
I will never have what I need in order to feel prosperous and well cared for.

WORTHY TRUTH:
Who I am is something that is so much bigger than the systems around me. I am intrinsically a part of the abundance of the universe and have all I need.

+

The Faces of Abundance

We can't tap into abundance until we confront our feelings and stories about scarcity. A scarcity mindset is characterized by the belief that we don't have enough resources, internal or external, to meet our needs. It can manifest in the fear of living from paycheck to paycheck (which many Americans and people around the world do) or the belief that no matter what we do, we'll never be able to exist with comfort and ease—we have to stay on our toes, in case of the next crisis or recession.

The scarcity mindset is often accompanied by either over-consumption or a sense of denial and deprivation (often, the same person can swing between both extremes). The thing I find so sad is that the scarcity mindset doesn't exist only among those who are truly living in poverty. It exists in the middle class, and even among the wealthy. I've met many well-to-do people who still wear clothing that's decades old, who save useless appliances, and who pinch pennies in order to feel secure—and this comes from a place of self-denial, not joy. This is not true abundance.

Many metaphysical teachers describe abundance as a flow of energy—and when we are tightly holding on to our resources instead of sharing them freely, we tamp down on the flow of energy. It's almost like we're creating a kink in a garden hose to keep the water from freely flowing, in an attempt to take it all back for ourselves. But when we do this, we're not actually storing up more water, we're just preventing ourselves from watering the garden of our abundance.

There are lots of reasons for a scarcity mindset that go beyond our individual experiences. For example, financial trauma (which may be intergenerational), a history of poverty, media that conflates what one has with who one is, and societal expectations about what our lives "should" look like can contribute to the kind of despair that makes us feel like we don't have enough . . . or that we ourselves just aren't enough.

As we learned in Chapter 2, we have the power to break generational cycles by choosing to do things differently, and this is just as true in the arena of abundance as it is in the arena of peace. First of all, we must start questioning the voices and forces that keep us under the toxic spell of believing that we'll never be "enough": not pretty enough, not smart enough, not wise enough, not confident enough, not rich enough, not young enough, and the list goes on. Enough is enough!

I think that, rather than swinging between the extremes of deprivation and self-indulgence, what we really want to aim for is sufficiency. Sufficiency means that we are enough and we have enough. It means that we don't project our sense of unworthiness out into the world or use it as an excuse to act irresponsibly. It's not about cutting down every tree in the forest so we can have shelter; it's about working with the sacred reciprocity of nature, which gives so generously and also replenishes its supply. It's our task to respect this.

Sufficiency is about learning to recognize that abundance exists in so many diverse forms. When we live intentionally from our inner worthy woman, we understand this and start to take actions and form new beliefs that coincide with our new understanding of abundance. This can look a lot of different ways, such as:

* Empowering ourselves to learn about our finances and build our wealth from a stable base, instead of succumbing to cycles of "feast and famine"
* Interrogating the beliefs conveyed by our language around abundance (e.g., instead of saying, "I'm broke," you might say, "I'm choosing to put my resources toward something else right now")
* Actively choosing where to spend our resources (which include not just money, but also time, energy, and attention) rather than feeling "compelled" by external forces

* Enjoying the gifts of nature by getting our hands into the dirt, growing food, or simply spending more time in beautiful natural environments where we can start to see sacred reciprocity at work
* Engaging in community mutual aid—a collaborative model in which people exchange resources and services for the benefit of all community members, and to meet one another's needs with what we already have
* Having "no spend" days when we immerse ourselves in what we love (e.g., walks in the park, cooking with friends, going to museums on "free" days)
* Creating something with your hands from items you might already have (e.g., a scrapbook, a piece of art, a culinary dish)
* Making something to give to someone else (remember, abundance is currency, and we are always giving and receiving—the trick is to be conscious of this when it's happening, and to be more intentional about the energy we're putting out and taking in)
* Paying it forward—that is, repaying the kindness you receive by offering it to someone else (e.g., paying for the groceries of the person in line behind you, making a donation on behalf of someone else)

Please feel free to add to this list of suggestions. I honestly feel that it's medicine for the soul when we start to tap into the many faces of abundance. It teaches us to move beyond our scarcity-based beliefs and to connect to a well of self-replenishing joy that already lives inside us.

For example, one of my clients was struggling to find work. She had a very specialized skill set, and there were literally fewer than a hundred people in her particular industry—so when she left her job due to mismanagement by the organization's leaders, she found herself in a painful and isolated place, where she constantly questioned her worth and wondered if she'd ever find gainful employment again. At some point, she realized that she needed to get out of the rut she was in, so she started volunteering at a community garden in Brooklyn. Over time, she made lots of new friends, many of whom encouraged her newfound passion for sustainability and ecology. One afternoon, after bringing home an assortment of flowers, fruits, and vegetables from the garden, she looked at her table, covered in nature's bounty, and burst into tears of gratitude.

"It was like I was seeing the rainbow of abundance in front of me, and it hit me for the first time that I was always taken care of, even if it didn't always feel like it," she explained. "I was overwhelmed by gratitude. For the first time in a long time, I felt . . . full. Like I had more than enough to sustain me, and I didn't actually need anything more."

She ended up changing careers and now works with a nonprofit that encourages communities across the country to build gardens where residents can learn to grow their own food and embrace sustainability as a way of life that helps them to collectively reenvision their neighborhoods as places where they can plant the seeds for everyone's highest potential.

I loved my client's observation about accessing the "rainbow of abundance," especially because it helped her connect to a worthiness she hadn't felt in so long. Nature gave her a beautiful and much-needed reminder that she could start to use her "currency" with the utmost respect and care, recognizing that it reflects the natural laws of the universe. As a result, she started to really get that abundance goes beyond material wealth, status, and other people's perceptions of us. It's about our connection to our own aliveness, to nature, to community, to the love and vitality that are our own inner spring of aliveness. From this place, miracles happen. We stop fixating on the matter of whether we have enough or are enough—it becomes self-evident that this is the wrong thing to focus on, because it's based on lies. Instead, we let ourselves receive the beauty that is already always surrounding us, which changes our perspectives and invites new possibilities that start to mirror our inner worthiness.

Worthy Work:
From Scarcity to Abundance

For this exercise, spend some time at your worthy woman altar and journal on the following questions:

1. What were some of the things I learned from my family of origin about scarcity?

2. What did I learn about abundance?

3. How did these perspectives impact my life as an adult, and the ways I give and receive?

4. Where in my life do I feel abundance?

5. Where do I feel scarcity, doubt, and disbelief that I can have what I want?

6. What are some of the things I most appreciate in my life?

7. What are some of the things I take for granted?

8. What are three tangible things I can do to welcome abundance into my life?

After taking time to journal, sit in silence for five to ten minutes, acknowledging all the abundance you already have. This might feel challenging if you're going through a rough time, but it's when the going gets tough that your inner worthy woman has the opportunity to open more deeply to true abundance.

Visualize yourself surrounded by a warm cocoon of rose-gold light. Feel yourself surrounded by your loved ones, as well as healed ancestors and spirit guides. As you mentally list everything in your life that feels abundant and life-affirming, imagine that your loved ones are showering blessings of care and goodness all over you. This has the impact of making you feel even more abundant.

Give yourself permission to be free from a scarcity mindset, for it is our mindset that dictates our reality. When you feel abundant, what you place your attention on will grow—a metaphysical phenomenon that many of my clients and community members have seen blossom into unexpected miracles. Feel abundant, and this will become your truth. Acknowledge the goodness in your life, and even more will flow in your direction. Appreciate the blessings that are already here, and more will come. Step into your true worth by welcoming the beauty that is already here, and abundance will grace your life in ways you'd never previously imagined.

Working with the Flow and Energy of Money

I want you to take some deep breaths, diosa. I'm not gonna lie: No matter how they're presented, topics like money and abundance can be challenging for many of us. Oftentimes, we can become physically and emotionally constricted around it, especially since many of us have been taught to equate money with "worth," and many of us have also lived through periods of poverty and lack—which isn't good news for our beliefs about worthiness. So I want you to take a few moments to breathe. Fill your lungs completely on the in breath, and let them deflate like a balloon on the out breath. Repeat this a few times. I hope you're starting to feel a little freer and more easeful. I want you to know the air flowing through your body is just one example of the extraordinary abundance that's all around you.

But what about money? Again, I know lots of conscious people who tend to be wary of money: of wanting it too much, of letting it corrupt them, of exploiting others to get to the top, of amassing ill-gotten riches, and so on. We live in an exploitative economy, so the hesitation to get too caught up with money is perfectly understandable. But it is absolutely possible to welcome comfort and wealth, to care for ourselves and others, to be happy and content, spiritually fulfilled, and socially responsible. Money is not good or evil; it's neutral. Because our main system of exchange, capitalism, tends to value profit over people, we've come to conflate capitalism with money. But when we extricate ourselves from any negative associations with money, we can actually start to work with it—for the purpose of building not just wealth, but true abundance.

We can start to work with the flow of wealth in simple ways. For example, our worth goes beyond the money we have, but we can affirm our worth by agreeing to work for and with companies and organizations whose values we align with, and who value us enough to pay us beyond a mere living wage. We can release our resistance to wealth pouring in, not from a place of ego or entitlement, but because we know we can use it to help ourselves and others. (A trick I sometimes share with clients is this: When you're asking for a raise, enter the conversation with an awareness of how more money will enable you to help so many people and contribute to so many causes you're passionate about. This often increases your confidence, especially if you have a difficult time advocating for yourself.)

Another area where it's so important to start cleaning things up is debt. So many of us in the U.S. are in debt. Sometimes we have no choice, such as when paying for education or medical care. Other times we run up credit card debt on items we don't truly need. Either way, owing money can generate fear. Often, people with long-term debt start buying stuff they don't need in order to assuage the fear of having nothing—which only incurs even more debt. This creates a vicious cycle of lack.

I want to offer a powerful refrain: I don't necessarily consider debt a bad thing. I say thank you for the ability to pay for things with my credit cards and loans, knowing I will make more money and pay it off when that season comes. This is why I highly encourage everyone in debt to reframe their relationship to debt. First, get grateful for the opportunity to be able to buy things and experiences with the supportive tool of credit. Then get clear on if and why you desire to no longer have the credit cards or unpaid loans. Then make a plan to pay it off—not because of shame, but because it's the right choice for your specific situation. Sometimes the shame around debt is more unhealthy than anything else. Shame won't help; empowerment will. Be empowered as you make a new choice—that's all it is. Diosa, you deserve to live with freedom around money, and you get to not shame yourself on your way to financial freedom.

I am reminded of one of my clients, a Latina therapist and entrepreneur who kept shaming herself for having debt. I told her, "Do you know most white men in the U.S. have debt? But they don't fear it—they use it as an advantage in their taxes and then pay off things as they need to. You got to go to school and become a therapist with those loans and credit cards, and now you will focus on making more money to pay it off because you desire to—not because you're bad or irresponsible." She felt a massive release and felt empowered instead of shamed. She actually started looking forward to making her credit card payments every month, and when she did, she would send out a prayer to the universe: "Thank you so much, spirit, for giving me the means to make more in my business as I pay things off because I choose to and desire to." When she did this, she smiled to herself as she thought of what her life would look like on the other side. Amazingly, she was able to increase her income and buy her home—and is on track to earn even more.

I always encourage women to get really proactive when it comes to learning about saving, retirement, and wealth building, as too many of us leave our money matters on the table and remain in a state of unnecessary confusion. Dear one, you are worthy of knowing everything there is to know about your finances! We've been brainwashed to think we can't handle wealth. No, diosa, no. The priestesses in these matriarchal societies were the ones managing money. We are meant to make and manage wealth, boo.

Your financial education might look like reading books about finance to learn the rules of money. It might also look like working with people at organizations like Ellevest, which offers wealth-building services and one-off classes and coaching calls to help women navigate their finances, or finding a money witch to do money mindset work. When I started taking steps on my financial journey, I did a lot of mindset work, reframing things like I shared above, but I also got practical support with a bookkeeper, who helped me look at my numbers and organize things well. Sites like NerdWallet offer great monthly budget planners that can help you track all your expenses and set goals for savings. All of it is valid. All of it will help you direct the flow of your energy and shift your mindset from one of lack into one that embraces social responsibility and the life you want to live. This is when synchronicity starts to kick in: When you take a step closer to abundance, it'll take several leaping bounds toward you.

The benevolence of the universe is limitless, and money is a part of this. We have to be willing to step outside our conditioned and colonized beliefs about money, and to think and dream bigger. I'm a huge proponent of finding a money mentor—preferably someone who has overcome the odds and who has a healthy, conscious, socially responsible perspective on wealth.

I think of all the miraculous things I've manifested over the years (not all of them material in nature), and I know without a doubt that the riches of life can arrive in a millisecond if you have the willingness to embrace them. When you start to work with the flow and energy of money, you will step even more decisively into your worthy woman. You'll allow yourself to move toward your grand visions instead of remaining small, afraid, and worried that your dreams aren't realistic.

Remember, you are already a part of nature—and nature is unabashedly abundant. When you allow yourself to dream with all your senses, the universe will respond in kind. When you honor your inherent inner abundance, you will find it easier to unapologetically draw money and wealth to you. Again, this won't be from a place of ego or entitlement (which, as we know, are not aligned with our inherent worthiness), but from a place of deep trust and the willingness to experience all the goodness this life can bring to you. Just remember, your soul wants to experience everything it possibly can in this body, and you are just as deserving of the good stuff as anyone else.

Worthy Work:
A Meditation for Manifesting

This exercise consists of three parts:

1. Take time to write down at least one vision you have for each of the main areas of your life. Be as descriptive as possible.

2. Next, create a vision board—a collage of words and images that represent your highest vision of wealth and abundance. You can do this on a large piece of cardboard or a whiteboard, using images cut out from magazines, or you may wish to gather images from Pinterest and arrange them using a program like Canva. You might want separate vision boards for each area of your life, or just one. You may choose to focus on a single area of your life right now, to build your manifesting mojo.

3. Place your vision board(s) somewhere where you'll see it every day. I highly recommend coming back to the meditation, or even taking a few minutes to visualize what you wish to manifest. The key is to do so as if it's already happened—because in metaphysical terms, time is an illusion and everything you can imagine has already occurred in some reality within this vast universe! I like to add "this or something better" to every manifesting session, because it can be just as amazing to let La Diosa surprise us with unexpected forms of abundance!

Peace/Mental Wellness:

Spirituality:

Rest/Relaxation:

Abundance/Money:

Career/Soul Purpose:

Health and Physical Vitality:

Personal Development/Growth:

Community:

Fun/Pleasure (Hobbies and Extracurricular Activities):

Love (Romance and Sexuality):

Using Your Privilege for Good

Sometimes it can still feel tough to square the idea of building wealth with the reality that there are so many people in the world who go without—not due to any personal shortcomings, but because of systemic poverty and the exploitative aspects of living under capitalism. I would argue that those of us who have any degree of privilege—on the basis of nationality, race, gender, ability, generational wealth, or anything else—must use it responsibly.

A lot of people react to the idea that they have privilege with defensiveness. "I've had to work for everything I have!" is a common response I hear. But this concept isn't meant to deny the hard work you've put in or the ways in which you're *not* privileged—it's simply meant to acknowledge that we seldom start out on an equal playing field. I urge you to see whatever privilege you might have not as an indictment of your work ethic or character, but rather as a blessing that you can use to pay it forward. A lot of people feel guilty or bad about having privilege, but in truth, having privilege means you probably have the means to help many, many people. You can, in fact, use your privilege for good—especially if it's connected to money, which has the potential to contribute to many beautiful endeavors.

Diosa, let yourself be empowered to become a massive conduit for universal abundance. Dream beyond yourself, and think of the causes you'd like to contribute to. Here are some possibilities:

1. Tithe a percentage of your income to a charitable organization. Although tithing is most common in the church, you can choose to give a percentage of your income to any cause you feel passionate about. Ten percent is typical, but if this feels like a stretch, that's okay. Just remember that all that you give will absolutely find a way back to you. That's the universal law of sacred reciprocity!

2. Instead of investing in stocks and bonds and building your wealth by supporting companies whose ethics you

might not even know, consider investing in individuals and organizations who are doing good work, as well as in local businesses. Allow yourself to make a difference close to home.

3. Join a mutual-aid hub or community self-support project. They exist in most communities and can be great ways to build trusting, supportive relationships with others. This can look like sharing baby clothes and children's toys, fundraising for individuals in your community, identifying specific needs in your community (such as elderly residents who might require help running errands), and building a network of people who are able to respond to those needs. The sky's the limit! Start small and enlist the support of your neighbors.

4. Consider paying voluntary land taxes to the Indigenous people who have stewarded the land you live on. (Native-Land.ca is a great website for identifying which First Nations people lived on the land you're on.) Most Americans live on stolen land that was forcibly taken from Indigenous groups, who were killed or moved onto reservations. The Indigenous peoples who lived on the land you inhabit may have been forced onto a reservation in a completely different location decades ago, but in many cases, their descendants are still around and would appreciate acknowledgment and respect. Voluntary land taxes recognize that we are accessing stolen Indigenous land. They can be directed to an Indigenous nation or organization of your choice. Land tax programs exist across the nation, and they can be a wonderful way to recognize the material needs of our Indigenous siblings.

5. If you're further along in your career, contribute to leveling the playing field by mentoring or sponsoring someone in your industry who is at a junior level. It would be especially helpful if you did this for someone who has experienced systemic disadvantages. Help them to feel more seen and heard, and to own their inner worth.

Worthy Work:
Gratitude and Generosity Practice

Gratitude can be a wonderful way to step into a greater sense of our worthiness and inherent abundance, as you've already seen. But we're going to take it a step further. Beyond just being grateful for all the abundance in your life, you are going to become the abundance—and offer it to the world with gusto and generosity.

For this practice, you'll keep a gratitude-and-generosity notebook. Every night, take a few minutes to note all the things that brought you joy. That might be as simple as holding your partner's hand as you ran errands together or sitting with a steaming cup of tea as you watched your puppy play. Observe the tiny things and the huge things. Be grateful for the beauty, as well as the painful moments that might serve as important lessons for you on your path.

At the end of the week, read over everything you listed. Truly feel the abundance that is the universe's gift to you. To honor it and be a part of it, write down two acts of generosity you'll take to pay it forward. The first act will be for you, and the second will be for someone or something else. Be creative!

What counts as generous? That's up to you, but I suggest anything that helps you remember the resource pie isn't finite. Most of all, it should come from a place of love, where you aren't forcing anything. This is about being generous not only with your money or material resources, but also with your time, energy, and attention. Spending an evening babysitting your best friend's kids so she can enjoy her first night out in months is probably going to feel more meaningful than making a big donation to a charity of your choice, although you're welcome to do both!

I encourage you to pour your generosity not just onto others, but also onto yourself. So often, the scarcity mindset can cause us to unknowingly deprive ourselves of some much-needed TLC. Are you in need of your own time, energy, attention, and money? This doesn't have to be extravagant (although I know many diosas who could stand to buy a round-trip ticket to paradise!), but it should be intentional.

✳ **Worthy Affirmations** ✳

◎ *Abundance flourishes inside and outside me—it is the nature of the universe, and it is also my true nature.*

◎ *I am enough, exactly as I am.*

◎ *Money and abundance flow easily and effortlessly my way.*

◎ *Good women with good intentions deserve the money and wealth to continue doing good work in the world.*

◎ *I deserve to be paid abundantly for my work.*

◎ *I am worthy of receiving nature's bounty and abundance.*

◎ *I continually manifest opportunities for prosperity and flow.*

◎ *I was born to be prosperous and to share my riches with others.*

◎ *I am generous with myself and my loved ones.*

◎ *I use my privilege responsibly—by intentionally choosing the ways I share my time, energy, attention, and money.*

◎ *I am grateful for the wealth that flows into my life every single day.*

You Are Worthy of Living Your Soul Purpose

Reexamine all you have been told in school or church or in any book, and dismiss whatever insults your own soul.

—Walt Whitman

I remember when I was first starting out in the wellness/personal development world, I attended a number of networking groups with mostly white women. While they were all nice and did nothing to make me feel unwelcome, I began to notice that most of them were primarily from the Upper West Side and Upper East Side—for those of you not familiar with New York City, these are some of the wealthiest neighborhoods in the entire country. I couldn't help but feel insecure in their midst. Whereas most of them had grown up with a natural sense of their own worthiness, I could feel my energy shrink every time I entered a room and noticed that I was the only woman of color—and very likely the only one who'd grown up in a different socioeconomic class.

Without realizing it, I began to dim my light. I started to feel not as smart—not as secure in my medicine, my voice, and my worthiness. I could feel myself simultaneously playing small and also playing up certain "exotic" aspects of being Latina—almost as if I were tokenizing myself. Under the white gaze, I could be invisible, or I could make myself more prominent for being "different," but I didn't believe that I could just be me . . . and that it would be enough. Beneath the white gaze, the shadow of my cultural insecurities loomed larger than before.

Luckily, it didn't stay that way. I'd done enough personal work to remind myself that these insecurities and judgments were not the result of my shortcomings. There was a reason they were in place—a reason that lay at the intersection of personal trauma and cultural indoctrination. Instead of taking any of it at face value as the "truth," I slowed way down and asked myself: "Why am I having these negative thoughts about me? What is this *really* about?"

I recognized that, like so many other BIPOC, I'd grown up with this idea that I needed to erase all signs of my "otherness" in order to feel worthy of success. Even my parents held similar views and would aim to have me be "less Latina," for fear that I wouldn't be seen as educated or good enough by white American culture. I realized that I was still carrying some wounding from my worthiness that had caused me to react to white women with distrust and discomfort. It wasn't easy for me to look at all this, but I knew I had to be brutally honest with myself. As I watched some of the women around me skyrocketing to success and living out their dreams of the perfect career, I found myself not standing in my full power and worth.

But I realized that nobody else's judgments of me mattered. What mattered the most was that I had to unlock my gifts—not by hiding who I was, but by reclaiming it and allowing it to shine forth from me. I understood that my self-judgment was coming from the conditioned, colonized part of myself, who had disowned her wholeness—which included her cultural heritage and all the wonderful resources she had inherited from generations of beauty and resilience.

Again, worthiness is an inside job, and it requires a willingness to disentangle ourselves from self-judgment and recognize the bigger message behind our feelings. When I faced my feelings of jealousy and being "less than," or when I ended up comparing myself to one of my colleagues, I made it a practice to honor my "why." Why did I feel that way? What was the source of my insecurities? As I began to dig myself out of the web of lies that had ensnared me, I reminded myself that I was protected by my healed ancestors, that my medicine was deep and valid, and that I was a gift in the room. I was dishonoring myself by hiding or attempting to be like anyone else. I was a wildflower in a bed of roses—and that was perfectly okay.

When we are willing to identify our divine gifts, this is when we catalyze our own Goddess-given purpose—the one each of us came into the world with, the one that cannot be compared to anyone else's because it is uniquely our own.

This chapter is about your medicine, as well as your purpose. Most of us start wondering what our soul work in the world is, because we are eager to be of service to our communities. We want to be blessed with opportunities for meaningful work that we enjoy and that is of benefit to others. When we find ourselves faltering, the individualistic, pull-yourself-up-by-your-bootstraps overculture often tells us that it's our fault. However, it's important to recognize the insidious effects of the cultural systems that most of us have been drinking for years, often distilled into messages around not being resourced enough, smart enough, beautiful enough, white enough. Over and over, our ability to bring our Diosa-given gifts to the light of day is sabotaged by the indoctrination that only some are worthy of sharing our purpose with the world.

This isn't true. Purpose is something that is ingrained in us. The divine plants a seed within each of our hearts—and that unique seed contains our soul stamp, which is our singular expression here on Earth.

Our first soul purpose is simply to be, to learn and grow, to evolve and share that love and growth with others. The reminder here is that we are human *beings*, not human *doings*. And walking back into a sense of purpose is inextricable from claiming our innate, just-because worthiness, which nobody else has the power to take from us.

You and Your Soul Purpose

I remember walking down Myrtle Avenue in Brooklyn with my mom and always seeing the same homeless man. We all knew him in our neighborhood. He suffered from some kind of addiction and mental illness. I grew up seeing him perched in the same spot in front of the same Duane Reade, day in and day out, opening doors, smiling, and asking for change. I would ask my mom if she could give me money to put in his cup.

There is a certain level of vulnerability that it takes to lose it all and still ask for help. Even at a young age, I understood this. There was something about this man's courage in the face of utter loss that felt strangely familiar to me. I could sense behind his smile the tug of loneliness and despair, as well as the desire to be assured that he was worthy of love.

He didn't have to say a word—I could feel it in my soul. And I wanted to help.

One day, I asked my mom for permission to talk to him, and she said yes. I asked, "Excuse me, sir, do you have a family? And how did you get here?" He seemed surprised to be asked about himself, but I could also tell that he was eager to talk. He said he did have a family, and that he was here because of "a lot of wrong decisions." He also gave me some general advice to be grateful for what I have and to do the right things and stay on the right path.

Long after that conversation, his words kept replaying in my head. I was shocked to know he had a family and humbled by the recognition that no matter what someone's life might be like, if you introduced addiction and mental illness and "a lot of wrong decisions," you could end up with nothing. I understood then and there that nobody was above it all. Even back then, there was a tenderness in me that was accompanied by the fire of righteous indignation at cruelty, injustice, and lack of care. I wanted very much to do whatever I could to right this wrong and all the wrongs of the world.

I knew I wanted to be a therapist well before I knew what the word *therapist* even meant. Perhaps that's because I was playing this role in my own home at an early age. I had been forced to act like an adult very early because the adults around me didn't fully know how to, due to the confluence of their own mental health and addiction issues. They didn't name any of this out loud, but perhaps I was drawn to the man outside Duane Reade because I could see echoes of my own family in him. Nobody at home ever talked about it, because our family's pain, addiction, and poor mental health were all much more buttoned up. Though many of us have different experiences on the outside, we can still identify with the same feelings on the inside.

I also believe that, even before experiencing the pain in my own home, my soul spark was committed to healing injustice. I believe that I came into this world with a deep sensitivity to and awareness of all the injustice and trauma that required healing and resolution. I came into the world with an intense passion and a voice that was meant to facilitate experiences of transformation on both the personal and the collective level.

Like many of us, the circumstances of my life simply gave me extra fuel to undo the toxic patterns and enact the change I sought—the kind of change that would enable all beings to step into their innate worthiness. When you know different, you do different—so I searched for different. As I've already mentioned, I sought to break the patterns I had grown up with by going to therapy healing groups, priestess trainings, and tantric workshops. I got healing bodywork and Reiki, in addition to having a regular practice of yoga, prayer, meditation, church services—you name it, I tried it, *because I just wanted something different.* I knew I needed to break free from toxic patterns and negative coping skills. And somewhere inside me, even in the midst of the drunken nights prior to becoming sober, there was a deep awareness. For as long as I can remember, I've heard the words "You are here to help" reverberating within me. And on a conscious level, I wanted to help so badly—to make my own pain disappear, to make the pain of the world disappear, and to assist other people who were struggling with pain.

Of course, pain is a fact of life, and it never completely goes away. But I understood that while pain might be unavoidable, suffering is always optional. I knew there was a better way, and I was committed to finding it. Today I understand that my soul purpose, what Buddhists and Hindus call dharma, or one's life's work, is all about undoing the toxic patterns in my lineage and integrating them in such a way that I can model a healthier paradigm. I want to show others what is possible, so I've done this by sharing tools and creating spaces where people can find their own inner worth, power, purpose, and truth. For me, one of the greatest responsibilities that each of us has is to unlock our soul purpose—because when the fire that lives within us is catalyzed, we have the capacity to change the world.

So much of the pain of the world is in deep need of transmutation. I guarantee that the strongest people you've ever met derived their strength from being able to transform their pain into something greater—into service, into truth, into joy and celebration. Your soul purpose is what helps you do that, because it exists not *despite* the circumstances you might find yourself in, but *alongside* those circumstances, in order to give you fuel to change them.

Some of us are born knowing our purpose in this lifetime with a heightened degree of clarity. For others, it takes more time. No one way is better. Every individual has their own unique journey, and all of us have our own path to finding our soul purpose. It is your destiny to explore the real reason why you're here and to live that reason every single day, with a commitment to uplifting yourself and others. For when we are clear that our core purpose is simply to be in communion with our truest and most authentic expression, we learn through life's ups and downs to be this true self in the world.

The great theologian Howard Thurman famously said, "Don't ask what the world needs. Ask what makes you come alive and go do it. Because what the world needs is people who have come alive." Your first and most important soul purpose is simply to be *you*, to know yourself from the inside out, to understand what makes you tick and what makes you light up. And, of course, the fuel for your dreams and desires is your sense of worthiness—and you need a full tank of it. This is the energy that will make your actions in the world feel soul-aligned and effortless. This is the energy that will enable you to go after the things you desire, and to let go of what isn't aligned. This is why, in so many spiritual and religious doctrines, the question *Who am I?* is one of the holiest questions you can ask yourself.

Understanding the most authentic expression of who you are is often the work of a lifetime. But it doesn't have to be a struggle. Instead, when you are soft and gentle with yourself, when you listen to the stirrings and whispers that come from within, you learn to embody your soul in the purest and most effortless of ways. From this deepened connection comes the expression of your soul purpose. Whether you desire to be a mom, a wife, an entrepreneur, a political leader, or anything else, awakening a true connection to your core essence will always connect you to your soul purpose.

Worthy Work:
The Biography of Your Higher Self

Who are you? I mean, really, who are you deep down, beneath all the disguises and masks you have been conditioned to wear on a daily basis? When you're that, when you're embodying that most essential core of who you are, what is your purpose? It's important to step into both your heart and your history when you ask these questions, for when you do, you will automatically sense when you feel the most alive and in your passion—when you are a living embodiment of your purpose.

1. For the purpose of this exercise, give yourself at least fifteen minutes to write down any memories or

awareness about when you feel the most alive and in your passion. This might be in the form of stories or bullet points that help you identify specific activities and circumstances under which you feel your life energy in the most palpable way. A lot of times, our aliveness and passion are things that we don't necessarily stop to consider when we're actually in the midst of feeling them, so we end up taking them for granted.

2. Now take at least fifteen minutes to write down your gifts. Again, this might take a bit of digging, since we're not accustomed to claiming what makes us beautiful and unique. You might be an amazing singer or dancer. Or maybe you have a knack for making people laugh. Or perhaps loved ones and strangers confide in you because you're warm, friendly, and nonjudgmental. All of these are incredible gifts. If it's hard for you to identify your own gifts, consider what other people might come to you asking for help with. What are you often complimented on? A lot of times, the compliments we receive tend to go in one ear and out the other—but they often shed light on the gifts we have that can bring the most benefit to others. And I promise you that the most powerful of these gifts will be the ones where your passion and aliveness intersect with being of benefit to others.

3. Now distill what you've learned so far and write down at least five of your divine gifts. A divine gift is the highest expression of your soul, because it's where your deepest authenticity meets the world. Our divine gifts usually signal where we can be of the most benefit to ourselves, our loved ones, and our communities. This might look like: "My extroverted and outgoing nature; my ability to tell stories that evoke wonder and hope; my great hostess

skills that make people feel at home and welcome; my impeccable attention to detail; my ability to help people identify their own gifts."

Overall, you're going to notice some common themes in the lists you just made. Take the examples I just offered above. Someone who has identified all those gifts might be a really excellent motivational speaker or community organizer who excels at bringing together people for the purpose of inspiring them to live into their highest aspirations.

Again, in the colonized world in which we live, which tends to assign more value to certain abilities and capacities, some of the divine gifts you identify may have been taken for granted. I want you to forgive yourself, my love, if you've ever not seen your own brilliant nature. Now it's time to truly absorb each one into your heart space. I recommend writing down your gifts on an index card and placing them on your worthy woman altar. Let yourself acknowledge your own unique, divinely given power and beauty.

4. Finally, take another fifteen minutes or so to write the biography of your higher self based on the gifts that you've identified. The biography of your higher self isn't some kind of CV where you're trying to impress anybody with all of your accolades and the things you've accomplished. Rather, we're going to the soul level— beyond titles, roles, and relationships to others.

My biography of my higher self says: "I am a cosmic soul learning and growing through my human experience. My purpose is to heal through relationships. I express this purpose by being a mama, a lover, a priestess, a healer, a poet, a gatherer, an empowerer, and a writer. I am meant to share my real, raw, vulnerable experiences with others, and to create community and safe spaces for Latina women and women who desire to deeply connect with themselves, to share, to remember who they are, and to own their worthiness in life, love, business, family, and all domains. My purpose is to be a bridge between the mundane world and the spirit world, between individuals and communities. I am a cosmic bridge and a soul mentor."

I see this statement every single day when I open my computer and get to work. It also lives on my altar, alongside the card that contains a written description of my divine gifts. Yours doesn't have to be a complicated statement. It could be a single sentence, as long as it's one that rings true in your heart of hearts.

Breaking Free from Imposter Syndrome

According to a survey conducted by the American Psychological Association, women are more likely than men to report stress related to low self-esteem. The survey found that 60 percent of women reported experiencing stress related to their own negative self-image, compared to 47 percent of men. Additionally, a study published in the *Journal of Social and Clinical Psychology* found that women are more likely than men to experience imposter syndrome, which is a feeling of inadequacy or self-doubt despite evidence of success. The study found that 70 percent of women reported experiencing imposter syndrome at some point in their lives, compared to 50 percent of men.

Clearly, low self-esteem and feelings of unworthiness are common among women. That's why it is especially important for us to recognize and challenge these feelings, and to culti-vate a strong sense of self-worth and self-love.

So many of us are taught to feel unworthy of our dreams because they simply feel too big. We haven't been taught to hold and incubate our dreams and to feed the fire of our soul desires. A lot of women in particular are told to be small, compliant, and modest, and to refrain from getting a big head. Is it any wonder we end up asking ourselves: "Who am I to do this? Am I deserving of a life this good? Am I going to be rejected for shining this way?" There are so many uncon-scious beliefs that can sabotage our dreams and our sense of self even before we've taken the critical steps to move toward what we most yearn for.

I work with a lot of clients who have this sinking sensa-tion that they've gone too far. This is often true when we have family members and friendship circles who don't recognize and uplift each individual's higher potential. I call this the "crabs in a bucket" mentality: If you watch crabs in a bucket, one that attempts to climb out will be pulled back in by the others, which leads only to the collective ruin of the entire group. The truth is, when any one of us makes it out of the status quo and achieves something amazing, we show others what's possible.

There's something that's known as the Roger Bannister effect, which is named after the first athlete to run a mile in under four minutes. Before that, people believed that run-ning a mile in four minutes simply wasn't possible. But once Bannister broke that psychological barrier, a huge number of runners were able to do it. In the same way, the idea that our dreams are unreachable is ludicrous. Think of all the Roger Bannisters of the world: innovators who changed the game and moved the benchmarks in every area.

One of the most important aspects of reclaiming your

innate worth is adopting a mindset that welcomes the impossible—one that says our dreams, even if they seem out of reach, are always closer than we think . . . because that which we most desire, from our true core essence, is always seeking us! Our mental models tend to hold us back and make us feel like unextraordinary little beings. But you are a diosa! You don't have to accept the limitations of what's known as conventional wisdom. Your task is to be a warrior in the Worthy Revolution, and to be part of transforming people's ideas about what is possible.

How do you do this? First, you have to identify the limiting beliefs and stories that are keeping you stuck in your colonized and wounded self. These limiting beliefs will be unique, based on your own experiences and circumstances. For example, you might feel that you don't have the education to do anything meaningful with your life, or that you're not talented enough to pursue the things you're most passionate about. Ask yourself: "Is this really true? Where did I inherit this belief?"

I often tell my clients that for every limiting belief we've unconsciously taken in, we must counter it repeatedly with a more empowered belief that exudes hope, possibility, and positive self-regard. I never suggest an affirmation that feels too far afield, because our brain is automatically trained to disregard and disbelieve anything that doesn't fit our reality. I usually find that instead of countering a limiting belief with a positive affirmation that says the opposite, it's important to choose an honest statement about your strengths and hopes.

For example, a limiting belief that you're not educated enough to do anything meaningful can be countered with something like "I lead from my heart, and it is my heart and not my intellect that feeds and nurtures those who need it most" or "I am curious and motivated, and if there's anything in my skill set that I'm currently missing, I can easily find a way to learn it." In contrast, a statement like "I *am* educated enough to pursue the goals I want to pursue" might sound good on the surface, but your mind might reject it if, on some level, you actually do need further education to do the things you want. The key is to be both honest *and* kind with yourself.

When we do this work of reclaiming our worthiness, we often uncover limiting beliefs we didn't even realize were present. I remember talking to one of my clients who couldn't seem to get past her imposter syndrome—during every conversation we had, she would say something self-deprecating. After a few sessions, she recognized that a limiting belief she had was a fear of success. When I gently pressed to ask what success looked like for her, it was living in a joy-filled environment, with close friends, community gardens (she was a talented community organizer), and everyone getting their needs met.

"That sounds beautiful!" I said. "So what's the problem?"

"Every community I've ever had has fallen apart," she explained. "I really want to be able to bring people together, but I guess I have a fear that I'm just setting myself up to fail because of what I've experienced in the past. And that manifests in me doubting myself, maybe as a way of keeping myself safe from disappointment."

As my client found, we stay constrained when we listen to the misguided part of us that believes staying right where we are will keep us safe from any number of fears—loneliness, new enemies, being isolated from our family, working longer hours, being asked for favors or money, falling further when we make a mistake.

We don't claim our divine gifts on our own, however. We do it by taking time to be with ourselves and the diosa within.

We also do it by finding mentors who support our dreams and desires, and who are able to mirror back to us our highest potential. At a certain point in my career, I realized that I had to stop seeking the advice of people who simply didn't believe in what I was doing. This wasn't because they were "bad" people, but was usually because they were nursing their own wounds and remained stuck in a colonized mentality that kept them from pursuing their dreams—and that gave them a "crabs in the bucket" mentality when it came to witnessing others who were attempting a different approach. Instead, I sought out powerful, wise women who were allowing themselves to actualize their dreams, from a place of innate worthiness and the desire to be of service to the world.

Who are the people you know who are living out their dreams in a powerful way? Find them. Talk to them. Remember that you are not alone.

UNWORTHY LIE:
I am not good enough, smart enough, or talented enough to fulfill my dreams, so maybe I should stop trying and just be content with what I have.

WORTHY TRUTH:
I was born with divinely given gifts, and it is my right and responsibility to use them in ways that brighten my life and benefit the world.

It's About Being, Not Doing

One of the things that I think a lot of people forget when they're looking into their soul purpose is that it's about being, not doing. Remember, your primary purpose on this planet is to be who you are, with all of your quirks, all of your unique talents, the perspective that only you can possibly bring to any situation. It is your uniqueness that the world needs most. It's ideal to have a livelihood and activities that align with what your soul purpose is, but this is going to shift from time to time, and your purpose is so much bigger than any particular job or role.

This is also where I want to say that no purpose is better or worse, bigger or smaller, than another. Because every single one of us is different. There are some people who feel that their soul purpose is to be a stay-at-home mom and others who believe that their soul purpose is having no kids but being of service to the world in a way that involves greater numbers of people. It could be that you're happy with a nine-to-five job that you don't feel super-passionate about because you're much more interested in the ways you spend your time when you're not working. Or it could be that whatever you do for a living is the very thing that fuels your fire and makes you feel the most alive. The most important thing is to stay connected to what you really want.

And this can change at any given point in a person's life! I've had many clients who were much more focused on externally facing work, such as being the leaders of organizations, when they were younger, only to realize that they were moving in a direction that was asking them to focus inward more later in life. Sometimes, it's the reverse.

The important question to ask yourself is: *How am I being me?* This isn't about being good, successful, or worthy according to somebody else's measure of any of those things. It's about being in your own wholeness and worthiness from moment to moment, and recognizing that even as your needs and desires shift over time, the core of who you are is always going to be the same.

I recall working with a client who was having some difficulty with her job. She worked as a lawyer, helping large businesses maintain ethical, environmentally sustainable practices. She loved her work, and all of the organizations she worked with loved her, but over time, it felt like something was missing. She realized that while the objectives she was aiming for were important, she wanted more connected, heart-centered relationships with her colleagues, and this just wasn't going to be possible in the corporate world she inhabited. She decided it was time for a shift, but that shift was extremely challenging. She didn't know whether a new career would allow her to do other "big, important" work.

When we dug into her definitions of importance, we realized that, as a first-generation Caribbean American woman, she was still looking at her success from the vantage point of how other people would judge her. But the truth was, as I shared with her, her dissatisfaction with her high-powered career was actually a sign that she was ready to step into her worthy woman, who was asking her to define success in a brand-new way: on the basis of how it felt rather than how it looked.

It took her a while to figure out her "what's next." Today, she is nurturing beautiful connections with others in her work as a professor at a small private college, inspiring a new generation of young people who wish to bring sustainability directly into their communities. Her work with young activists gives her a sense of deep meaning and service unlike anything she's ever felt before. Today, she is truly living from her worthy woman self and being the woman she's always wanted to be.

Your Greatest Service

Dear one, I want you to take a moment to stop and think about your greatest contribution to society—what I call your legacy work. Perhaps you believe it exists in your creative dreams and desires, or in your children, or in a product or service you've created that makes other people's lives more fulfilling. Perhaps you have a special talent or skill that has proven to be beneficial to others. Well, I'm here to tell you that no matter what you think it might be, and despite the great care you've put into considering how you would like to contribute to the world, none of the things you've thought about can possibly come close to encapsulating your greatest service to the world: living from your deepest truth.

I once had a client who looked at me like I was crazy when I told her this. "Isn't that selfish?" she asked.

I shook my head. "No way. Your authentic essence might be self-full, but she is definitely not selfish. Because when we are selfish in a way that's all about getting ours at anyone else's expense, that's not our core self. That's our colonized, wounded self who thinks she's separate from others. Everyone's greatest truth is an expression of the divine. It is an expression of love."

Honest-to-goodness truth must acknowledge that all of us are interconnected and we do not live in a vacuum. Your greatest truth isn't just about making as much money as you can, because that kind of reductive end goal is driven by fear and scarcity. Your greatest truth is intrinsically connected to service, to living in ways that are authentic and that have ripple effects on the world.

Like I said, anything you *do* (like writing a book, building an organization, or starting a movement) is secondary to what you are letting yourself *be*. Your essence is love, and that is what you are meant to offer as your greatest service. In the words of Mother Teresa, "There is more hunger for love and appreciation in this world than for bread." When we offer ourselves and our service from a place of love rather than a place of fear, we have the distinct experience of being a conduit for divine love.

There are so many beautiful examples of parables and fairy tales in which poor but loving people generously offer what little they have—and what little they have magically multiplies, because the act of giving comes from a place of love, and the desire to truly be of benefit. Usually, in the same stories, there is a character who is wealthy but stingy, who gives what they have with the expectation of receiving something in return. In true fairy-tale fashion, such characters end up having their comeuppance, and the world mirrors back to them their own disdain and lack of care.

Our service to the world should overflow from us as an act of genuine goodwill and generosity, not because we think we have to give it, but simply because we want to give it. In order to give with love, we must remember that we ourselves are the ultimate embodiment of love. This means that we need to once and for all let go of feelings of unworthiness, which come from a place of fear, which is the polar opposite of love.

Please allow yourself to understand that relinquishing unworthiness is one of the greatest acts of service you could possibly do for the planet. The span of a human life is short. Are we going to live it from a place of fear, scarcity, and hiding? Or will we bravely step into our truth, which is love, and offer whatever we have to give—not because it is perfect, but because our generosity will set the world free?

Worthy Work:
Feeding Your Dreams

For this exercise, you'll start by looking at a typical day in your life and considering your activities, as well as how your time tends to get taken up. Do your activities align with your soul purpose, or do they feel disconnected? What can you actively do to ensure that you're embodying your soul purpose at every moment? Don't worry—when you start to do your Worthy Work with greater intention, your soul purpose will simply radiate through you. But it's important to gain awareness of where that purpose does not feel aligned with what you're doing and to create some tangible steps to start living your purpose every single day.

What does success look like to you? Feed this vision by closing your eyes, and for at least five minutes imagine a typical day in your life when you're embodying the biography of your higher self. What are the specific things you see yourself doing? These are things that should nourish your soul. There should be a sense of higher purpose, emotion, feeling, and fire. Without that, achieving your goals will feel very difficult.

Now I want you to take your vision and actively breathe life into it. You're going to identify at least one goal that is associated with an activity you would be doing if you were embodying your soul purpose. The following example is one that has been guiding my own life over the past several months of writing this book. As you can see, I use the framework of a SMART goal. This is an acronym for specific, measurable, achievable, relevant, and time-bound. Defining these parameters as they pertain to your goal helps ensure that your objectives are attainable within a certain time frame. Instead of keeping your dreams in the realm of fantasy, you begin to actualize them.

My Soul Purpose	Specific	Measurable
To embody the wisdom of my intuition, and to allow the realms of the invisible to impact the way I live my life daily.	I will write a book that inspires women to access their own personal magic and creativity.	The book should be about 80,000 words long; I want to write at least 5,000 words a week and spend ten hours a week working on it.

Achievable	Relevant	Time-Bound
I've written a ton of blogs and have a social media following that is hungry for this book, so I know I have what it takes to achieve my dream.	This would embody my soul purpose of living intuitively and helping others who feel lost to do the same.	I will do all of this in one year.

I recommend starting with one goal, but you can have up to three at a time. You may wish to break down the goal even further, noting any milestones you'd like to achieve in one month, two months, three months, and so on. Be sure to check in with your goal on a regular basis to see if anything needs to shift. Don't let the assumption that you are "failing" sabotage you! It may just mean that it's time to take a different tack or to ask for help.

✳ Worthy Affirmations ✳

◎ *My highest purpose is to embody my most authentic soul expression.*

◎ *The world wants and needs the medicine that is uniquely my own to offer.*

◎ *I live from and embody the truth of my soul, and it is my birthright to express this truth.*

◎ *My actions are in perfect harmony with my soul purpose.*

◎ *I deserve to express my soul purpose, and the universe supports me in bringing it to life.*

◎ *Every day, my soul purpose becomes clearer, and the right actions to align with it come easily and effortlessly.*

◎ *My greatest service to the world is doing and being what lights me up and fuels my inner fire.*

7

You Are Worthy of Health

*Communities and countries and ultimately the world
are only as strong as the health of their women.*

—Michelle Obama

The female body is sacred because it is intrinsically connected to the cycles and seasons of our beautiful Madre Tierra, our Mother Earth, to whom we owe our life and our vitality. This is true for all women on a spiritual level, whether they have a menstrual cycle or not. But the dis-ease and imbalance that run rampant on our planet—in the form of wars, pandemics, chronic illness, addiction, and so many other factors that demonstrate how out of whack things are—are mirrored in our attitudes toward our own bodies.

We are all worthy of experiencing health and harmony in our bodies, minds, and spirits. And yet many of us have been harmed by a culture that sexualizes those of us who live in feminine bodies without honoring our full humanity and divinity, our reproductive rights and bodily autonomy, and the sacred wisdom that lives inside our wombs.

In order to come back to our full, Diosa-given health and vitality, we must recognize the role of the sacred. A number of peer-reviewed studies have demonstrated that a connection to the sacred directly correlates with better health outcomes. Why is this? I think it's because so many of our mental and physical afflictions are the result of our broken hearts and spirits—of the fragmentation we encounter in the face of shame and our stolen sense of worth. The syndrome of separation and unworthiness has done a number on our overall well-being, and it's time to say "Fuck no!" to the status quo, which encompasses our broken healthcare system and a great deal of misinformation about who's worthy of good health, who isn't, and what it takes to get there.

Denying the sacredness of the body goes back to many of our origin myths. Eve is said to have committed the original sin, which is the reason why women experience the pain of childbirth. In this story, the female body is the scapegoat that carries the stain of our "sinfulness." This condemnation exacts a heavy price for all humans, but especially women, whose wombs and menstrual blood are seen as proof of the "curse" that has befallen us.

Thankfully, there are many other archetypal stories that honor women and the body, that view pleasure as a life-affirming, holy right that each of us has. In the Sri Vidya tantric lineage, which I've studied in depth with my teacher Amma and the late Psalm Isadora, we are given a path to integrating the power of shakti, or the divine feminine, which allows us to experience God/Goddess in our own body.

Each of us is a vessel for divine energy, but it's impossible to feel worthy of health when we aren't raised with the awareness that our body is our temple—not a temple in which we must undergo penance and strict rules and shame and the weight of original sin, but a temple in which we can pay homage to La Diosa and bask in the holiness of pleasure.

Our mental, physical, spiritual, and emotional health are all housed in this holy temple called our body. But how many of us can truly say we view the body as holy? As women in particular, we've been taught to fear it, to hide it, to mistrust its wisdom, to treat it with suspicion, disgust, and disregard. We have been robbed of our holy awareness, which matriarchal scholars insist was widespread in many cultures before the rise of patriarchal, monotheistic religion.

We have been robbed of the belief that this body is worthy of devotion. Thus, we suffer from a collective amnesia, which has manifested in a general disconnection from nature (as well as her holy remedies) and our own worthiness and primal wisdom. The true power of the female body has been ignored by commercialization and consumerism, which uses beauty and sexuality to sell us everything from clothing to cars.

I know that I came into a new understanding of my own health when I reclaimed the sacredness of my blood, of home birth, and of breastfeeding—which are all powerful rites of passage. Of course, like most women, I wasn't taught to honor these rites of passage, but to be fearful of them. As I learned more about the ways that traditional cultures did pay homage to the sanctity of the female body, I wondered: What would happen if we were taught from a young age that when we return our blood back to the earth, it makes the soil fertile and rich because our blood is so magical and potent?

I regained my period about two years after I gave birth. One thing I was sure to tell my daughter when she saw me bleed for the first time was that this blood was special, sacred, holy—blood that flows out of the bodies of grown-up women. I put the blood on my face to demonstrate the ancestral practice of sacred painting with menstrual blood. My Taíno ancestors also intentionally fed their menstrual blood back to the earth, so doing the same thing affirmed my connection to them.

I knew that I wanted to be an example of what it looks like to fully honor the female body. I had done this with my home birth, by choosing to forgo medications and to convene with midwives in the sacredness of my home, activating the beautiful ceremony of giving life. I was surrounded by birth affirmations, as I danced and swayed and breathed alongside my partner. In many ways, my birth was an ecstatic experience. I had my partner suck on my nipples as my daughter crowned, because that was what my intuition told me to do: to bring in pleasure as a holy and sacred aspect of this important experience.

In addition to all of this, I continued to breastfeed my daughter past her early infancy, but I didn't refer to this as "extended breastfeeding," even though that's what people called it. I found that to be a disdainful label, mired in taboo. In truth, breastfeeding creates a strong bond between mother and child, and is a deeply nutritive experience that boosts the immune system, lowers the risk of certain diseases, and soothes the nervous system. However, our capitalistic system often urges women to detach from their children early on so that they can go back to work, be productive, and work around other people's schedules. This can be detrimental to our health in deep ways.

I knew that reclaiming these pieces of my worthiness was my way of reintroducing the divine feminine into the major initiations I was going through. This was also my way of tangibly reclaiming the sacredness of my body and to live in and through the archetype of La Diosa. In this way, wherever you are in your life and on your journey, my desire for you is that you also reclaim your health and feminine power.

Honoring the Menstrual Cycle

Why do so many women see menstruation as a curse rather than as a mysterious rite of passage that connects us with the liminal spaces between heaven and Earth? Across so many ancient cultures, menstruation was seen as a time during which women's spiritual powers were heightened, and their ability to peer into present, past, and future sharpened. The idea of the "curse" of menstruation received more traction when patriarchy and monotheism replaced matriarchy and its ways of flowing with the seasons.

Diosa, how do you relate to your menstrual cycle? If you no longer have a menstrual cycle, what was your previous relationship to it?

A dishonoring of our menstrual cycle can be a way that women might not feel worthy. Many of us are trained to talk about our period in disgusted whispers or to refrain from discussing it in mixed groups. Although menstruation is literally the fluid that harbors the potential for life, we are taught to treat it with disdain and secrecy. We probably all remember the time that Donald Trump disrespectfully characterized Fox News host Megyn Kelly as having "blood coming out of her wherever," to discredit her, make her seem "less than," and suggest that she was not fit for a position of authority. This attitude is hardwired into patriarchal culture, but we have the power to change that.

When we don't honor our menstrual cycle, we end up denying an important aspect of our feminine power and wisdom. Menstruation is a time when our bodies are naturally shedding and releasing, and it can be a powerful time for introspection, reflection, and renewal. By ignoring or suppressing our menstrual cycle as a source of our feminine power, we lose the opportunity to connect with our inner wisdom and power, which are deeply sourced in La Diosa.

Additionally, a failure to honor our menstrual cycle can lead to physical and emotional discomfort. This is meant to be a period of time for rest and deep listening, and when we don't take care of ourselves during our menstrual cycle, we end up experiencing more severe cramps, mood swings, and other symptoms. This can cause cyclical feelings of frustration and unworthiness, as we may feel like our bodies are betraying us or not functioning properly.

Honoring your menstrual cycle is really all about recognizing and celebrating the power and wisdom of your body. A lot of times, we're taught to place external value on our female body—it's worthy only as long as someone else thinks we're sexy, pretty, or fit. Menstruation is a physically and spiritually internal process that is all about developing a strong core of internal worthiness that connects us to Mother Earth. It involves taking care of ourselves physically, emotionally, and spiritually during this time and recognizing the importance of self-care. By honoring your menstrual cycle, you experience a deeper self-love that cannot be taken away.

We know that menstrual taboos that cast women as impure second-class citizens are all around us—and that modern culture has done a lot to whitewash the "inconvenience" of menstruation in order to make women into more productive, efficient members of society. But what's really missing is an archetypal connection to the sacred aspects of menstruation that tap into our innate worthiness as feminine beings with the holiest gift of all: the gift of life, which surpasses the birth of a child and takes us into the essence of creativity itself.

The negative associations and religious taboos around menstruation in various cultures are well known. Women may be prohibited from sexual intercourse, banned from places of worship, or segregated in special huts. Theories about these restrictions range from false beliefs that menstrual blood is toxic, to fears that the blood triggers castration anxiety in men, to beliefs that the smell of the blood disturbs animals and interferes with hunting.

However, I have been invested in finding myths and archetypes that restore menstruation to its holy place. For example, Itiba Cahubaba, or Great Bleeding Mother, is a revered ancestor spirit of the Taíno. Itiba dies in childbirth, but she gives birth to four sons, who are the creators of the ocean and land. In her sacrifice, she makes humanity and the universe itself possible. In Cuba, Itiba is connected to pregnancy, labor, delivery, and the matron saint of the island: the Virgen de la Caridad del Cobre. To this day, pregnant women and mothers attend the Virgen's shrine in gratitude and prayer. Taíno people from the Sagua-Baracoa Mountains also continue to make offerings to Itiba, to bless their crops and ensure that their herbal medicines are potent.

In addition, honoring the menstrual cycle has proven to be a powerful way for women to connect with one another. Though menstruation huts are stigmatized in some cultures, Ulithian people in the Pacific Islands treat them as places for menstruating and breastfeeding women to convene in a spirit of celebration. Similarly, there are cultures around the world that celebrate menarche, or a girl's first period, as a rite of passage into womanhood. For example, in Ghana, girls receive gifts beneath ceremonial umbrellas.

There's also a beautiful site in India known as Kamakhya, in the hills of the state of Assam. This site is believed to be the place where the womb and genitals of the goddess Shakti fell after her body was divided and scattered across the planet to bless the Earth. In the temple of Kamakhya, there is no depiction of the goddess, only a yoni-like stone over which a pure spring of water flows. Three to four days out of the year, during July, the menstruation of the goddess is honored during a festival known as Ambubachi Mela. Throngs of people gather to receive blessings from the yoni, and to strengthen women's connections to their bodies' ability to give life.

That's not to say that any of these cultures don't have their own problems with misogyny, but all of this is extremely different from the idea that we are "cursed"!

Creating powerful rituals to honor your menstrual and reproductive health is so important, especially in the absence of a sacred framework for our feminine processes. I recommend integrating some of the following practices into your life to honor your period:

1. **Menstrual journaling:** Set aside dedicated time during your menstrual cycle to journal about your experiences, thoughts, and emotions. Reflect on how your body and mind feel, and explore any insights or patterns that arise. This practice helps cultivate self-awareness and strengthens the connection with your menstrual cycle.

2. **Create a menstrual altar:** Designate a small space in your home as a sacred altar for your menstrual cycle. This can be a portion of your worthy woman altar, or somewhere else. Decorate it with meaningful objects like crystals, flowers, candles, or symbols representing fertility, rebirth, and feminine power. Visit the altar during your cycle to offer gratitude, to set intentions, or simply to meditate and connect with your body.

3. **Connect with other women:** Start a "red tent" circle, a place where women can connect (perhaps during the full or new moon) and share stories about menstruation, fertility, childbirth, menopause, and the rites of passage

that connect us to our cycles. This can be a safe space for women of all sexual orientations and gender expressions to talk about their sacred connection to themselves.

4. **Ritual bathing:** Take a ritual bath during your menstrual cycle as a way to honor and cleanse your body. You can add soothing herbs or essential oils to the bathwater, light candles, and play soft music to create a calming ambience. As you soak in the water, visualize it washing away negative emotions or tension, and embrace a sense of renewal.

5. **Moon gazing:** The word *menstruation* is linked etymologically to the word *moon*. The ancients connected the menstrual cycle to the moon cycle, as both are about twenty-eight days long. A great way to honor this mystical connection is to spend time bathing in moonlight during your menstrual cycle. During a full moon, find a place to rest and observe it. Connect with the moon's calming energy and presence, and reflect on the powerful connection between your cycle and the lunar cycles, which have been revered as sacred the world over since time immemorial.

6. **Offering ceremony:** Prepare a simple offering, such as flowers, herbs, or a handwritten note, and choose a serene outdoor location. During your menstrual cycle, go to this spot and offer your gratitude for the wisdom, strength, and transformative power of your cycle. Express any intentions, desires, or emotions you wish to release or transform.

7. **Dance or movement:** Engage in mindful, intuitive dance or movement during your cycle. Choose music that resonates with you and brings out your deeper emotions.

Move your body freely, allowing yourself to feel and express whatever is within you. This practice can help you connect with the primal creative forces of your menstrual cycle.

Feel free to mix and match, and to adapt these rituals according to what you most need. You can also create your own rituals. The idea is that you commit to regularly creating a sacred space where you can literally flow with your life blood and engage in powerful self-reflection and empowering ceremonies that help you embrace your body's innate wisdom.

Activating Womb Energy

Regardless of whether or not you menstruate, and whether or not you have given birth, the womb, or uterus, is a powerful and potent home for your creativity, self-expression, and overall health. When we are in a body that contains a womb, our spiritual initiations live in this potent center. We experience initiations through bleeding, giving birth, nourishing our children, and going through menopause. In this way, our womb health carries us through the maiden, mother, and crone phases of our life.

A soul sister and teacher of mine, Mali of Sacred Woman School, graced me with this wisdom, and I want to share it with you. Mali has extensively shared that the womb is a place to create and to birth—and this goes beyond the creation and birthing of babies. In fact, you may be a woman who no longer has a physical womb, or a woman who was not born with a womb. This doesn't matter; your feminine essence rests in your energetic womb.

The energetic womb goes from the pubic bone all the way up to the sternum in a spiral formation, and it is a doorway through which we receive source energy and information from the matrix of life itself. However, the womb, just like any portal, requires great respect and constant attention. How does one tend to the portal of the womb? My teacher Laura Mar has shared ways to connect to the energy of the womb by recognizing where in our cycle we are. This is a process of deep honoring that helps us recognize the creatrix who lives within our bodies and our feminine consciousness. This is also a way to honor the portal, no matter where we are in our menstrual cycle, or even if we menstruate at all.

A Journey Through the Menstrual Phases

The following pages offer a journey through the menstrual phases, but even if you do not bleed, you can hearken to the season, the phase of your life you're in, or the phase of the moon. Also, don't think it's necessary for your menstrual cycle to literally sync up with the moon phases; every woman has her own unique cycle, her own moon, her own seasons. Don't feel this process of attending to and activating your womb has anything whatsoever to do with "getting it right." This is your reclamation of your unique womb energy, sis! Trust your intuition and use this as a map for honoring and activating womb energy and ripening the fruit of your own intuition.

Menstrual Phase | Dark Moon / New Moon | Winter

If you see red blood, this is considered Day 1 of your menstrual phase. At this time, hormone levels in the body drop, and energy levels do the same. The cervix is slightly open, which allows blood to flow from the uterus freely. This is a time that is typically marked by a sense of withdrawal and attunement to one's inner voice and self. During this time, the barriers between the conscious and subconscious minds are lowered, which helps you open up to all levels of your awareness—through dreams, intuition, synchronicities, and direct engagement with the wisdom of your body. The wise crone is the archetype most associated with this phase.

Follicular Phase | Waxing Moon | Spring

During this phase, follicles in the ovaries ripen and secrete estrogen. The cervix is closed, and thick mucus plugs the cervical passage. There is a sense of energy beginning to rise up from the depths; a new beginning is afoot, and there is a sense of lightness after the menstrual phase. This period of time is associated with the innocent and buoyant maiden archetype.

Fertile Phase | Full Moon | Summer

During this time, estrogen rises and signals to the uterus that it's time to build a new blood-rich lining. The cervix produces fluid that ranges from creamy to gel-like over many days. The vagina is lubricated by this fluid, which demonstrates that ovulation is about to happen. At a certain point, estrogen peaks, and the egg (ovum) is released from the ovary and travels into the fallopian tube. If it isn't fertilized, it disintegrates within twenty-four hours. Your fertile phase is your own sultry summer. This is a period of ripeness and bringing life into being through your own creative endeavors. As such, it can be an extremely productive time, full of energy and creativity. The mother archetype is the one most associated with this phase.

Luteal Phase | Waning Moon | Fall

The corpus luteum (Latin for "yellow body") is the empty follicle from which the ovum bursts. It stays on the surface of the ovary and acts as a temporary endocrine gland that produces high levels of progesterone, which increases your temperature and dries up cervical fluid. The corpus luteum peaks at about six days after ovulation; at this point, hormone levels decrease. The corpus luteum lasts sixteen days at most; after this, your uterine lining gets released, which triggers your period. This is often a dynamic time during which the heat of summer gives way to the long exhalation of early autumn. Your intuition is especially heightened at this time, and you might long for spiritual nourishment, time alone, and authentic relationships and communication. This is a soulful time that exists between the activity of the mother archetype and the deep going-inward of the crone archetype.

Worthy Work:
Clearing the Energetic Womb

It is crucial to periodically clear your energetic womb. A woman's womb is a sacred center of consciousness that holds so much information. This is also the place where you might be holding repressed emotions and other people's energy in the form of past sexual partners, children, friends, or even ancestral wounds. This part of you might also harbor wounds and internalized toxic beliefs about your femininity and sexuality, as well as birthing trauma, abortions, miscarriages, grief, and sexual wounding.

I received this powerful tool from my teacher Mali, who helps her students release and clear toxic emotions and beliefs in this area of the female body where our power has been suppressed and denied. I suggest finding time and space to sit before your worthy woman altar (or your menstrual altar, if you created one) to drop in and feel your feelings.

1. Tap into the energy in your womb. Notice any emotions or sensations. Even "numbness" is a sensation, so acknowledge it if it's there.

2. Visualize the energetic portal of your womb as a spiral that spirals inward.

3. Humbly request that your energetic portal open up to you. Now, if you have any questions, ask them. These might be questions like: "What do I need to do to heal from my past relationship? What is the energy I'm suppressing in my womb? How do I activate your guidance and wisdom? How do I generate a stronger connection with you?"

4. What you'll be shown may surprise you, so be sure to come to this exercise with a beginner's mind. Be open to what you receive, which may come in the form of sounds, body sensations, images, or other symbolic information.

5. Thank your womb for what she has shown you. Clear the space of your energetic womb by using your hands on that area, spiraling counterclockwise at least three times. (To activate rather than clear your energetic womb, make the same motion but spiral clockwise at least three times.)

6. Take time to journal about your experience.

Although this practice doesn't have to be time-consuming, I suggest spending at least twenty minutes being with yourself in a sacred space. Over time, your sessions might be shorter, and the communication may come more quickly and easily as you build trust with yourself and get to know the sacred region of your energetic womb.

Regaining Vitality

Diosa, I want to take a moment to acknowledge that every single one of us is on our own unique health journey with respect to our mental, emotional, physical, and spiritual well-being. In my community, I work with countless women who've experienced everything from optimal vitality and physical radiance to serious illnesses that Western medicine could not diagnose. I think it's important to bridge the gap between holistic and Western medicine, and not to deny the benefits of either. It is absolutely true that our healthcare system is broken and has also encouraged a broken relationship between us and our bodies. At the same time, all too often in the wellness world, people are blamed for their ill health.

I have worked with so many women who've been through autoimmune disorders, cancer, diabetes, and heart disease, as well as chronic and what would be considered terminal conditions. Every single one of us has our own story to tell, and none of these stories can be contained in the reductive idea that our health is purely of our own creation. There are so many systemic and other factors outside our control; too many people have little to no access to proper healthcare, paid time off, parental leave, affordable housing, and healthy food options. This is precisely why it's so important to create a society of worthy women who will be the champions and ambassadors of our collective well-being! It isn't about blaming or shaming ourselves for health problems, but about empowering ourselves with awareness that helps us to come into balance with our bodies and the world around us.

Every single one of us is worthy of experiencing optimal health and vitality, which is going to look different from individual to individual. And, of course, our unique journey to getting there must be taken into account. We can use our so-called obstacles to strengthen our connection to ourselves and to spirit. I have worked with a lot of women for whom illness became a powerful spiritual initiation that helped them to face and confront certain aspects of the self and the soul they might have previously disowned. If you are currently going through illness, consider the ways in which this might be catalyzing you into a deeper experience of yourself and your true worth. Let it be an opportunity for you to shower yourself with exquisite care and to find powerful new ways to dialogue with your body.

I recall working with a client who went through an autoimmune disorder that took a couple years to diagnose. She felt demoralized from her experiences with doctors, as well as her sense that she should have somehow been able to prevent the experience. It took her some time to come back to the idea that her body was worthy of love and care, because she had been viewing it through the lens that her body had failed her. We worked together to unpack some of her negative feelings toward her body, which were sourced in childhood and the message that she was less than for being overweight. We also looked at how, in the years before getting her diagnosis, she'd been numbing her pain with medication, food, and sex that didn't actually make her feel good. We worked with customized affirmations and meditations that helped her, on a subconscious level, to recognize that her body is her temple. Gradually, this enabled her to accept that she deserved to feel good and to give herself all the good things that life had to offer.

We also worked a great deal with helping her to identify tools for her well-being, including preventive measures that would support her vitality. This encompassed finding a functional medicine doctor who empowered her with different pathways to caring for herself. Of course, she was still struggling with the obstacles that most Americans dealing with a broken healthcare system struggle with, such as high deductibles and copays and difficulties with her insurance company. At the same time, she realized that by focusing on some of the factors she *could* control, she was able to actively advocate for her health and stand up for what she needed, while getting the support she deserved.

Like my clients and community members, I've had to embark on my own personal journey toward good health. A lot of times, small daily tasks connected with our everyday functioning can be challenging for people (especially the high-powered women I work with) because they seem so minor and are all too easy to put on the back burner. Personally, I had to honor myself with the utmost gentleness and compassion and understand that part of my own journey toward regaining vitality and respecting my health had to do with investing in my oral health and hygiene. After all, poor dental health can have truly serious consequences, including infections in other parts of the body and painful or even disabling health conditions that can end up being extremely costly. I bought a new electric toothbrush and really nice floss and toothpaste to make the journey more pleasurable for myself. These days, I also make sure to brush my teeth with my daughter to model good oral hygiene for her.

I want you to think about some of the things you wish to do in order to take your health and vitality into your own hands. It's also important to recognize that taking a holistic approach is beneficial. After all, your health is not just your body—it's also your mind and your mindset, as well as your capacity to set conscious intentions to care for yourself in the ways you need.

We know that exercise, sunlight, and fresh air increase serotonin levels in the body and give us a natural sense of joy and connection to ourselves. Are you getting fresh air at least once or twice a day? Are you making sure to give yourself breaks if you spend a lot of time sitting at your computer? Perhaps you can use a timer that reminds you to get up, put on a fun dance song, get into your body, and shake it out. Maybe finding greater balance means playing meditation music as you shower, making sure that you're getting therapeutic support for yourself from loving and trusted professionals, and going to sleep at a set time every night. Perhaps it looks like meal prep at the beginning of the week, scheduling regular checkups, and doing the more practical things that are easy to forget. Make a list for yourself and put it somewhere visible. What is it you need in order to honor the temple of your body?

UNWORTHY LIE:
I am a machine that's meant to look and feel good and be "working" at all times, no matter what—otherwise, I'm not living my best life.

WORTHY TRUTH:
I honor the temple of my body and recognize that my health is a multidimensional aspect of my aliveness that must be honored through cycles of rest, care, and exquisite self-compassion.

✦

Worthy Work:
Care for Your Temple

You are worthy of attending to and caring for all aspects of your health! Take some time to connect with your heart and journal about the various areas of your health, using these questions to guide your inquiry.

* **Physical health:** *Am I getting enough sleep? Am I getting enough exercise? Does my nutrition help me to care for my vital energy? Do I feel connected to the messages my body is sending me (in the form of things like aches, pains, and exhaustion)?*

* **Emotional health:** *Do I have outlets for releasing and processing my emotions? Do I honor my personal moods and seasons, doing what I can to care for myself no matter where I am? Is my inner dialogue compassionate and kind?*

* **Mental health:** *Do I experience a proper work/life balance? Do I feel mentally stimulated in my life? Am I feeding my mind with nurturing influences (in terms of things like the media I'm taking in, the words I'm speaking, the influences I allow to enter my life)?*

* **Spiritual health:** *Do I regularly nurture a connection with the sacred? Do I make time to go inward with activities like meditation or prayer? Do I feel a sense of connection to a soul-led life purpose?*

* **Social and recreational health:** *Do I feel connected to a healthy and supportive community? Am I spending enough time with friends? Do my friends nurture my deeper sense of connection to myself? Am I making time for fun?*

* **Environmental health:** *Is my immediate environment clean, clear, and healthy? Do I surround myself with objects that reflect my deep connection to myself? Do I feel at home and held in my environment?*

Now let's go a little deeper. Based on your answers above, journal about your answers to the following questions:

* What did I learn about health from my caregivers?
* Where do I feel worthy of claiming health?
* Where do I feel unworthy of claiming health? Where do I have the most difficulty caring for my temple?

Next, commit to creating a plan for your health, based on where you feel most worthy and where you know you still need to reclaim worthiness. I encourage you to choose concrete, actionable commitments like the following examples:

* **Tending to your physical health:** *I commit to getting medical checkups once a year and visiting the dentist twice a year to care for my oral health.*

* **Tending to your emotional health:** *I commit to engaging in compassionate self-talk in front of the mirror every morning for five minutes, to cultivate self-love.*

* **Tending to your mental health:** *I commit to weekly sessions with my therapist to find ways to bring greater balance to my life, and to heal from past traumas.*

* **Tending to your spiritual health:** *I commit to meditation and prayer twice a day, which will help me connect with La Diosa in more intentional ways.*

* **Tending to your social/recreational health:** *I commit to joining a women's circle that helps me to connect with other women who are on a path to healing and connection with themselves and others.*

* **Tending to your environmental health:** *I commit to cleaning my home once a week (and making it a fun ritual for myself) to clear the space of energetic and environmental clutter, and to make my home a healing place.*

Embodying a Well Culture

We've talked a lot about individual health, but how do we create a culture that is healthy from the inside out and that encourages a deeper relationship to our well-being?

The Indian philosopher Krishnamurti famously said, "It is no measure of health to be well adjusted to a profoundly sick society." This is why the journey toward discovering and reclaiming our worthiness is all about deconstructing the rules that have been handed down to us.

Do those rules really serve us? A lot of times, they're just ways to get us to be more productive, efficient, compliant workers. We have to start asking ourselves: What is the culture we want to create when it comes to our collective health and well-being?

I recall finding out about "blue zones," which are areas of the world where entire communities are known to live better and longer. Studies have indicated that genetics play only up to a 30 percent role in ensuring our longevity, and deeper studies of these blue zones demonstrate that it's our lifestyles that largely determine our quality of life. Even simple things like living in a place where a sense of purpose is encouraged among all age groups or being in a town with numerous green spaces have huge benefits, driving home the fact that our health requires us to acknowledge that we are all interconnected.

In addition, we need to encourage a culture of greater preventive health and of vibrant foods (including eating the foods of our ancestors and not just processed foods for convenience). We also want to live in a culture where we all actively contribute to being positive and empowered in the conversations we're having about our bodies. Instead of complaining about our aches and pains, or talking about our aging and broken-down bodies, we must normalize the processes of aging and actively share information that helps us to be at our best without any shaming. We can also put more pressure on our government officials to do things like abolishing food deserts in our urban communities, creating more community gardens, and allocating funds toward building local parks and walking trails.

What's important to you when it comes to community health? Use that as a starting point for being part of the change you wish to see or supporting the change that is already happening.

For example, I had a client who, out of her personal interest in natural remedies, entered a two-year apprenticeship to learn about herbal medicine. She fell deeply in love with it and decided to create an herbal medicine clinic for her community, where people could come in and receive specialized herbal remedies that they would purchase at a sliding scale. She also taught classes where people could learn about using the natural remedies in their midst to care for themselves. Overall, she found a powerful way to support the life of her village and to address the needs of her community.

I also firmly believe we need to do what we can to support low-income women of color who are taking on a great deal of the work around caring for our elders. There is such a thing as caregiver burden (as studies demonstrate that caregivers can end up getting stress-related chronic disorders), so we must be proactive about ensuring that the people who are providing care to the most vulnerable in our society are also being lifted up and honored.

This is the meaning of mother medicine. The divine feminine recognizes that every single one of us is needed on this planet, and nobody deserves to be overlooked. We cannot fulfill our true collective holy work if our bodies are diminished, overworked, and not cared for—and if some people are seen as more deserving of health than others. True health means that we look on a systemic level at all the ways we have been living out of balance with ourselves, with one another, and with nature. Embodying a well culture means that we go back to the source and that we model a reality in which all lives are seen as sacred and deserving.

It's time to come back to Mama Earth—to come back to what *feels* good and *is* good for all of us, and to share as exuberantly as we can so that all beings around us can partake of a culture in which we and our health are the priority. Overall, creating a true culture of health means that we see and know ourselves as interconnected parts of a holy whole.

Worthy Work:
Diosa-Made Herbal Elixirs

Traditional herbal medicine can be a powerful way to gather the wisdom of Mother Earth. Crafting holistic remedies ourselves is a beautiful way to honor our connection to La Diosa and to the holistic and multifaceted aspects of our being.

Herbal elixirs have been used the world over for centuries to address root causes rather than just surface-level symptoms. Many individuals and communities are reclaiming the power of herbal medicine to promote health, and to also prevent and cure disease. Here are some powerful herbs you can use, depending on the physical and spiritual properties you seek. I highly recommend buying herbs locally, from a community-based herbal apothecary, to ensure that you are getting them from a reliable, ethical source. Please check in with your doctor or medical provider before using these herbs, as some interact with certain medications, some are not appropriate for pregnant or breastfeeding women, and so on.

Herb	Physical Properties	Spiritual Properties
Arnica flowers	Treats bruises, sprains, and muscle aches	For trauma healing and reconnection with the spirit
Burdock root	Has anti-inflammatory, antioxidant, and antibacterial effects	For clarity, protection, courage, and vitality
Calendula flowers	Helps wounds heal more quickly; aids in skin hydration and elasticity	For good luck, perspective, and rising above perceived challenges
Cayenne powder	Addresses stomach problems; resolves circulatory issues; combats poor appetite	For removing mental/emotional obstacles and blockages
Chamomile flower	Heals hay fever, inflammation, muscle spasms, menstrual disorders, and insomnia	For purification, protection, and good luck
Chickweed	Has anti-inflammatory, antiseptic, and antifungal properties; great for addressing skin ailments like eczema	For love, dreams, and moon magic

Herb	Physical Properties	Spiritual Properties
Comfrey leaf and/or root	Supports the respiratory system and helps to heal broken bones; ideal for "antiaging"	For overcoming difficulties
Echinacea herb and/or root	Boosts immune function; relieves pain; reduces inflammation	For creating healthy boundaries
Ginger root	Raises the body's temperature; boosts metabolism	For generating greater energy and experiencing more security
Goldenseal leaf and/or root	Helps with respiratory infections; addresses digestive upsets, such as diarrhea	For prosperity, protection, and healing
Lavender flowers	Lifts depression and eases stress and anxiety; aids in sleep	For purification, grace, serenity, and devotion
Licorice root	Treats the common cold; promotes a healthy liver	For love and sensuality
Nettle leaf	Helps with skin and bone health; also has antihistamine and antibacterial properties that help treat acne and skin problems	For awakening creativity and bringing newness into one's life
Plantain leaf	Great for skin irritations, cuts, insect bites, burns, and colds	For healing and strength
Raspberry leaf	Ideal for menstrual cramps and promoting fertility and clarity of mind	For love, fertility, and protection

Herb	Physical Properties	Spiritual Properties
St. John's wort	Fumigant for home purification; soothes wounds, bites, digestive disorders, and depression	For protection, blessings, and alleviation of heavy energy
Thyme leaf	Helps with respiratory illnesses and colds; good for healing acne	For beauty, happiness, good health, and psychic ability
Violet	Calms the nervous system	For protection, healing, money magic, and peace
Yarrow leaf and flowers	Anti-inflammatory; heals wounds	For courage, healing, and love

With this knowledge in mind, here are two recipes that include rose—one for a salve (external medicine to be applied to the skin) and one for a tea (internal medicine to be ingested and circulated through your cells). Rose is a gorgeous flower and a symbol of femininity, love, divine connection, and beauty. Among herbalists, roses are loved for their diuretic, anti-inflammatory, nutrient-rich properties. Rose is wonderful for healing everything from PMS, to sore throats, to grief. Roses can be used in tinctures, teas, honeys, hydrosols, essential oils, and so much more. Again, please be sure to check in with your doctor or medical provider before using these elixirs, especially if you're breastfeeding, pregnant, on any medication, or dealing with any kind of illness.

Diosa Rose Salve

For this simple yet effective salve, you'll need the following:

Rose petals	Beeswax
Other herbs of your choice from the previous table (I recommend using no more than three)	Coconut oil
	Small containers
Olive oil	

If you're using fresh rose petals, allow them to dry out overnight by placing them on a table or counter. Fill a jar or other container about halfway with dried petals and pour in just enough olive oil to cover the petals fully; at this point, you'll want to add any other herbs you're using.

Fill a large pot with several inches of water, then place a smaller pot or container on top of the water; transfer the olive oil and rose petals into that smaller pot. Simmer the water over medium-low heat; basically, the water in the large pot should be just hot enough to warm the olive oil without burning or boiling it. Gently heat the oil and rose petals in this way for one to two hours, then remove from the heat. Let the olive oil cool until it's safe to handle, then strain out the rose petals from the oil and keep your new rose petal oil.

In a separate pan, melt down the beeswax and coconut oil (do not boil it, just make sure it's melted down). Use 2 ounces of beeswax and 2 tablespoons of coconut oil for every 4 ounces of rose petal oil. When you're done melting the beeswax and coconut oil, pour this concoction into the rose petal oil and gently stir to combine. Pour the resulting liquid into small containers; the salve will harden over a few hours. Feel free to gift some of the containers to your loved ones!

* * *

Diosa Herbal Tea Blend

For this soothing yet invigorating tea blend, use the following ingredients in the following proportions:

6 parts rose petals

4 parts raspberry leaf

3 parts chamomile flower

2 parts any herb of your choice (depending on the physical and magical properties you desire)

1 part ginger root

1 part licorice root

Place all the ingredients in a large teapot. Pour 4 cups of boiling water into the pot and allow the ingredients to steep for 30 minutes. Then drain the liquid into mason jars, straining out the solid waste of the herbs. You can choose to make this an iced tea by refrigerating it, or you can heat it up again to enjoy a warm beverage.

* * *

✴ **Worthy Affirmations** ✴

◎ *I am worthy of feeling good in the temple of my body.*

◎ *I deserve the utmost nourishment and healing.*

◎ *I am radiant, whole, and full of vitality.*

◎ *I am in harmony with my body, and I nurture it with compassion, care, and love.*

◎ *I am gentle and patient with myself as I navigate my unique journey of health.*

◎ *I am balanced and well.*

◎ *I experience optimal well-being in all aspects of my health.*

◎ *My womb and my blood are clear symbols of my connection to all that is holy and sacred.*

8

You Are Worthy of Growth and Flowing with the Seasons

Every season is one of becoming, but not always one of blooming. Be gracious with your ever-evolving self.

—Brittin Oakman

One of the most important things I've learned on my journey of worthiness is that growth—the burgeoning of the soul on its unique voyage through life—is not always an obvious process. In many ways, I have most learned to flow with the varying internal seasons during my rite of passage from maiden to mother of my daughter. There is a very special coming undone that happens when a woman becomes a mother. It is not just a physical breaking open, but also an emotional one that extends to all aspects of one's life.

My experience was that my baby became my world. There I was, tending to this perfect little being, not sleeping much, and, in my case, nursing around the clock (joyfully and also exhaustedly!). It was an enormous transition, but to add to that, a few months after my daughter's birth, my partner developed a rare illness that caused him to start limping and also took away his ability to walk or even speak. My anchor during this time was my self-sourcing, my spiritual practices, my breath, my understanding that life can be hard and chaotic . . . but I still get to choose to my best ability how to hold the grief and the calm.

I learned to create a sense of inner security in the midst of the falling apart. I found ways to ask friends and family for help. I found ways to feel held by spirit, even when I was scared and overwhelmed. There were times when a part of me longed to turn back the wheel of time and go back to the way things used to be. But I'd done enough spiritual work to recognize that our growth into our true, worthy self—the one we've always been, deep down—requires moving forward, not back. In the words of the prophetic African American science fiction author Octavia Butler, "All that you touch you change. Change changes you. The only lasting truth is change. God is change."

When we open up to change, we open up to our own evolution into our highest wisdom and most worthy self. My friend, I know this isn't always comfortable. But growth means leaning into our edges and recognizing that everything we encounter is an opportunity to ground ourselves in the seen and unseen sources of support around us. I think of it this way: We come into this world a tight bud, and every experience we have has the capacity to make us either close more tightly or to open up. As we open, we bloom into our full potential. We encounter our beauty, our resilience, and parts of ourselves that maybe we didn't even know existed! This is *good*. It's like we are giving space for all aspects of self to breathe.

And while we must do what we can to source our lives in an unshakable inner peace that is part of our birthright, we'll definitely have those moments when life *lifes*—when arguments, conflicts, and difficult situations come filtering in. We can learn to find our center no matter what, but part of growing into our worthy wisdom is flowing with the seasons.

And that's exactly what I did. I could feel it. I was smiling, and I was also giving myself space to cry. I was letting myself feel my edges—the incredible joy of the new life I was holding in my arms, as well as the grief of sudden loss through my partner's illness. I committed then and there to give my all to my baby, myself, and my partner, which required a ton of small and big changes. Easy? No! But possible? Yes!

We all go through times of ascent and descent. Every life is punctuated by peaks and valleys. In the cosmic dance of our existence, we are intimately entwined with the rhythmic patterns of the universe. Fertility and creation encompass the cycles of life, death, and rebirth. As women, our bodies mirror the cycles of the moon, the tides, and the seasons. Reclaiming our worth entails honoring these sacred rhythms, granting ourselves permission to ebb and flow, to ride the waves with acceptance. As I discovered, we do have support in these places, but we also have to be willing to open up to it . . . and to accept inevitable change. By aligning with the cosmic rhythms, we harness the power of our cyclical nature, embracing our worthiness with grace and surrender.

We see firsthand that rushing a process or trying to stay in one leg of the journey goes against nature. It takes time to grow a crop. And then, when a fruit or vegetable is ripe, it's ripe for only a time. When we reconnect to the innate intelligence of our bodies, hearts, and spirits, we become part of an endless cycle of giving and receiving. As long as we stay open, we realize we don't have to hold on to "the way things used to be," which is another manifestation of the scarcity mentality. We can't manipulate nature in order to be in the perpetual summer of youth or fertility. We respect the periods of fallowness and loss, as well as the ones of abundance and gain, as we know they're two sides of the same coin.

Of course, we live in an immature culture, given our general obsession with the pleasures and freedoms of youth. But opening up to being worthy of growth means we welcome the cycle from maiden, to mother, to crone (what is known in many pagan traditions as the three faces of the goddess). We honor our journey and what our worthy woman self is telling us needs to happen in order for us to gracefully flow with our own true nature.

Dear one, I take this opportunity to remind you that you are nature—you are not separate from the Great Mother and her cyclical, regenerative properties. So, throughout this chapter, if you notice yourself feeling resistant to the realities of your own cycle, wherever you may be in your life (in the maiden, mother, or crone phase—it's all welcome), I urge you to be gentle with yourself. Please remember that you've already been through so many changes, and you managed to navigate them to the best of your ability.

The opportunity now is to claim your worth in the midst of the changing seasons, and to learn to flow with all the ups and downs, with fluidity. I remember one of my clients, an older woman in her seventies, giving me the most beautiful smile and saying, "It really is a blessing to be alive, to have lived this long, to have seen and felt and known everything that's crossed my path. How amazing that I get to do this!" The wisdom of her observation gave me chills. My hope is that we can all receive the same medicine and greet the changes with eagerness and grace. Because, diosa, we get to do this amazing thing called life. And no two seasons are ever the same.

Embracing the Glorious Mess

Growth is never linear. In fact, it's damn messy most of the time! It's a constant process of expanding and contracting, blooming and decaying. Two steps forward, one step back, often with a face-plant right in the middle to add some frustration and humility to the mix.

The journey of development means there's bound to be messiness. It's inevitable! We are going to continually create and destroy, become and unbecome. Although this can sometimes be a downright pain in the ass, the power of staying present is that we get the precious chance to watch the miraculous process of change, of our soul's evolution. It isn't the superficial Instagram version of becoming our best self. (In fact, these moments are likelier to end up in the virtual trash bin because they're not usually our most glamorous or graceful!) Rather, it's about recognizing the forces of nature that shape us, that allow us to become more than we ever thought possible. There's a method to the madness, and the messiness has a purpose: to nurture us more deeply and to give us opportunities to live a more soul-aligned life.

I always wondered who made the PSA that we're supposed to have it all together and miraculously create a sense of order and harmony—as if any of us came out of the womb fully formed, with the skills and wisdom to build the life of our dreams! I also get super-frustrated when I get wind of the level of spiritual bypassing that permeates the wellness community. It can sound a little something like "If you're not happy all the time, you're doing something wrong." As if we were meant to thrive in every season. As if growth were about constantly being on the up-and-up, without running into any bumps whatsoever along the way. I suspect that consumerism and advertising myths are behind this idea that life is always supposed to look generative and comfortable, but obviously, this isn't true.

Being on this beautiful planet means accepting that we ourselves are a part of nature, and that there is a season for everything. We must understand that creation and creativity have their built-in cycles, their peaks and valleys. With this understanding, we allow ourselves to make mistakes and learn as we marvel at the beauty and complexity of life's nonlinear trajectories. When we are always searching for sunlight, summer, and perfectly manicured lives, we block our potential for true happiness and true growth. In fact, we become stagnant automatons constantly searching for pleasure without recognizing that pleasure is only one aspect of living a truly meaningful life.

Like many of the women in my community, I'm sure you've dealt with your fair share of turmoil—illness, breakups, loss of jobs and friendships, and even the sense that you are simply running in place, not getting anywhere. I remember an older friend looking at me with a smile and saying, "One day, you'll miss even the things that you used to curse and want to wish away. You'll remember they're all a part of what it means to be alive." My friend understood that it's all about perspective. All our pain, our uncertainty, our mistakes are opportunities to show up with more grace and presence. When we step into our worthy woman self, we automatically bust the myth that we're not supposed to fuck up, get it wrong, or slip up. Instead, we reframe it and embrace the very essence of life.

What happens for you when you start to shift your ideas about failure and making mistakes? What opens up for you when you recognize that there are no failures or mistakes, only endless opportunities to step up to the plate and try, try again? For me, I feel a wave of forgiveness and grace that allows me to see how far I've come, and how far there is to go.

Our spiritual purpose on Earth is full of lessons. You can think of this earth plane as a school with endless opportunities to learn and grow. In many ways, the messiness of our human circumstances is an initiatory path that takes us into the PhD level of Earth School. We flow with the individual circumstances of our lives and the massive collective changes that every generation is called to face. We have no choice—we can't run away from it.

But as I've learned, stepping up to the messiness is not about being good or perfect or right. Our growth edges are not here in order to mold us into cookie-cutter images of perfect women. They're here to break our hearts open and to unleash our full human and spiritual potential. The most important thing we can do in the midst of all of this is to simply *be*, to observe ourselves with the utmost compassion and recognize that we are enough; to open our hearts and allow ourselves to bloom right where we've been planted.

I think of the process of embracing the glorious mess as one of massive grief and growth because it contains the full spectrum of what it means to be human. I know that I have grown leaps and bounds in my journey of motherhood. I gave birth not only to my beautiful daughter, but also to myself. And in many ways, I still consider myself a newborn. The process of becoming is the process of constantly arriving in a new phase of our development. And I know for sure that every day, week, and month brings a new lesson that keeps me on my toes. It is an immense responsibility to embrace this kind of growth. Alongside the well-being of my precious little one, I am also nurturing the well-being of my own wild, worthy woman within.

I have found that from season to season, the things that I need might be different, but the care I give myself never changes. Sometimes it looks like stealing a nap with my daughter, or finding moments to cry, or expressing gratitude out loud to the people in my life, or writing like a badass as I sit there in my pj's with breast milk spilling all over me.

You can be a badass, too! And I'm here to say a badass isn't just the person who quits her job and travels the world to find herself on some kind of life-altering adventure. The life-altering moments are often quiet and unglamorous. You might be in a state of utter exhaustion as you live those moments, but all the same, you're more than willing to show the fuck up as you embark on the next phase of your life.

Again, giving yourself grace is the most important thing you can do. I mean, could you possibly imagine a beautiful tree getting down on itself when its leaves start to fall off in autumn? We must be like the tree and embrace the essence of life, which will take us down many paths and on many different journeys. And while we may have a good amount of control over our perspective and how we frame our experience, it's important to be patient with ourselves when life doesn't seem to be going our way. These are the moments when we are often on the cusp of a breakthrough.

Shame has permeated the lives of so many people I know, and I believe that we are ready for a new pattern of growth—one that isn't rushed along or held in a stagnant state of suspension, but that is allowed to unfold in its own time, at its own pace.

Just like you, I'm a work in progress, and I'm not done yet. I'm constantly training myself to welcome the glorious mess, because I know that it is one of the most beautiful parts of my inheritance as a divine human being.

Dancing Through the Elements:
Seasonal Rites of Passage

We're always in a process of growing, but certain stages of our growth can be more momentous than others. These stages include birth, puberty, marriage, and death, but they also encompass other moments in our lives when we go through powerful changes that alter the course of our journey forever: our first period, our first experience of sexual pleasure, our first encounter speaking truth to power, the first time we feel we've mastered something we're truly good at, and even the first major disappointment that teaches us to temper our expectations with patience. All of these are rites of passage that mark the important moments and help us to cull a deeper wisdom that determines how we navigate life.

Since time immemorial, we've had rites of passage to mark important points in our human evolution. This has been our culture's way of recognizing that we are not meant to remain the same from moment to moment. We are meant to flow through the stages of being the maiden, mother, and crone—not just for ourselves and our own soul growth, but also for the enrichment of our societies and communities. Unfortunately, rites of passage are few and far between in our lives, and even when we experience them, they tend to lack the sacred rituals that work to activate our power and give us the strength and spiritual support to show up with our new identity in the world.

In many ways, cultural critics and spiritual teachers have noted that we are living in a time of soul immaturity, of arrested development that keeps us caught in Peter Pan syndrome—reluctant to grow up and take on the mantle of greater responsibilities. A true rite of passage connects us not just with our world, but also with Mama Nature and her glorious seasons and cycles. It gives us the chance to wake up from what Dr. Clarissa Pinkola Estés refers to as "psychic slumber," which keeps us stuck in a spell of sameness, in a spiritual torpor that prevents us from genuine soul growth.

For me, one of the most powerful ways of acknowledging our personal rites of passage (especially in the absence of formal cultural rituals) is working with the four elements: fire, water, air, and earth. These four elements are the building blocks of nature, and they exist symbolically and literally in our makeup.

For me, the elements in a state of balance represent the natural equilibrium of our inner worthy woman. The thing is, balance is going to look different in different moments of our life. A fire phase of life might look extremely extroverted, dominated by passionate activity and a more external orientation. A water phase might look like paying attention to our emotions, our inner world, and our ability to heal. An air phase could entail welcoming an influx of new ideas and inspiration. An earth phase might mean settling down and building a stable home base for ourselves and our loved ones. Each of us has a unique mixture of the elements at any given stage, and some elements may be more activated than others.

In many traditional practices, from traditional Chinese medicine to Ayurveda to alchemy, each element is associated with a specific season. In this way, the elements give us a beautiful metaphor for the variegated wisdom of the Earth and her cycles and seasons. They help us to see that life is meant to be cyclical. There is a time for joy and celebration, and a time for going inward—entering the garden of the soul in the midst of winter.

The elements have been a really important way for me to understand my own true nature, and to honor that I may not be in the same place that I was ten, five, or even two years ago. I am constantly in a state of change—like our planet, like our sun, like the galaxies themselves. And the less I resist, the more attuned I will be with my own worthiness.

Where are you with respect to major or minor changes you might be navigating? Are you in one season or in between seasons? Using the following table, consider how you might be able to dance through the elements in this moment of your life, allowing your dance to be a testament to your resilience and all the lessons you carry with you.

Season	Element	Qualities
Spring	Air	Freshness, clarity, insight, new ideas, massive change, inspiration, sudden epiphanies, endeavors like starting a new business, getting married, or birthing something new into the world (can also be associated with qualities like being overly spacey, escapist, in one's head)
Summer	Fire	Desire, motivation, passion, intensity, fervent emotion, love, romance, socializing, active engagement with the world, physical vitality (can also be associated with qualities like physical depletion and burnout from overwork or challenging relationships)
Autumn	Water	Intuition, healing, nurturing, psychic ability, spirituality, dreams, cleansing, clearing (can also be associated with qualities like chaos, being overly emotional, and seesawing between emotional states)
Winter	Earth	Stillness, cycles coming to an end, hibernation, going inward, connecting with ancestors, building something that endures (can also be associated with qualities like rigidity, antisocial behavior, and obeisance to outdated traditions or ways of being)

Our overculture is obsessed with vitality, with youth, with constant positivity. It has accordingly dishonored the mysteries of aging and death, or, as Sarah Durham Wilson calls it, "saging." The irony is that when we glamorize eternal summer, what we get is stagnant death energy. One of my mentors, Aimee Aroha, says we are living in a death culture, a culture that is orienting us toward destruction and zapping us of our true life energy. You see, if we fail to honor the seasons and cycles of life, we experience soul death. Without honoring and tending to the mother—both Mother Earth and the women of the world—we die. The beauty and potential of the elements within and without are neglected and left to languish and decay.

The feminine understands that life is cyclical, that the sun rises and sets, and that just as we move through the seasons, we must revisit lessons in order for learning to occur. When we follow the wisdom of the elements and their attendant seasons, we are consciously choosing to navigate transitions with grace and ease, and to lean in to whatever season of growth we may be in.

UNWORTHY LIE:
In order to be happy or to be seen as worthy,
I need to remain youthful, beautiful, and
desirable to others.

WORTHY TRUTH:
My true beauty and power rest inside my
capacity to welcome the coming and going
of the seasons, recognizing they all have
their own unique wisdom.

+

Worthy Work:
Marking Time

It can be difficult to honor important rites of passage in the busyness of our lives, but it's extremely crucial. As the old adage goes, we can't know where we're headed unless we know where we've been.

For this exercise, take at least an hour to create a time-line of your life, marking the most important moments of your journey. I advise you to include at least one experience for each year of your life (and you may discover that certain years were more eventful than others!). The way you determine these moments is going to be unique to you, but consider the following questions:

1. Did I emerge from this experience a different person? If so, how?

2. Did I consider this experience to be positive or negative?

3. What were the sacred lessons that I received from this experience?

4. Where was I during this experience (in a spiritual spring, summer, fall, or winter)?

Consider the phase you are currently in. What can you do to honor this moment of your life? For example, I have a client who has been in a winter/earth phase in the wake of a painful divorce. She is becoming her own stable rock by taking time to go inward and to love up on herself. Although things may look slow and uneventful on the outside, she has gone through a series of powerful perspective shifts. She's also learning to practice the sacred art of rest—something that living inside the construct of capitalism often prevents us from doing. As she flows with this particular season, she is learning to step outside of the artificial constructs of time that cause us to be busier than we need to be. For the first time in her life, she is getting eight to ten hours of sleep per night, filling her house with sunlight and candlelight in lieu of lamps and overhead lighting, and connecting with nature in a more intentional way.

What is it time for you to do, in order to more easily flow with the season you're in? Write out a list of at least five self-honoring ways to mark this period of time in your life, and commit to doing them.

The Story of Inanna: Initiation into Your Mature Worthy Woman

One of the most important stories of growing into our authentic self can be found in the ancient Sumerian myth of the Descent of Inanna. In this story, the goddess Inanna, the Queen of Heaven, travels to the underworld to pay her respects to her sister Ereshkigal, the Queen of the Dead, who has been recently widowed. Ereshkigal is not happy about her sister's visit and doesn't allow her to enter the underworld at first. Finally, she lets Inanna in on the condition that she strip off an article of clothing or piece of jewelry at each of the seven gates she passes through. By the time Inanna reaches Ereshkigal, she is completely naked. Then Ereshkigal fixes her sister with the gaze of death and strikes her dead.

When Inanna's Father God, Enki, hears what has happened, he sends two androgynous beings to the underworld to retrieve her. These messengers see a distraught Ereshkigal, and they offer her deep sympathy for her grief. In return, the

Queen of the Dead offers to grant them whatever they wish, and they ask for Inanna's corpse.

Inanna is resurrected with the food and water of life but must find someone to take her place in the underworld. When she returns home, she discovers that her sons and servants are all mourning her death—but her lover, Dumuzi, is not. Inanna is infuriated and immediately sends him to the underworld in her stead. However, Dumuzi's sister offers to go in his place; it is ultimately decided that Dumuzi will spend half the year in the underworld, and his sister will take his place the rest of the year.

So, how do we make sense of this complex story? Many historians and mythologists recognize its resemblance to stories like the myth of Persephone (which also explains why we have spring/summer for half the year and fall/winter for the other half). However, a lot of feminist psychoanalysts, like Marion Woodman and Dr. Clarissa Pinkola Estés, refer to the story as a classic heroine's journey. In this story, the protagonist, Inanna, must descend into the underworld in order to be made whole. Many view Ereshkigal as the underworld version of Inanna. In many ways, both goddesses must undergo a kind of soul death (Ereshkigal through the death of her husband, and Inanna through her own murder) in order to be resurrected (Ereshkigal is "brought back to life" when she receives empathy from the messengers, and Inanna is revived by the food and water of life).

This is an important story—not just because it is one of the oldest myths of the world (and one that's centered on a strong, worthy-ass goddess who knows that, even though she's divine, part of her journey has to do with dying to her old self), but because it's a metaphor for the moments of reckoning we must all go through in order to become *more* of who we are. By the time we get to the end of the story, Inanna has gone through a major change—one that has helped her to know she's capable of doing the hard things and that makes her damn sure she is worthy of being honored (bye-bye, Dumuzi!).

We all have these deep moments of entering the underworld and a part of our nature that can be scary to face: one where we are asked to confront our "darker" aspects and to grieve what we have lost. This is a myth for all diosas to honor and to take into our hearts. Yes, it can be scary as fuck, but there is great wisdom and power in the darkness, which is no different from the holy darkness of the womb—the gateway to every birth and rebirth we will experience.

I also love the story of Inanna because it reminds me that growth is a spiral. We might be the Queen of Heaven in our lives, but the larger cycles of growth always include an ascent and a descent. We might find that it's necessary to shed certain aspects of our identity in order to uncover a new aspect of our power. This might mean letting go of intimate relationships, friendships, careers, and other things that no longer fit into who we are becoming. This is something that spiritual "doctrines" like the so-called prosperity gospel or the law of attraction fail to take into account. Such doctrines tend to simplistically suggest that the difficult or painful moments of our lives are the consequence of "negative" thoughts, not taking into account that our proudest moments are often preceded by loss, grief, and confusion.

I know I've had my fair share of moments when I believed that I had it all figured out, only to be humbled like Inanna and brought to my knees so I could kiss the earth and remember the parts of me I'd forgotten. The story of Inanna helps us make sense of these moments when we forget who we are, and it encourages us to cultivate the faith to lean in to the mystery, to die to who we used to be, to allow new aspects of who we are to come shining through.

Sister, all the challenges in your life are dark soil for new initiations. Divorce? Betrayal? Death? Isolation? The feeling that your life is falling apart and you just don't know who you are anymore? The experience of heartache and disappointment over what could have been? Some might call it a quarter-life crisis, a midlife crisis, or something else, but when you reenter sacred time and honor the cycles of your life, which are full of unexpected rites of passage, it's all fertilizer for new realizations.

Remember, even goddesses die. But the purpose of death is to remind you of your resilience, your eternal nature, your enduring identity as a phoenix plunging into the flames and rising from the ashes of circumstance into your true worthy self.

The Phoenix Process

The idea of the phoenix process comes from the guided imagery pioneer Dr. Gerald Epstein, who believed we can navigate transformation using the metaphor of the phoenix, a mythical bird that bursts into flame and is reborn from the ashes in an ever-renewable quest for its true self. The idea is, when you experience loss or change that causes pain or anger, instead of fighting against it, you can embrace it as an opportunity to burn away that which is no longer serving you and transform yourself into who you are meant to be. Other teachers, including Elizabeth Lesser, have referred to the phoenix process as a necessary journey through transformation: Instead of being dragged through the painful turning points of our lives, we willingly plunge ourselves into the fire to be born anew, and to be initiated into our eternal nature.

The thing that sets apart the person who signs up for the initiation from the one who goes through it reluctantly, complaining every step of the way, is the awareness that the pain has a purpose. Even if we don't know what it is, we descend into the depths of our grief and loss. We go all the way in, even though it hurts, even though we have no fucking clue what will happen next. We stay in the depths with our broken-open heart, recognizing that whoever we are meant to be on the other side is being birthed within this sacred, spiritual darkness. Often, we discover that there's really nothing left to lose except for the illusions that kept us from living from the deepest, rawest, most truthful core of who we are.

Every single diosa in this world is a unique soul whose journey will look a special way, depending on the lessons she is most meant to integrate. I have clients and friends whose phoenix process entailed everything from excruciating illness, to confronting and eradicating toxic generational patterns, to stepping into a more authentic love after decades of heartache and disrespect. Please don't compare your journey to anyone else's. Think of the ways you have danced the dance of the elements and seasons in your own life. Think of the lessons you have learned, and the ones that have been most difficult to integrate. If you find yourself spiraling back to the same painful lessons, consider that your full acceptance of the situation and your willingness to love yourself up in the midst of it are part of the transformative process.

Of course, riding the wave of change is easier said than done. I recall a client I was working with who discovered that not only had her husband of thirty years been having multiple affairs throughout their marriage, he'd also lived a double life, with another partner and two children. "It was like something out of a soap opera," she told me. "I didn't want to believe that this was my life, because it made me feel weak, stupid, oblivious to what had been going on behind my back for so long."

In fact, even though this information had come to light when the other woman contacted her to tell her the truth, she chose not to confront her husband for more than a year. "Some part of me thought that if I didn't talk about it to anyone, least of all him, then maybe it was just a bad dream that would go away on its own," she said. But her denial only made things worse. She was having panic attacks on a weekly basis, and she was overtaken by a depression that left her physically and emotionally debilitated.

But we worked together to help her move in the direction of change, and as the tears flowed, something inside her thawed. She eventually filed for divorce and moved into a new phase of growth and possibility. She learned that relinquishing the "dead weight" of our life—letting go of the things that no longer serve us and that, in fact, block our connection to our truest and most worthy self—is necessary.

Diosa, I want to acknowledge that this takes courage. It doesn't always look pretty or orderly. As you know, change is messy, and there may be some aspects of who you are, who you've learned to be in order to get by and survive, that need to be kicked to the curb. This is part of the process. It might mean learning to ask for help, to address problems in a more constructive and direct way, to question the parts of your identity that you've taken for granted as intrinsic aspects of who you are.

If you find yourself in the midst of a phoenix process, please take heart. This is an opportunity to be reborn as your worthy woman self, as the powerful goddess you've always been. It is in moments like these that you are given a potent gift: to uncover who you really are, past the relationships and accolades and layers of illusion that the overculture places on all of us.

I also want you to remember that transformation isn't all death and destruction. Remember, Inanna's journey into the underworld wasn't only a descent; it was also an ascent back into the world. Sometimes we forget that winter always gives way to spring, to possibility, to new hope—but an important part of honoring the seasons is recognizing the stirrings within us and breaking free from the egg that's incubating our new self.

I know for myself that part of my phoenix process has been about stepping more decisively and publicly into my spiritual and intuitive gifts, without guilt or shame. I've had my fair share of raised eyebrows from people who didn't understand why I was doing the things I was doing, especially in the wake of my sobriety, when some people accused me of becoming a totally different person. The truth is, I was becoming more comfortable expressing the parts of myself that had always been there, but that had been under wraps due to self-consciousness and self-doubt.

It's true that some of the things you may end up doing in your transformative phoenix process will seem strange to other people. But that's perfectly fine. You're the main character in your life, and it's up to you to flow with your seasons in the ways that make the most sense to you. The beautiful thing about this journey is that it will break you open to your deeper knowing. And from there, you will have the most reliable compass anyone could possibly ask for: your own worthy heart.

Worthy Work:
Dying to Be Reborn

This is a powerful ritual of death and rebirth that will take you on a journey into the parts of yourself that are ready to be awakened, that are waiting to share their power with the world. Please give yourself at least an hour, in a private and well-contained space, to go on this quest into your true self. You may wish to do this ritual while naked, as a celebration of your essential nature. Or, in the rebirth section of the ritual, you may wish to put on a garment that symbolizes the queenly being you are ready to transform into. Surround yourself with the magical tools and objects that will support you the most on this descent into the underworld and reascent back to a new reality. Many of us also come from ancestral traditions with ties to rituals and ceremonies that have been long forgotten. If you wish, welcome your roots into this exercise—perhaps through dance, prayer, chanting, or anything else. Explore and reclaim the rites of passage that your ancestors wove into their lives.

1. Take a few moments to breathe and get quiet. You can light a candle, burn some incense, put on some meditative music, call in your wise ancestors and spirit guides, and do anything else you need to in order to set the space and center yourself. This should be a space where you're free to be vulnerable and express yourself however you want to: screaming, stomping, dancing, crying, and so on.

2. Next, take a piece of paper and separate it into three columns. The first will be "What I'm Letting Go Of," the second will be "What I Fear About Letting Go," and the third will be "The Wonderful Things That Are Possible When I Let Go." Check out the example on the next page to get a sense of what this might look like. Do not censor yourself here. Tune in to your heart and write down everything you can think of as truthfully as you can. You'll want to have at least seven entries under each column for the next part of the exercise. Here are a few potential examples.

What I'm Letting Go Of	What I Fear About Letting Go	The Wonderful Things That Are Possible When I Let Go
Shame around my sexuality (which is wrapped up in negative sexual experiences with abusive boyfriends)	Being alone, inviting negative attention from others (especially men), being perceived by others as slutty or desperate	Great orgasmic sex, being confident about what does and doesn't turn me on, more respectful and communicative partners, greater confidence in myself
Allowing my boss and colleagues to talk down to me	Being disliked or seen as bitchy, being told I'm overly sensitive and an angry woman of color, being out of a job, being seen as too high-maintenance	Being respected for standing up for myself, teaching others how I will and will not be treated, using my voice to advocate for others who don't feel seen and heard
Trying to please my family members by avoiding difficult conversations	Getting into major arguments, having estranged relationships, feeling endlessly guilty	Creating more honest and authentic relationships, getting deeper with others, breaking patterns of family dysfunction and avoidance

3. Read over everything you've written. Feel the pain and the possibility in your situation. Remember that you are capable of birthing your true self many times over.

4. Now allow yourself to enter into a meditative state. You'll visualize yourself walking through the seven gates of the underworld, just like Inanna did. Each of these gates is a portal to your true, worthy woman self. At each of the seven gates, determine what you are

ready to put down, based on the list you made. Again, these should be things that have deep meaning for you or that have characterized your identity up to this point, but that you acknowledge are no longer serving you or helping you to be your worthy woman self. Feel yourself literally shedding the dead weight of the past, and say aloud, "I am freely putting down [whatever it is you're letting go of]. I am surrendering control and opening to what is."

5. After you have passed through the final gate, visualize yourself dead, similar to Inanna. (If you've ever had suicidal ideation, please skip this step. The purpose here is to envision not a literal death, but a symbolic one. In many spiritual traditions, envisioning your death is a way to step across the threshold of your current life and into a new one; it is not a way to bypass the pain of your circumstances or escape into an exalted afterlife. Please be gentle with yourself here and remember that this is not meant to be a literal experience.) Feel what it is to die to your old self, and to hang in the state between death and rebirth. Feel all the feelings in your body and give space to your emotions and however they may wish to be expressed.

6. You will know intuitively when it's time to be reborn. Feel your body stirring awake. You may wish to sing, chant, dance, or move in a new way. Feel yourself rising, rising, rising . . . out of the darkness of the underworld and into the light of a new dawn. You have been born anew! Gaze at yourself in the mirror and greet your resurrected self. How beautiful she is! She is the eternal

face of the goddess. She is the phoenix who rises, over and over, from the ashes of her life. You may wish to say to yourself, "I am the goddess, I am the phoenix, ever birthing myself anew." As you close your ritual, you may wish to offer prayers for your new life, for new and beautiful possibilities.

7. Finally, seal your Worthy Work by doing something that honors your rebirth. This may look like having a delicious, healthy dinner with a friend or taking yourself out on a date. Whatever you do, do it in honor of the new incarnation of your worthy woman self, who is ready to take on the world.

✳ Worthy Affirmations ✳

◎ *I am meant to flow and grow with the seasons.*

◎ *Reclaiming my worthiness as a cyclical, holy woman is a revolutionary act.*

◎ *I am a part of nature's cycles and evolution.*

◎ *I continue to expand into the most soul-aligned version of me.*

◎ *I am a phoenix rising from the ashes and gracefully entering the next phase of my worthy woman self.*

◎ *As I expand, I make room for more goodness and relinquish that which no longer serves me.*

9

You Are Worthy of Community

*I am often struck by the dangerous narcissism fostered
by spiritual rhetoric that pays so much attention to
individual self-improvement and so little to the practice
of love within the context of community.*

—bell hooks

These days, loneliness is an epidemic of heretofore-unseen proportions. Despite the fact that the digital age means most of us are hyperconnected through social media, people are feeling more disconnected than ever before. According to a Meta-Gallup survey, 24 percent of people aged fifteen and older reported feeling very or fairly lonely. A recent Harvard study also notes that 36 percent of all Americans (including 61 percent of young adults and 51 percent of mothers with young children) experience serious loneliness.

How did we get here? In an era of convenience, in which technology seems to have figured everything out, why do we still feel so damn alone? Throughout most of human history, people have coexisted in tight-knit multigenerational villages (literal or figurative), where they depended on one another for survival. But modern Western life is more atomized than ever. We laud rugged individualism, picture-perfect gated communities, and the isolated nuclear family unit that lives far away from extended family. Industrialization and its attendant creature comforts have made life "easier" in some respects, but harder in others. After all, our hearts, minds, bodies, and spirits are wired for connection, which for most of us, especially since the pandemic, is severely lacking.

We are in times of massive change that can feel alternately transcendent and chaotic. We might have been indoctrinated with the idea that we can face the whole shebang alone, but the mental health crisis and extreme loneliness that so many of us are facing is telling us a different story. The overculture isn't working. We are animals that require our pack in order to thrive and create a world that allows each of us to embrace our worthiness. We are nature, and nature is filled with symbiotic relationships that reflect the potential for what human community can look like.

Poet and naturalist Alison Hawthorne Deming writes:

The human community is interwoven with, and ultimately is a subset of, the biotic community. If the biotic community takes a dive, so does the human. In such a place, stewardship of resources is in everyone's self-interest. And the place feels like a community. Neighbor befriends neighbor, tomato seedlings are exchanged in the spring, jam jars in the fall, and local story links everyone together like threads of mycorrhizal fungi in a forest. Everyone knows everyone else's business—to their joy and grief—and the sense of belonging is a genuine and stabilizing factor in the face of change.

Belonging is the ground of our true nature, which is woven into our ecosystems. We are all interconnected links in a grand chain of being that is becoming less and less obvious to us as we are sold the lie that we need to be self-made instead of community-made and community-nurtured. No matter what you've been told or how self-sufficient you've been taught to be, you, diosa, are worthy of community.

I started my Diosa community during a time when I craved a sisterhood of conscious, spiritual women of color. At the time, I'd only come across groups of mostly white women, and while I deeply benefited from the teachings and friendships I found in these spaces, they were lacking the cultural context and depth I needed in order to feel seen, heard, and validated in my experience. Because I didn't hear stories from people who'd specifically experienced some of the things that I had, I realized that I needed to create a community in which my stories and experiences were reflected—and where other women of color similarly felt mirrored.

As my community grew, miracles happened. Many sisters came together to hold space for one another. Lots of women reported feeling happier and less isolated, as all of us shared resources to support one another's growth. I even met the doula who helped me give birth to my daughter, right in my community! She came to my first Diosa retreat. As she thanked me for holding space for her, I said, "One day in the future, you're going to be there for me, literally holding me and helping me birth my daughter into this world." And she did!

Even though I began the Diosa community as a leader who was there to hold space for other women to come together and be supported, I quickly came to understand that I also get to be held by my community—something that too many facilitators and space-holders forget.

During the first year of my daughter's life, my partner came down with a rare illness that caused him to lose some of his essential functions. This meant that the responsibilities of caretaking and tending to our family's financial needs fell on me. Moreover, we'd just moved to NYC to be closer to my mother and to attend to some of his issues with his declining health. With all the stress of being a new mom, caring for a young child and an infirm spouse, and simply taking care of day-to-day responsibilities, my business became unmanageable.

I recall my dear soul sister Linda García, author of the amazing book *Wealth Warrior: 8 Steps for Communities of Color to Conquer the Stock Market*, telling me, "I'm ringing the alarm, babe. You need help!"

Even though I'd been doing community-building work for so long, there was a part of me that felt ashamed to ask for help. I was accustomed to getting women's circles going and encouraging the participants to be there for one another, exchange resources, and hire one another for their services—but I had never thought to take a dose of my own medicine. So I put together a GoFundMe that shared what was going on at home and admitted that I needed some serious help, as insurance costs and doctor's visits had turned my family's finances on their head. It was a big, vulnerable ask.

Another dear soul sister of mine, Nisha Moodley, affirmed this by saying, "You get to be held by your Diosa community now. You've helped create this beautiful web of support, so now you get to have it support you."

It was a humbling experience that still brings up a lot of emotions for me, but I'm grateful I had the opportunity to put down my ego and simply be loved in a way that helped my family to build ourselves back up.

We are taught in this hyperindividualized world that we

must do all of it on our own—even the moments that require the multidimensional wisdom of the collective, which is the greatest blessing I can think of. Enough is enough. We must return to our roots. We must water them with care and diligence, and do the soul work that is necessary to reach out beyond our isolated bubbles; to say, "I need you, and you need me"; to recognize that community is not a luxury—it is our worthy birthright.

Community Care Is Self-Care

You've probably heard the proverb "It takes a village to raise a child." But today, the village is becoming increasingly uncommon. Instead of growing up with tons of relatives across the generational spectrum, with friends and family members spilling into the doors of our homes on a daily basis to share food, laughter, news, or support, many of us get what we need through transactional relationships: by paying for support or buying stuff online. Today's communities aren't necessarily held up by heart connections, but by a global economy and next-day delivery. At the same time, we yearn for ancestral memories of the village, of the tribe that comes together through times of harvest and of lack, to celebrate and to grieve. Some part of us intuitively knows that community care *is* self-care.

In a time when we tend to measure our worthiness by our job titles and how much money we make, I think it's crucial to bring this idea of the village back into public awareness. The village is where our most enduring values—kindness, compassion, mutual aid, generosity, and openheartedness—are cultivated. It makes me think of the Bantu term *ubuntu*, which often gets translated as "humanity," but more specifically means "I am because we are." We are all part of an interconnected ecosystem of relationships that nurture the soil from which our life grows and flourishes.

In some ways, I wonder if the breakdown of local villages is asking us to reconnect to the greater global village. Yes, we're all individuals with our own thoughts, beliefs, histories, and embodied experiences, but we also belong to a complex world that is overflowing with struggle and beauty. We can choose to redirect our attention from our isolated lives and into a planet that needs our love and our gifts. We can choose to stand up against oppression of all kinds and to embody a way of being that says, "All beings are a part of my village, and nobody deserves to be excluded." We can choose to step into our worthiness so that we can rebuild local communities that are linked to this larger global village and that are robust enough to weather any crisis.

Of course, while I want to acknowledge that this is a grand vision I hope all of us can start to live into, there is no one-size-fits-all when it comes to community—and everyone's situation is unique. I've worked with diosas who live in big cities, midsized suburbs, rural areas, and even secluded ashrams and monasteries. Some of them have enormous groups of friends and family; others only a few. Some mostly talk to people online, and still others consider the surrounding plants, trees, and animals to be their primary village.

All of us are faced with unique circumstances, and we all have unique relationships to community, as well. For some of us, community is a source of ease and joy; for others, it is tied to experiences of pain, disappointment, and rejection—especially if we grew up in traumatic households that encouraged conformity and obedience over self-expression and genuine connection. Most of us have experienced a blend of the two. And as much as we may long for a village like the ones our ancestors had, it doesn't always feel safe. We might long for a tight-knit circle of family and friends, but if we are cycle breakers, it may not be healthy for us to have some of them around, tending to our children and potentially spreading their toxicity.

Still, we are not meant to do all the things alone. We are meant to find our soul family, no matter how big or small it might be. Because without it, we can't thrive.

During COVID, larger groups of people came to recognize this as an undeniable truth, and many of them engaged in acts of mutual aid—which occurs when everyday people unite to care for one another and pool their resources together to help those in need. Mutual aid during the pandemic was also a political statement—a way of acknowledging that we are not served by the current systems and powers that be, so we must learn to lean on one another. My GoFundMe was a striking example of mutual aid in the face of a broken healthcare system.

Mutual aid is not to be mistaken for charity. Mutual aid involves recognizing that it is advantageous to lift your community up and to build relationships of symbiotic trust, respect, and generosity. And it can look a lot of ways, aside from giving money. It could be as simple as inviting a friend with no close family nearby to share a holiday meal, or sharing words of encouragement with a stranger, or taking time to teach a group of people a practical skill that will make their lives easier. Even though we live under capitalism, mutual aid is something people—especially those of lesser socioeconomic means and those who come from historically marginalized communities—have been practicing forever. The idea that we should compete for resources is ludicrous when mutual aid is a way better and more efficient method of resource-sharing and living the values we'd like to see reflected in our society: justice and equality, empowerment and dignity.

Unfortunately, these days, carrying and supporting one

another through mutual aid is undermined by the phenomenon of disposability, which has many people treating relationships and objects as commodities of convenience, as if the only reason other people are around is to serve our needs, as if we have no responsibility to them whatsoever.

Nobody is disposable! Of course, that doesn't mean everyone you meet has to be your BFF or that you have to love absolutely everyone. It just means that the beings around us are deserving of dignity and respect. We might not connect with everyone on the level of soul, but we can find ways to honor everyone in our lives. Each of us has a meaningful role to play, after all. For example, I have a neighbor who has very different values from mine—and yet, she is so kind and sweet to my daughter, which sends a message of positivity and solidarity; this reassures me that we have each other's backs, even if we don't see eye to eye on everything.

I think of community as existing in concentric circles and layers. This looks different for everyone. Our closest circle, which is at the center, is likely to be the smallest—this is the one that consists of our "inside" crew, such as our spouse, kids, and dearest friends and family members. The next layer might contain friends who aren't quite as close, or family members we love but to whom we might not necessarily spill all our secrets. The layer after that might include colleagues, collaborators, and neighbors. And after that, there might be people we see in our community, like the man who owns the bodega down the street or the person who delivers our mail. The point is, we're all connected, and we can choose to the best of our ability to see the light in everyone we meet—or to at least acknowledge the fact that they, too, are souls worthy of compassion and care.

One of my dear colleagues, Dra. Rocío Rosales Meza, advises us to "decolonize and dream in the New Earth." She writes, "The New Earth is not new age. It is rooted in Indigenous wisdom. Train your vision so that you can see more than this dying paradigm. Decolonize so that you can dream in the New Earth . . . In the New Earth we get to weave together again, we are stronger together, each of us sharing our love and gifts and building together and supporting one another." We must incubate the dream of what we wish for our communities to be. And then we must birth what we wish to create. Our dreams of community must be fueled by love and justice—by the recognition that we need one another if we are to survive and thrive in all the ways.

UNWORTHY LIE:

*Community is a luxury—it would be nice
to have, but at this stage in my life, it doesn't
feel essential or realistic.*

WORTHY TRUTH:

*Community is a necessity—it helps me to know
that I am connected to everything else in
this world, and it reminds me that I am
worthy of love and support.*

+

Healing the Wounds of Sisterhood

There's so much power in sisterhood, which I define as the sacred bond that unites women across time and space. Sisterhood is so necessary in the Worthy Revolution because we're stronger together than we are alone and apart. Together, we are capable of rising above our circumstances and building a monument to our collective worthiness from the rubble of oppression, by supporting, uplifting, and celebrating one another. Together, we magnify our individual and collective resilience.

Since antiquity, women have gathered together in circles to steward one another through important rites of passage, offer empathy and support, and share in practical ways the burdens and joys of their lives. Unfortunately, patriarchy has severed us from our sisters. Over time, as our communities have grown smaller and more isolated, sisterhood was taken away from us (although it certainly didn't disappear altogether—we are too powerful for that!). I believe that patriarchy has always been onto the fact that when groups of women gather together, enormous power is incubated. And, of course, that's bad news for those who have sought to keep us down.

I believe that patriarchy is the source of the sisterhood wound, which I see as the painful or ambivalent relationships we develop toward other women. Some of these come from our own personal experiences, but, by and large, they come from the poisonous stereotypes about women and femininity that we have internalized from our culture. Together, they form a toxic root system that can keep us from growing the kinds of fertile and meaningful relationships that would serve as powerful mirrors of our own divine femininity and worthiness. They keep us in a state of comparison, fear, jealousy, and downright vitriol when it comes to relating to other women.

A lot of times, we're not encouraged to see women as our sisters who are engaged in the same struggles and challenges as we are. We forget that honoring other women is a way of honoring the goddess. Instead, we have internalized patriarchy's objectification of women and started to view other women as being either way above us or way beneath us. This often occurs across racial and class lines, as in slave-owning white women's treatment of enslaved Black women in the antebellum South, or even in some upper-class women's exploitation of female domestic workers today.

I believe all of this is by design. If women are expending all our energy fighting one another, we can't address the conditions of our continued oppression. Some of us may be overly focused on individual gains instead of recognizing that it's our collective responsibility to fight for all the women of the world. When we don't recognize how patriarchy keeps us apart—through suspicion, competition, and internalized stereotypes—we can't see the forest for the trees. And we miss the opportunities to build bridges with the people who could be our staunchest allies and advocates.

Unfortunately, most of us have experienced mean girl syndrome, whether it's been directed toward us or we've directed it toward others. In middle school, high school, and even college, I saw how commonplace it was to be hyper-judgmental of other women—to refer to them as bitches, sluts, and any number of words that degrade the feminine in our society. I saw how easy it was to judge women's appearances, as well as the strength and credibility of their ideas. From an early age, however, I resisted this idea that I should see other women as my enemies. I felt an affinity for women, because some part of me knew that connecting with them was an aspect of connecting with the divine feminine.

However, many of us who are indoctrinated into belief systems that cut the divine feminine out of society altogether may not realize what we're doing. Sometimes we don't even recognize we're perpetuating a system that is at its core disrespectful to women. As Margaret Atwood observed in her phenomenal book *The Handmaid's Tale*, women themselves can be the most effective foot soldiers of patriarchy. Often, we turn against one another for our own survival. However, in the immortal words of Audre Lorde, "The master's tools will never dismantle the master's house. They may allow us temporarily to beat him at his own game, but they will never enable us to bring about genuine change."

Healing the sister wound means that we need new tools—which, for me, are actually ancient tools, sourced in our female ancestors' wisdom and strong connections with one another. It's also about recognizing that we are not separate. It's about cherishing the great diversity in our midst. It is about being antiracist, antiableist, and unswerving allies of our LGBTQ+ sisters and brothers, and anyone else who dares to break out of narrow social norms. Healing the sisterhood wound means that we start becoming savvy about the ways oppression actually impacts our lives, by questioning the norms we have around female friendship and reconnecting to rituals and ceremonies that give us the chance to connect with one another in deep and soulful ways.

I really love the idea of building revolutionary relationships, which Black feminist scholar Toni Cade Bambara wrote about in her essay "On the Issue of Roles." When we start to question these roles, we naturally step into new relationships that can uplift all of us.

Here are some ways to transmute the wounds of sisterhood into a community of diosas, connected to one another through bonds of love and revolutionary friendship:

1. If you find yourself repeating stereotypes about women ("Women are catty," "You can't trust women because they're two-faced," etc.), ask yourself where these toxic generalizations come from. Often, it's a combination of extrapolating from personal experience and drinking the poisonous waters of our misogynistic overculture. See if you can reframe every stereotype to highlight the positive attributes of women ("Women are great listeners

who can be so empathetic to one another," "Women are able to swim in emotional territory in a deep and meaningful way," etc.). The aim isn't to come up with more generalizations and stereotypes, but to rewire your mind to focus on qualities that encourage and magnetize trusting relationships with other women.

2. If you have a tendency to blame and shame women for acting out of line with classically acceptable norms around femininity, ask yourself where you learned those norms. Most of our ideas about who we should be as women come from patriarchy, and when we see women "disobeying," it can trigger an ancient fear that makes us feel unsafe. Instead of considering that patriarchy has created that lack of safety, we might lash out at the women who step outside the box. If you find yourself doing this, ask yourself how you can be an ally to women whose expression of womanhood may be less traditional than yours.

3. If you consider yourself "a guy's gal" or "one of the boys" because you "don't get" other women, write out a list of what makes you uncomfortable about womanhood. Women who feel pressured to conform to standards of femininity might instinctively shy away from other women, but what if you were to embrace your own unique expression of womanhood and give other women permission to do the same? In addition, see if you can expand your circle to connect with a diversity of other women. Every woman is a snowflake in the best possible way—no two are alike.

4. If you notice you're comparing yourself to another woman in ways that make you feel bad about yourself, see if you can simply allow yourself to admire her

qualities instead. I've found that if I'm able to see something beautiful and powerful in another woman, it's because I already have those qualities within. Be grateful that she's reflecting something back to you that you have an opportunity to catalyze in your own unique way. At this stage in my life, I give genuine compliments to women profusely and often. I love the feeling of a woman lighting up when she's offered sincere praise, and it makes me feel better about myself, too.

5. If you've ever distrusted women who are "too much" (too pretty, too loud, too sexual, too smart, too opinionated), check where your judgments are coming from and consider that patriarchy has conditioned all women to tone themselves down in order to be acceptable. Have honest conversations with other women about where they've been judged as being too much, or where they've done the judging. Reframe your discomfort so that you can find something to admire in these women (while also being emotionally honest with yourself if you need to maintain a distance from people who are engaging in inauthentic or harmful behavior).

6. If you've engaged in gossip or shit-talking with other women (which, to be discerning, isn't the same as discussing the impacts of another woman's truly harmful behavior), challenge yourself to stop. If others around you are doing this, don't participate. You may even wish to advocate for the woman who's being slammed in conversation, noting that patriarchy often pits us against one another and sends us into ad hominem attacks against women's character. Again, it's possible to have a genuine grievance against another woman (such as someone who's abusing a position of

power or who has acted in damaging ways) without tearing her down, while taking into account that patriarchy has done a number on all of us—which means that many women might be engaging in toxic behavior in order to "get ahead" in the overculture.

7. If you've felt jealous of women due to perceived differences in power or status, purposely seek out role models and inspiring stories about women who have jubilantly claimed their worth. Allow their stories and journeys to ignite the fire within you. In addition, celebrate and advocate for other women in your life who may not be as far along in their journeys as you are. Life is not a zero-sum game, and there's room for everyone's brilliance.

8. If your relationships with women have mostly been based on commiseration and complaining, find ways to shift your conversations into what's going well and how you want to bring your dreams into fruition. This ain't about toxic positivity, which is a way of skating on the surface and avoiding difficult conversations. However, constant complaining gets really old really fast. I once had a friend who always wanted to vent about how shitty her life was. I loved this woman very much, so I'd listen for a while, then I'd shift the conversation into what she wanted to do to transmute those experiences into something positive. Once she understood that I wasn't around to merely listen to her complain, she became more reflective. This might not always be the case with your friendships, so decide on whether it's time to set a boundary or change the terms of your connection.

9. If you've had a tendency to end relationships over perceived slights, upsets, or the inability to deal with

conflict, practice relationships of repair rather than disposability—call people in to engage them in deeper reflection and a movement toward shared understanding instead of calling them out, which usually means letting someone know their behavior is unacceptable and must be stopped. Although calling someone out can sometimes be useful when someone is engaging in harmful activities, it can be more restorative to start with calling in, to develop a basis of shared understanding.

Worthy Work:
Pulling Weeds and Planting
the Seeds of Community

The following exercise is intended to help you be intentional about crafting a community that sees, knows, and values every single one of us. Building meaningful community is an ongoing process, so please be gentle with yourself and go slow. You might find yourself coming back to this exercise throughout your life, as you change and grow.

Part 1:
Community Red Flags

Take time to write out your red flags when it comes to friendships and community. These are warning signs that can signal dysfunction in the near future or down the line. For example:

1. You can't be yourself or express your opinion without being attacked.

2. You're in a community that feels overly hierarchical, where one person's needs, opinions, or ideas take precedence over everyone else's.

3. You're in a high-pressure environment where you feel coerced into conforming to a particular set of standards, which might include the way you talk, dress, think, or act—or cutting out other people or activities that are outside the community's interests.

Once you've written down your red flags, take time to journal on the following questions:

1. Based on your red flags, are there any relationships or communities it may be time to let go of because they no longer feel aligned? Write them down.

2. Who do you need to distance yourself from? It's okay to outgrow relationships and let them go with love.

3. Who do you need to set better boundaries with? If there are specific people and communities you don't want to let go of completely, it may be necessary to maintain specific and respectful boundaries.

4. Are there specific qualities you identified that feel depleting or that don't serve to nourish you? What are they?

5. Are there conversations you need to have in order to navigate growth and move into the next chapter? What are they? What kind of support can you receive around having them, if they might prove to be hard?

Part 2:
Community Green Flags

Take time to write out your green flags when it comes to friendships and community. These are acknowledgments of positive, healthy qualities and behaviors that help you step into even more of your worthy woman. For example:

1. You can be your full self in this environment without fear of being judged or shunned.

2. When conflict comes up, you can address a problem with grace and clarity, and trust in your deeper sense of belonging.

3. The people in this community are steadfast, reliable, and keep their word when they say they are going to do something.

Once you've written down your green flags, take time to journal on the following questions:

1. Based on your green flags, are there any relationships or communities it may be time to commit to in a deeper way, because they support your worthy woman? Write them down in your journal or the notes section of your phone.

2. How do you typically cultivate community? Do you usually wait to be invited in, or are you the first to reach out, offer assistance, and so on? How can you be the one to initiate new friendships? And if you tend to be the one who usually initiates, how can you cultivate more reciprocal relationships?

3. What are your hobbies and interests? What is your soul calling you toward? This is good information that can offer insight as to where you might find soul family.

4. Which of your gifts would you like to give (and how)? And what would you like to receive in return?

Part 3:

Friendship Contracts with Those Closest to You

With my closest and dearest friends, I love creating mutually reflective "friendship contracts" that help us to really articulate the unique beauty of our connection and how we can use it to help each other grow. This isn't about putting your friendship into a restrictive box or forcing someone to do what they said they would do; instead, it's a guide that helps you come back to your commitment to each other, over and over. I've found that it can be especially powerful in times when the relationship is sticky or communication is tough.

I suggest getting together with at least one of your BFFs. You can also do this with a spouse/partner, close family member, beloved colleague, or anyone else you want to. Have fun with it! Draw, paint, dance, put on music, cozy up over yummy food and tea, and dive deep as you nurture the garden of your connection.

You can come up with your own questions, but I like the ones below.

1. What are the things we deeply want for our relationship?

2. What resources do we need in order to accomplish those larger desires?

3. What personal resources/gifts/superpowers are we individually bringing to the relationship?

4. Together, what can we do as a team?

5. What are the ways in which we might individually self- or other-sabotage (and what are the gentlest and most effective ways for us to call the other in when this happens)?

6. What are each of our fundamental beliefs about relationships that might affect how we connect with each other?

7. What are our fundamental beliefs about this relationship?

8. What are the best ways we can support each other?

Culture as Community

Growing up in New York, one of the most beautifully diverse place in the world, I had the honor of witnessing communities made up of so many different kinds of people. I loved walking through my neighborhood and hearing Spanish, Korean, Urdu, Tagalog, and even hybridized forms of English melded with other languages. I know it's a privilege to have grown up in a place where so many rich cultures intersect, and I don't take it for granted for a second.

In fact, the diversity of NYC has helped me to recognize and take pride in my own Nuyorican heritage. Nuyoricans (people of Puerto Rican descent who live in New York City) have a rich creative, spiritual, sociopolitical legacy, dating back to when we began forming barrios across the Bronx, Brooklyn, and East Harlem (commonly known as Spanish Harlem). Today, there are roughly two million Nuyoricans in the city, and we've carved out a vibrant cultural identity that spans everything from literature to civil rights. One thing I've come to realize is that an essential aspect of my community is my Puerto Rican pride and culture. My roots extend all the way from that beautiful island to the streets of NYC, and they run *deep*.

I understand that this is a privilege that not all American-born BIPOC—or white folks, for that matter—have access to, especially if they've lost a sense of connection to their family's cultures and languages due to assimilation into the dominant culture. But I also know plenty of adoptees, multiracial folks, and white people whose ancestors have been in the United States for generations and who've found ways to resist assimilation and celebrate their ancestry. We are multidimensional beings who often live at the intersection of a complex constellation of cultures, so we are waaaaaay more than our skin color, race, ethnicity, and other markers of identity. But at the same time, in the words of Maya Angelou, "You can't really know where you are going until you know where you have been." When we become separated from our ancestral traditions, we become separated from an integral aspect of our personal autobiography, whether we know it or not.

Celebrating our ancestral traditions is an important act of resistance—one that says we will not simply conform to what we are told to be in order to be seen as worthy of belonging. In addition, a lot of traditional non-Western (and even Western) cultures are bastions of values that so many of us yearn for today: connection, social cohesion, the ability to break bread and grieve and share our joys together, and the capacity to engage in soul-transforming rituals that enable us to come home to ourselves.

I know that for many BIPOC in particular, there can be a strong sense of loss when it comes to the cultures of their families. I have plenty of first-generation BIPOC clients who have felt pressured to choose between the dominant culture and that of their families. Sometimes they've actually been actively encouraged by their family members to spurn their ancestral culture and assimilate, to essentially "act more white" in order to succeed in a country where racism still rears its ugly head. Often, they grow ambivalent about their ancestral cultures due to a variety of mixed messages. They might be told to take pride in where they come from, while noticing that their parents deliberately didn't teach them the languages or traditions of their culture. Or they might be taunted for being neither "American enough" nor connected enough to their ancestral culture. Other times, they might seek to go against certain cultural norms—for example, I've had plenty of BIPOC clients who felt that their family's culture held a lot of harmful attitudes about gender roles, which they wanted to move away from.

When it comes down to it, I believe that integrating the best aspects of our ancestral cultures is a way of growing our own worthiness—but we have to be able to do it on our own terms, without the pressures of family or the overculture bearing down on us. In order to develop a more honest and loving relationship with our culture, it's important to disentangle from the ways we've been colonized by external ideas about who and how we should be.

I once worked with a client who was a strong, beautiful, driven, and successful Filipino American woman. But some part of her felt a void. She didn't have strong ties to her culture, as she'd left home at an early age and carried wounds from her highly traditional, patriarchal, Catholic upbringing. However, she also felt estranged from the predominantly white community in which she lived. As we started to work through some of her feelings of confusion and loss, she discovered a strong connection to shamanism. Synchronistically, she also learned about the legacy of the babaylan, shamans from the Philippines with precolonial origins who work with nature spirits and communicate with the spirits of the ancestors. This was an extremely healing connection for her. As she learned more about the ways in which the Spanish conquest had shaped her people and how the babaylan modeled spiritual resistance against the conquerors, she developed a new sense of pride in Filipino culture, which made it easier for her to reconnect with her family on new terms. She began apprenticing with a babaylan and started a Filipino American cultural alliance in her town that brought many generations of Filipinos together and encouraged them to define their culture in new and intentional ways.

As she came to see, it's so freaking important to acknowledge both the "good" and "bad" aspects of our cultures—and to acknowledge the complex weave of both powerful and life-affirming traditions, as well as cultural norms that feel overly restrictive. Instead of walking away from all of it, which the overculture *wants* us to do, we can actually start to work with what's there: lifting up and honoring the parts we want to cherish and pass down to the next generations, while also being the lightworkers and lightning rods who work to question, heal, and transform what may no longer serve us or the collective.

Remember, your family and lineage carry gifts of healing and wholeness, and it is your birthright to claim them, all in honor of the worthy woman within!

Worthy Work:
Connecting with Healed Ancestors

Within our bones, the memories of our ancestral lineage lie dormant, waiting to be awakened. Those memories are not merely traumatic or wounding, however. Our ancestors weathered storms, fought battles, and birthed the flame of worthiness within us. By honoring their struggles and embracing their triumphs, we forge an unbreakable bond, drawing strength from their resilient spirits.

This exercise will help you connect to what I call your "kind ancestors"—that is, those ancestors who lived fruitful, loving lives, or who experienced the healing of trauma in the realms after death. Specifically, it will focus on find-ing a kind ancestor you can connect with anytime you want to address the unhealed wounds of your ancestors, which could be playing out in subtle or overt ways in your life—or when you want to celebrate and express gratitude for aspects of your lineage that have contributed to the beautiful, wor-thy woman you are today. This healed ancestor, who may be male or female or Two-Spirit/nonbinary, will be someone you can call on in meditation or just in your day-to-day life. They can always be invoked as a trusted part of your commu-nity and as a benevolent link to the beauty of your culture.

1. Clear your mind and take some time to imagine your kind ancestor. What does this person look and feel like? If you wish, you can draw an image of them to place on your altar.

2. What is the primary message you think your healed ancestor wants to send to you—through words, images/symbols, or just a felt sense?

3. How can you honor your kind ancestor's message in a tangible way (e.g., through specific changes you're committed to making in your own life that celebrate your worth and the worth of your people)?

✳ Worthy Affirmations ✳

◎ *Loving connections enable my full self to bloom in beautiful and unprecedented ways.*

◎ *I deserve support.*

◎ *I am worthy of a healthy, loving community that fully honors my authentic self-expression and my gifts.*

◎ *My community nourishes and uplifts me.*

◎ *Community is a source of healing, fun, love, and abundance.*

◎ *I honor the flow of connections in and out of my life, and I trust that the right people will come at the right time.*

◎ *I let myself ask for help and offer my gifts, in a mutual reciprocal flow of energy.*

◎ *My community encompasses the medicine of my culture, my wise and resilient ancestors, and the more-than-human world.*

10

You Are Worthy of Fun and Pleasure

*Pleasure is not one of the spoils of capitalism. It is what
our bodies, our human systems, are structured for; it is the
aliveness and awakening, the gratitude and humility,
the joy and celebration of being miraculous.*

—adrienne maree brown

What brings you pleasure, diosa? What makes you light up? What sends you into a state of pure flow so that you're fully in the zone, in a place of sparkling wonder, in that gorgeous bubble of being where your body and soul are in perfect unison? What makes you feel like you were born to receive the caress of the elements and take in the beauty of the universe as it cradles you like a precious child? What makes you feel ecstatic as fuck?

I hope these questions bring to the surface a range of luscious answers that help you to feel the bliss you've already experienced in this lifetime and that you know to be possible. And if you find yourself drawing a blank, that's okay, too. This chapter will be an initiation into the pleasure that every single one of us has a staggering capacity for. Because it is our birthright. Pleasure is not a fleeting indulgence, but a gateway to self-love. By embracing fun and pleasure, we embark on a sacred journey of self-discovery and self-acceptance. Pleasure is the magic ingredient that helps us to expand beyond our limits and relax into the mysteries of the cosmos.

True pleasure is very different from the depleting forces of hedonism and indulgence, which, for me, are about constantly seeking excitement and avoiding pain. Pleasure is not about having the grandest, most expensive experiences; it's about opening up to the beauty and magic that is intrinsic to life, appreciating and loving what is right here in front of you. When we open up to pleasure rather than going on a relentless hunt for it, we become more comfortable with its ebb and flow. Easy come, easy go. Pleasure is always available to us, from the simple enjoyment of savoring a strawberry to the satisfying ache of giant belly laughs with our bestie. When we realize that the nature of life is pleasure, we don't have to stress ourselves out in order to find it.

I've always hated watching zombie-apocalypse media, which seems to be extremely popular these days. I don't know about you, but seeing people go into hyperdrive survival mode ain't my thing! What I want is to see people come together, even in adverse situations, to sing, dance, laugh, pray, comfort one another, and love. I know from the resilience of my ancestors that the capacity to recognize and capture the beauty and wisdom of nature, of the mundane moments, is a skill all of us need to cultivate. I know that my ancestors went through an inordinate amount of suffering in order to survive the overculture of capitalism and colonization, but I also know that in the midst of this all, they had tools and rituals that helped them feel alive while navigating deadening situations.

This is why I declare: *Pleasure is radical.* And while I believe we are meant to grow, evolve, and expand, doing this solely through suffering cuts us off from one of the most important dimensions of our worthiness. Capitalist propaganda may condition us to believe we're merely units of production, not souls that are meant to have ecstatic experiences, but in reality, attuning to pleasure is one of the greatest tools I can think of for our long-term survival (despite what the zombie movies might have to say!).

In her Substack newsletter *The Queer Agenda*, Shohreh Davoodi writes: "Prioritizing your pleasure is a radical act in a world that regularly reinforces the idea that only the pleasure of a select few matters. What if you viewed your pleasure as an act of resistance against the status quo? A tangible way of aligning with your values? Would you be more likely to prioritize it? If your body is the epicenter of the oppression enacted against you, then reclaiming your pleasure in defiance of that oppression is a middle finger to the system and all who uphold it." I absolutely agree that queer bodies, femme bodies, differently abled bodies, and BIPOC bodies especially need to understand that we spark a revolution when we love ourselves so much that we aren't willing to let the denigration of the overculture suppress our capacity for fun and pleasure. We harness what it is to feel good in our bodies and souls, because we know that this has ripple effects.

I've learned that my pleasure is *not* separate from my worthiness. We are so accustomed to believing that we must work hard in order to experience enjoyment, but in truth, pleasure—a sacred path of La Diosa—is one of the foundational touchstones of existence. It may not feel like it, given the self-imposed rules and hardships that humans have created, but I'll say this one more time: *Sister, you are not here to struggle. You are here to thrive and flourish.*

This is not about getting somewhere or accomplishing something. Just as flowers bloom, birds sing, and the earth engages in a sensuous dance—you are here to experience pleasure in every cell of your body, just because. No strings attached, nowhere to go, nothing to be. Pleasure is simply a part of your essence. And as you intentionally immerse yourself in pleasure, you cultivate a deep love and reverence for yourself, honoring your worthiness in every breath, touch, taste, sight, sound, and smell.

I began to understand this shortly after I got sober. After my first year of sobriety, I realized that part of the journey of getting sober was learning how to live again. Of course there were happy moments prior to getting sober, but a lot of the ways I dealt with my earlier childhood trauma and early-adult trauma entailed numbing myself—whether that was fucking over my pain, drinking over my pain, or repeating negative patterns that were unhealthy for me, and not really giving myself the space to be held in healthy ways. Sobriety gave me the clarity and space to consciously redo life in a way that was loving. I learned so many things, like how to stick to my word and my commitment to self. I learned how to care for my body and spirit, and to become the loving adult I'd always needed.

After a year of sobriety, I found that my mind, body, and spirit were clearer than they'd ever been before. I started to change my habits and my thoughts and my ways of loving me—and I started to feel more worthy and deserving of *actually feeling good*. I got to the point where I understood that I no longer just wanted to do the shadow work or excavate the sources of my suffering, which I'd always been so adept at. I also wanted (and needed) to do the reintegration work of living life well. In some ways, that was a greater challenge. I had to reconnect with what gave me joy, which went beyond my responsibilities and sense of purpose. I began setting up sober dates with myself to do things like sing karaoke, take more time for self-care, move my body, laugh, play, and be silly.

As women, we have been conditioned to deny ourselves the full panoply of available pleasure, believing that it is frivolous or undeserved. So many of the women in my community tell me, "I'd love to take a vacation, but I have sooooo much work to do and too many people counting on me!" It can feel irresponsible to spend our time on something "unnecessary"—but pleasure is absolutely necessary. Rest (which we explored in Chapter 4) and pleasure are the fuel that fills our tanks. My hope is that this chapter will help you shed the weight of societal conditioning and embrace the truth that you are deserving of joy, delight, and the exquisite dance of pleasure.

What Brings You Pleasure?

"What brings you pleasure?" I often ask my clients this question, and they all answer in a variety of ways.

I asked the same question when I met with one of my good friends, who had squeezed in time for a gabfest between doctor's appointments for her kids, a huge presentation at work, and hosting a number of out-of-town family members for an annual family reunion. She was one busy woman! But when I asked her this question, her eyes went wide and she made a sound that didn't need to be accompanied by any words, because it communicated an unmistakable vibe: *Girl, are you fucking insane?!*

She was resistant to answering. "I don't see how that's relevant," she snapped, crossing her arms over her chest. "I'm not here to talk about *pleasure*. I want to talk about how the hell I'm supposed to keep my head above water in a time like this. I thought you were gonna give me some tips about boundaries or whatever."

I smiled. "Nope, not today. Today, I wanna know what lights you up, what makes you feel like you're floating on air while staying grounded in the present moment. I wanna know what makes you truly feel like you're coming alive."

What ensued was a three-hour discussion about the place and importance of pleasure in a woman's life. For the last ten years, she'd been busy attending to her family and building a successful leadership development business for BIPOC women. She was soul depleted . . . but she didn't see any way out of it. When we got to talking more deeply, I learned that pleasure actually freaked her out. She explained that she'd been drawn to intense experiences and people in her younger years. For her, pleasure had been about living like there was no tomorrow—partying, drugs, whirlwind affairs that crash-landed before they even got a chance to get moving. (As I mentioned earlier, this isn't pleasure—it's hedonism, which can end up depleting us and eroding our capacity for joy real fast!)

She knew it was time to shift her pleasure compass, but she didn't know how. Because she'd been conditioned to seek out intensity, many would-be pleasurable activities just ended up making her feel bored and distracted. "You know, I guess the intensity helped me get out of my head, even though it wasn't good for me," she said sheepishly.

"Wait a sec, what if intensity isn't the culprit here? Intensity can be a good thing—like, the kind of intensity that gets you into flow and helps you feel alive. But maybe it's about shifting to a different kind of intensity. The kind of intensity that helps you slow down, savor the moment."

I explained to my friend that for many of us who crave excitement and equate it with pleasure, the experience of taking pleasure in is a lot like having a delicious-looking cake sitting in front of us—we get seduced into eating the whole thing really fast, which only ends up making us feel gross and nauseated. We can become addicted to our own habit of taking everything in immediately, with fervor, to the point that we don't even realize we're actually diminishing our capacity for pleasure.

"What if you were to take smaller bites out of pleasure?" I asked. "What if you let yourself get into your body and really savor what you were experiencing? In some ways, that would increase the intensity of the pleasure, because now you're actually letting yourself feel it."

Whoa. Mind blown. She looked at me for a while before sighing. "Yeah, you're right. I realize that even when I thought I was having fun, I was mostly just breezing through everything. I didn't want to slow down long enough to feel . . . because I was afraid of what I'd feel."

I nodded. "I totally get it. And savoring is also really tough when we're in a culture that's all about consuming more, more, more. But slowing down to feel ourselves, in this moment, is one of the best practices I can think of when it comes to expanding into deeper pleasure."

"How do you do it?" she asked.

I thought about it for a moment. "Well, over time, I realized I like giving myself space to romanticize my life a little more. When I'm feeling depleted, I like writing poems or reading them. I gravitate to simple stuff, too, like going into cute tea shops, people-watching, making time to daydream. And because I know these things give me joy, I try to make a schedule to prioritize this stuff when my life gets full."

We brainstormed ways she could prioritize pleasure and

joy, and by the end of our conversation, I could sense that a weight had lifted from her shoulders. I was really happy about that, because I could relate to her predicament in so many ways. Although I didn't have a problem with slowing down to feel my feelings, I had always been drawn to underworld goddesses and the process of purging trauma and pain. I knew how to die and be reborn, and I knew how to be a warrior, but I had forgotten how to be like Aphrodite—sensual, playful, joyful. After years of exhausting myself on powerful personal development work, I knew it was time to fill my pleasure tank. I was brought back to my roots of studying the Sri Vidya path of Tantra, which, in India, is the path of the goddess—the path of passion, pleasure, and activating our orgasmic power.

My friend and I talked in depth about what it means to romance ourselves and become our own beloved—to allow everything from our gestures to our jewelry to invoke the energy we wish to bring into our lives. I often find myself having these conversations with the women in my community, many of whom feel pleasure-starved because they're so accustomed to taking care of everything and everyone before meeting their own needs. As I always tell them, "Diosa, your foremost need is to honor yourself. You are worthy of worshipping at the altar of your own divinity! So slow the fuck down! Burn candles. Play music you love. Fill your space with fresh flowers and plants. Adorn your home and body in ways that reflect your soul. Make your life a sensual ceremony that activates all your senses and makes you feel fucking good!"

We may find all kinds of reasons not to prioritize pleasure, but here's the bottom line: Every single one of us deserves pleasure, which is a fundamental human right. We are not meant to slog through our lives with work as the only goal! Pleasure is as essential as breathing. This doesn't mean that we have to turn it into some kind of idealistic destination that we work all year to "earn." Pleasure is a process, not an end goal. It's always available to us, and we don't have to grind away or spend shitloads of money in order to have it. It is not a commodity—it is the capacity to savor the goodness and beauty that is always in your midst . . . because La Diosa is always here, in the blooming flowers, the echoes of birdsong, the busker in the subway who makes your day by singing your favorite song. Magic is all around us when we slow down long enough to perceive it—it's as simple as that!

As I share with the diosas in my communities, pleasure is about letting go of the shoulds driven by an overculture of consumerism, misogyny, racism, lookism, ableism, and so many other oppressive messages that tell us that we don't deserve to feel good unless (fill in the blank with your own set of BS conditions). Fuck that noise! Pleasure is a sacred responsibility.

I am especially committed to pleasure because I often think about the way my parents worked so hard and always worried about spending too much money. They seldom took time to do simple fun things, so even something like a backyard barbecue or going to the beach was a huge occasion for all of us. They had been conditioned to believe that life had to be serious and oriented toward work and austerity. I know this was a part of their own wounding. It's no wonder addiction ran in the family—with all the pressure they experienced, turning to something, anything, that would alleviate their burdens for even a minute was totally predictable.

Science has given us a better understanding of why things like rest, laughter, physical contact, play, and joyful movement have all kinds of health benefits and do wonders for our relationships. All of these things can strengthen our immune system, boost our mood, diminish physical and emotional pain, and mitigate the harmful impacts of stress. Researcher Stuart Brown, founder of the National Institute for Play, has said, "The presence or absence of play, particularly in child development, has a great deal to do with competency, resiliency, emotional health, [and] brain size." Moreover, play is "not just for kids, but something that is an inherent part of human nature."

When I'm with my daughter, I see how easy play and laughter are for her. She's focused, alert, and effortlessly connected to all of life. Why is that so hard for adults? Aside from the conditioning of the overculture, many of us experience significant ruptures during childhood—these might include our parents getting divorced, bullying, or just feeling alone and misunderstood. I've had a lot of clients and community members who felt disconnected from their creativity because they had a parent who emphasized perfectionism over curiosity and improvisation. It's little wonder that they feel stressed out by the idea of play; if they never had the proper resources to simply let go and be silly in the past, doing so now can feel more laborious than joyful.

I always encourage my clients and community members to, first and foremost, cultivate a safe place to connect with the inner child within them (and we all have this, even if it's been repressed over the years). We must, most important, meet our own safety needs so that we can slowly integrate simple things like play and laughter back into our lives.

We know that when we are healing from trauma and a stressed nervous system, certain forms of play—such as expressive arts therapy, sound healing, and other creative therapeutic modalities—can be extremely healing, especially when administered by a compassionate guide. If you feel that you've forgotten the role of play in your life, or that it brings up difficult memories or emotions, please take heart. With the help of a professional, you can bloom like a many-petaled lotus into the domain of play and pleasure.

UNWORTHY LIE:
Pleasure is just another frivolous thing I don't have time for—I have adult responsibilities to take care of!

WORTHY TRUTH:
Pleasure is a sacred responsibility; when I engage in it, I heal myself and my lineage.

$$+$$

Worthy Work: Your Relationship to Pleasure

This is a journaling exercise that is meant to help you get a deeper sense of what pleasure means to you. Come to your worthy woman altar. Light a candle and play sultry music that opens you up to your playfulness and your sensuality. Now respond to the following prompts.

1. How do you generally experience pleasure? You might use synonyms for *pleasure* to describe the different flavors of your own experience. For example: *Bliss. Wonder. Awe. Happiness. Contentment. Sensuality. Sex. Orgasms. Openheartedness. Laughter. Play. Surrender. Silliness. Discovery. Delight.* Write down whatever comes to mind and whatever feels true.

2. Using these words as a guide, think about your most recent experience of pleasure. Describe it in detail, being sure to note the environment, anyone else who was present, and what it felt like in your body.

3. Now we're going to get even more specific. Considering each of the categories below, write down anything that you associate with your own pleasure. For example, when I think of smells, I think of the scent of my skin after a shower. When I think of tastes, I think of the juicy sweetness of a perfectly ripe mango as it bursts on my tongue. Write down as much as you can before moving on to the next category.

    * *Sights*
    * *Sounds*
    * *Smells*
    * *Touches*
    * *Tastes*
    * *Activities*
    * *People*
    * *Places and environments*
    * *Works of art (books, music, films, etc.)*

4. Now read back over what you've written. Based on what's here, are there any specific themes that are coming to the forefront? (For example, when I did this exercise, I noticed that the ocean and tropical environments were a recurring theme. One of my clients noticed that children and nature threaded through almost everything she'd written.)

5. Write about a particularly pleasurable memory that you associate with your chosen theme. Be very detailed, using all your senses and the other categories in question 3 to bring this experience to life, as if you were living it in the present moment. If you choose, you may wish to read this out loud to a loved one.

6. Now notice how you feel in your body after spending all this time feeling into what gives you pleasure. What are the sensations and emotions you're experiencing? There is something remarkable that happens when we

start to focus on what gives us pleasure: We actually start to feel that pleasure, and to draw it to ourselves, which is one aspect of the creative genius of the divine feminine that we can all tap into!

7. If you'd like to dive into a pleasure practice in greater depth, start a daily pleasure journal that charts your daily experiences of pleasure, no matter how big or small. Remember, where attention flows, energy goes! The more we begin to notice and honor pleasure, the more we invite it into our lives.

8. Based on what you've discovered about yourself, put together your own "best of" list, which includes all your favorites—songs, foods, places, items of clothing, and so on. Put that list up somewhere prominent. Take a look at that list on a daily basis and find some way to take pleasure into your own two hands and give it to yourself as often as possible!

Claiming Your Sensuality and Orgasmic Pleasure

One of the toughest aspects for women when it comes to claiming pleasure is prioritizing their sensual and orgasmic pleasure. From my tantric devotional practices, I know that having an orgasm is just the tip of the iceberg when it comes to experiencing deep-down-in-our-bones, sustained pleasure. Still, there are too many women who don't experience pleasure at all during a sexual experience. In fact, in a study of more than 50,000 people, 95 percent of heterosexual men reported always or usually achieving orgasm during intercourse, while only 65 percent of heterosexual women said the same thing.

There is so much about this that points to an extremely fucked-up culture that diminishes women's sexual pleasure. We're also inundated by myths about sex that permeate our expectations. From an early age, we're told by movies and TV that a man and a woman are supposed to achieve simultaneous orgasm after zero foreplay and a few minutes of penis-in-vagina intercourse. This simply doesn't reflect reality. Sensual (relating to the body and the senses) and sexual (relating to physical intimacy that includes intercourse and genital stimulation) fulfillment can look like so many things: your partner feeding you chocolate-covered strawberries while you wear a blindfold, reading an erotic story, having someone run their fingers delicately across your skin, or skinny-dipping in a heated swimming pool by moonlight.

Our bodies are sacred vessels, adorned with curves and contours, and we have more pathways to sexual pleasure than we may be aware of. But just like all the other aspects of pleasure we've discussed so far, claiming our right to sensual and sexual pleasure (and toe-curling orgasms!) requires us to claim our worthiness and to embrace and respect the power and wisdom that reside in our sensuous forms.

I love the work of Black feminists like Audre Lorde and adrienne maree brown, who've written about the radical importance of claiming our erotic nature. Particularly for queer Black women, whose eroticism has been denigrated, marginalized, and fetishized by mainstream culture, it is necessary to name and claim what Lorde calls the "uses of the erotic." In a revolutionary essay by that title, Lorde writes:

The erotic is a measure between the beginnings of our sense of self and the chaos of our strongest feelings. It is an internal sense of satisfaction to which, once we have experienced it, we know we can aspire. We have been raised to fear the yes within ourselves, our deepest cravings. For the demands of our released expectations lead us inevitably into actions which will help bring our lives into accordance with our needs, our knowledge, our desires. And the fear of our deepest cravings keeps them suspect, keeps us docile and loyal and obedient, and leads us to settle for or accept many facets of our oppression as women.

The way that Lorde so courageously connects the suppression of our erotic nature (which she defines as our capacity to feel) with the oppression of women is still incredibly pertinent. I recognize the many ways in which I and other diosas have used our erotic power as a means to an end, a commodity, a way of navigating a world that tells us our bodies are desirable but not worthy of being honored. I don't fault us for this. People in femme bodies have done this for survival reasons since time immemorial. The only problem is that if we couch our sexuality inside this capitalistic perspective, which seeks to cordon off our power by turning it into an object or commodity, we become even more disconnected from our pleasure.

Again, some truth bombs from Lorde:

The erotic has often been misnamed by men and used against women. It has been made into the confused, the trivial, the psychotic, the plasticized sensation. For this reason, we have often turned away from the exploration and consideration of the erotic as a source of power and information, confusing it with its opposite, the pornographic. But pornography is a direct denial of the power of the erotic, for it represents the suppression of true feeling. Pornography emphasizes sensation without feeling.

So many of us have experienced trauma with respect to our sexuality. Healing through sexuality is absolutely possible (I know, because Tantra gave me this experience!), but it is the site of so much cultural bullshit for a lot of us. Our sexuality is treated with fear, disgust, sensationalism, fetishization, and a blatant disregard of the spiritual aspects of our erotic nature. And if we live in marginalized bodies (BIPOC, queer, fat, disabled), it can be an even more difficult journey, which is why I'm so grateful for the work of Black feminists in shedding light on how various forms of oppression can quash our erotic power, which is essentially our life force—the "yes within" that Lorde so eloquently wrote about.

If you have ever felt uncomfortable in your sensuality and sexuality, please know that you're not alone! However, a distinctly feminine path can help us to pay homage and respect to the body as a vehicle for experiencing ecstasy.

In the tantric lineage, your body is your temple—a gateway for sensational bliss, as well as for the divine to come rushing through. A pleasure practice for expanding into your sensual and sexual self, for loving the life-giving energies of your gorgeous body, is essential. This is how we open up to a full-bodied, full-hearted, full-pussied yes! When we are aligned with our yes, we are aligned with our sensual and sexual energy in a clearer way that helps us to bypass toxic cultural messages. But we also have to know our no—that which depletes our energy, life force, and imagination. In fact, I believe that recognizing and honoring your no is like putting up a stop sign at the holy pleasure gates of your body, so that you can incubate a sense of sacred safety in your eroticism.

There are so many reasons our bodies might not be at a full yes to sexual pleasure. These include but are not limited to:

* Fear of being labeled as a "prude" or a "slut." As divine diosas, we encompass the full spectrum of sexual expression—nobody is either "this" or "that," and anyone who has ever told you this is just dead-ass wrong!

* Disrespectful, demeaning, or demanding partners, or partners your body doesn't trust (listen to your body—she's wise beyond words!).

* The fear of pregnancy, STIs (sexually transmitted infections), or UTIs (urinary tract infections). I urge every diosa to educate herself on the ins and outs of safe, consensual sex.

* Insecurities about your body/internalized ideas about female body image (fuck that noise).

* The pressure to have an orgasm. Remember, relaxation and enjoying the journey rather than the destination is key!

* Getting in the mood when your mind is distracted or preoccupied.

* A cultural focus on male pleasure (again, fuck that noise!).

* Physical discomfort or pain during sex. I hear this all the time, and if this is ever the case for you, please stop what you're doing and communicate with your partner, so you can find a position that facilitates greater ease.

* Not enough foreplay prior to intercourse. Remember, people with vulvas often require ample time to "rev up" before penetration (*if* penetration is desired—there are plenty of ways to be sexually intimate without it).

* Emotional vulnerability. Because sex can bring a lot of buried emotions to the surface, I urge you to go at

the pace that makes the most sense to you and build an open dialogue with your partner.

* Unhealed sexual trauma. If this is you, please seek out a licensed professional who specializes in helping folks to move through sexual trauma to reignite pleasure and a sense of connection to their erotic power.

* Not knowing what feels good to you sexually. If this is true for you, I urge you to experiment solo and with a partner, and to try out the Worthy Work below!

Over time, as we honor the voice of our no and work to transmute our honest no into an actively aware and empowered relationship with our eroticism, we can experience more and more of our exuberant yes. We can become more adept at communicating our desires to our lovers and to ourselves. We can set more self-honoring boundaries and have more open conversations about consent and sexual exploration. From this place, sensual and sexual pleasure can expand beyond our wildest dreams so that awesome orgasms are just the cherry on top.

Worthy Work:
Breast Massage and Mindful Masturbation

In my tantric Sri Vidya lineage, as passed down by my tantric teachers Amma and Psalm Isadora, there's an enormous amount of information and practices centered on building our orgasmic capacity. When most of us think of orgasms, we think of a pleasurable release that usually leaves us feeling depleted. In Tantra, we build sexual energy so that we can facilitate moving it through the body to experience pleasure, presence, and healing. This leads to generating more energy, or remaining in a state of equilibrium where we feel a continued sense of relaxation and bliss. (You've probably heard about the seven-hour orgasms that some people have reported having during tantric sex!)

The following practice is broken into two parts, which you can do together or on their own. I recommend using these practices whenever you want to connect with yourself, increase your receptivity to sensation and pleasure, or recharge your vital energy. After practicing on your own for a period of time, you may wish to share these practices with a lover and incorporate them into your lovemaking.

Part 1:
Breast Massage

Tantric sexual practice isn't just genitally focused. A lot of attention is placed on the breasts, which are the gateway to the heart and to our capacity for love. The breasts and nipples are sensitive erogenous zones that are worthy of our attention. In Tantra, breast massage is connected with Shyama puja, a celebration of Shyama, who is known as the tantric goddess of the heart. Arousing pleasure through the breasts and nipples can awaken the heart, as well as our receptivity to love, bonding, and intimacy. Many people have reported experiencing orgasm through nipple play alone.

For this practice, you may wish to create a beautiful, sensual space around you, with exquisitely scented candles, soft and meditative music, and textures (like silk or velvet) that increase your receptivity to pleasure. You may also wish to use a natural oil, such as coconut or jojoba.

Find a relaxing reclined position. Lightly begin to touch your belly, stroking around your abdomen, rib cage, and between your breasts, almost as if you're teasing yourself. Allow the sensual energy in your body to build. The secret to this massage is the practice of "edging," which is remaining at the edge of pleasure rather than rushing toward a big finale. You want to keep teasing your body, increasing its responsiveness until you're practically begging for more. Go slow and savor the sensations.

Once you can't wait any longer, trace around your areolas with a feather-light touch until your nipples become erect. Then gently pinch your nipples. You can gradually build up to a firmer touch, kneading your breasts and nipples in circular patterns, alternating between moving outward from the nipples and inward from the outer parts of the breasts. However, there are no rules. As your body responds, experiment with what feels good. Continue to massage yourself while doing Kegels (tightening your pelvic floor muscles for several seconds before releasing them, and repeating several times). Imagine that light is circulating throughout your body. Keep drawing that energy into your breasts. When you intuitively feel it's time to stop, hold your hands over your heart and feel the beautiful sensations gathered there.

Part 2:
Mindful Masturbation

You can choose to do this practice as a stand-alone or directly following the breast massage. Visualize a golden light shining into your vulva. Allow yourself to breathe it in, pulling that light from your vagina all the way up to the crown of your head. As you breathe out, release the golden light back down through your body and through your sexual organs, feeling the warmth and love coursing through you. Continue to work with this stream of light that courses up and down through the pillar of your body, filling you with sensual energy.

Next, begin to touch your sexual organs. Experiment with touch, remembering that the purpose of this practice isn't to rush toward an orgasmic release; it is to build the energy in your body and to feel your orgasm as a continually expansive state that it's possible to simply remain in. As you touch yourself, continue to breathe deeply, allowing that gorgeous light to warm you. Know that this light, accompanied by your loving and attentive touch, is helping you in every way; it is balancing your body, magnifying your potential, and making you more receptive to the blessings of your life. Allow yourself to relish and bask in these sensations, as if you are relishing and basking in the touch of a sensitive and ardent lover. Feel yourself visualizing and welcoming the fulfillment of your deepest desires, bringing in all that you wish for, all that you are worthy of. Your sexuality is a pathway to ecstasy in so many different ways—enjoy it!

When you feel complete, place one hand on your belly and one hand on your heart, simply letting yourself rest in the afterglow.

✳ Worthy Affirmations ✳

◎ *I am worthy of savoring pleasure in every cell of my body.*

◎ *Pleasure is a spiritual responsibility.*

◎ *I allow myself to effortlessly make time for joy.*

◎ *My sensuality and sexuality are a part of the divine matrix of my body/spirit.*

◎ *I open up to my erotic innocence and orgasmic fulfillment.*

◎ *I use the portals of breath and sensation to experience greater aliveness.*

◎ *I open myself up to childlike play and wonder.*

11

You Are Worthy of Love

A hero is one who heals their own wounds and
then shows others how to do the same.

—Yung Pueblo

I just don't feel lovable." *Bam.* The words came out in a
tumble as she sat there before me, her face soaked in tears
and her eyes telegraphing a helplessness I'd never seen
before. In the six months of working with this client, it was
the first time she'd ever been so vulnerable. And, man, did
it hurt! I could feel her hurt emanating from her trembling
body, but I could also feel my own hurt as I listened to this
beautiful goddess disclose her deepest, most shamefully held
insecurity. In her, I saw every woman I'd met in my years of
therapeutic practice and space-holding who shouldered the
same burden of unlovability. The ultimate lie.

Love is the nature of the universe, and it is our most fundamental essence. That's why it's such a trip to consider how
few people truly feel worthy of love. It's as if we are con-

stantly finding ourselves in a drought, bereft of water, when a crystal clear, self-replenishing fountain is always bubbling up within us, urging us to drink from it!

Often, the problem lies in the fact that the overculture teaches us that love is external, or that it's purely romantic, or that we need to do certain things to earn it—as if there's a love-o-meter that's capable of measuring our (fucking infinite!) worthiness. We've been taught that love is conditional, not that it's at the bedrock of what it means to be a soul having a human experience.

Many women in particular have been taught to beg for the scraps of someone else's love, rather than making room to understand ourselves and our authentic desires, which I consider to be one of the most crucial and valuable demonstrations of self-love. Self-love is the most powerful compass I can think of when it comes to creating greater harmony in our lives. If love is interdependence, a reciprocal and mutual connection between self and other, we must start with ourselves. We must learn to be in flow with ourselves so that we can align with our true desires and join our river to the great oceanic reservoir of love that permeates all of life.

Diosa, as you read this chapter, I want you to consider what it would take to cultivate the devotion to meet yourself where you need to be met. How can you be your first and best lover? And beyond that, how can you develop the love that is necessary in order for you to step into the grandest and most fulfilling vision for your life—in such a way that you are not sidestepping or compromising your nonnegotiables, but are confidently stepping into them, recognizing that this is what's required in order for you to create the most epic love story of all?

As you already know, love transcends yet encompasses romantic/sexual partner love, friendship, parenthood, connection to community and purpose, and all the elements that make up the chapters of this book. Love is the backbone of your worthiness because it is the primordial source of the divine. You are never separate from it, and it is yours for the taking and giving.

Receiving the Gift of Your Love

In order to know true love, we must recognize that we are worthy of it, because at our very core, it's who we are. And when we stop trying to seek it from everything outside of ourselves, we discover, the same way Dorothy did in *The Wizard of Oz*, that it was in us all along.

I learned that the way I encounter love within myself is inextricable from the way I encounter love outside myself. My capacity for healthy love with a partner, which includes healthy boundaries, strengthened when I chose to love myself, to meet myself with the utmost compassion and reverence.

Sure, it sounds easier said than done, but I discovered that the secret to self-love is meeting all parts of myself—including the hurt, ashamed, rejected, rebellious aspects—with steadfast devotion. I had to learn to say, "I'm always going to be here for you," in the same way I might with my daughter. After all, every single part of us is worthy of love—not just the shiny, beautiful, externally impressive parts that we want to place front and center, and ideally want to be known and appreciated for. If that's all we are emphasizing, I hate to tell you, but that ain't genuine love! It's the kind of hollow, colonized substitute for love that insists we must "earn" our own positive self-regard. This is a widespread cultural poison that has turned us against ourselves and made us accept shallow, incomplete relationships out of the fear of being alone.

But if we are against ourselves, how can we truly *know* ourselves—or anyone else, for that matter? Each of us is filled with these bruised, tender, wild, and yearning parts that are seeking connection with us in the best ways they know how. And the most incredible form of love that we can hope to experience is self-acceptance, which is what allows us to offer acceptance to the people around us.

When we think of ourselves as containing a multitude of parts asking for their emotional needs to be met, we can be like loving parents to ourselves. In many ways, I discovered the depth of my own love when I began to make space for dialoguing with the parts of me that felt unmet, unloved, unworthy, and angry as fuck about it. I came to recognize that every time I felt disconnected from love—either because a partner was not giving it to me sufficiently or because I was feeling down in the dumps and separated from my goddess-given worthiness—it was time to stop searching outward and to come inward. I had to be the beacon bringing my stray ships in to shore.

Over time, as I trained myself to do this, I no longer depended on the external world to love me up (which, let's be honest, would never be enough in the absence of the deeper self-love). Every time my mood and behavior were out of alignment, I didn't engage in punitive or self-defeating inner dialogue; instead, I lovingly recommitted to all those parts of me that were yearning for my attention.

I also got really good about talking with them about my nonnegotiables—the things I needed from myself in order to ensure that, like a loving parent, I was taking care of all of us. As I did this, something awesome happened: They listened! And as they did, they became my biggest cheerleaders and allies, helping me to catch myself when I was about to get pulled into yet another unfulfilling intimate relationship, or urging me to set more solid and loving boundaries if someone in my life was trespassing on my sacred territory.

I discovered that when I love myself enough to show up for all my parts, they show up for me, too! And it's like a big, happy cacophony of voices telling me, "Fuck yeah! You deserve to learn and grow and love and be loved!" This unswerving foundation of support that came from deep inside is what helped me to evoke the royal energy of the worthy woman within, so that I could then call in relationships that reflected this.

This is what it means to decolonize our love lens and to source love from a more genuine place. In a society that profits from your self-doubt, loving yourself is a rebellious act. Like a garden awaiting tender care, your inner landscape flourishes when nurtured with love, compassion, and the willingness to keep coming back to yourself—to never fucking self-abandon! Reclaiming your worth requires tending to your inner garden, gently removing the weeds of self-doubt and cultivating the seeds of self-love. This is perhaps the most transformative thing you can do to honor the holy place of love in your life. It will nourish your soul and rekindle your worthiness.

Remember the client I mentioned in the beginning of the chapter, who admitted to me that she felt deeply unlovable? She worked with this practice of loving herself up on a daily basis. She shared that it felt "unnatural," and I explained that this is only because we live in unnatural colonized conditions where it seems normal to hate ourselves and to believe that we need to work to earn mere scraps of regard and kindness. We must bathe ourselves in the gentle waters of self-care—honoring our bodies, minds, and spirits, especially in the times when we feel like doing the opposite. This is what I like to call "tough soft love." By building a disciplined devotional practice of granting ourselves forgiveness, grace, and acceptance, we create an oasis of worthiness within, radiating love into the world.

Please be patient with yourself in this process. It took my client several months of daily practice before she could honestly say that she felt what she considered authentic self-love. Imagine yourself as a vessel; some of us start with a deeper vessel to hold love, and some of us start with a smaller one. As we clean up the residue of past pain, we make more space in that vessel to give and receive love. We are no longer content to outsource our power by constantly looking outside ourselves, because we have filled up with our own core essence. From such a place, we do not need anyone else to validate our feelings or tell us that we're worthy (although it's likely that we'll begin vibing with people who reflect our knowing back to us!). We won't need others to approve of our decisions before making them. We won't need others to back us in our ideas before getting behind ourselves.

This is how we take back our own divine power and receive the gift of our love!

Worthy Work:
Mirror, Mirror

Dr. Tara Well's wonderful book *Mirror Meditation* offers some mind-blowing information culled from studies about the simple act of looking into a mirror. Well shares that if we ever feel disconnected from ourselves, all we have to do is study our reflection in the mirror and we'll be able to gauge the truth of our feelings. This is a three-part exercise that'll help you practice self-love and self-trust.

Part 1:

Journaling

First, spend some time journaling on the following questions:

1. Where are you looking for approval, reassurance, and validation as a prerequisite for acting from your own gut and inner soul knowing?

2. How can you establish greater trust and intimacy with yourself so that you are not outsourcing your power to others?

Part 2:

Mirroring

Take some time to stand before a mirror and make sustained eye contact with yourself for five full minutes. You may be tempted to look away, but allow yourself to soften into your own gaze. What do you see that you might not have noticed before? What emotions are radiating through your eyes and your facial expression? How do you meet your own gaze? Does it feel strange or unnatural? Be patient with yourself. Practice speaking the Worthy Affirmations you'll find at the end of this chapter. You might not necessarily believe them at first, but that's okay. The eyes are the portals to the soul, and the more you practice connecting with yours, the more the vessel of self-love and self-trust will deepen.

Part 3:

Backing Yourself Up

Identify a couple areas in your life where you might seek validation or approval from others before allowing yourself to take action. For example, maybe something as little as sending the "right" text to a friend ties your stomach into knots, which makes you end up second-guessing yourself or asking for advice. There's nothing wrong with asking for advice, but when we practice trusting our gut, something magnificent happens.

Try this: Stand before the mirror, the same way you did in Part 2 of this exercise. Place one hand on your heart and the other hand on your belly. Breathe deeply for a few minutes so you feel your body rising and falling against your hands. Soften into your gaze. What are your heart and belly communicating to you around the situations you identified where you might have trouble trusting yourself? You might get a subtle tug of awareness or a very clear message. It's okay if it feels a little nebulous; self-trust is something that strengthens over time.

Now go out into the world and back yourself up, trusting your own gut and intuitive knowing. Once you do, make a note of it in your journal and write about how it felt. Celebrate your courage by sharing your experience with two trusted people in your life.

Healing the Lover Wound

I've met so many soulful, openhearted, beautiful, magical diosas in my life who want nothing more than to find a partner they can share their full hearts and lives with. Frequently, women who come to my community long to connect with themselves and the world on a deeper basis, and to experience the kind of love that most of us dream about. And so often, they are dealing with an unhealed lover wound.

Heartbreak is one of the most painful experiences a person can go through, and this is not to shame or blame anyone for not being "strong" enough to simply get over it. No fucking way! Our emotions are part of our superpower, and the only way to heal is to feel. The problem is, many women shut themselves off from surrendering to their emotions and being with themselves in times of heartbreak. This means that the lover wound never gets an opportunity to fully heal, and we may even find ourselves re-creating toxic old relationship patterns, such as:

* Chasing after someone who is emotionally unavailable, thinking it'll be different this time
* Idealizing someone who actually isn't all that great or supportive of a partner
* Accepting unreliability and half-hearted efforts as a form of "love"
* Making excuses for a partner's lack of emotional intelligence, even though they're a grown-ass adult who is more than capable of doing their own personal work
* Not fully showing up as yourself in a relationship, out of fear that the other person will leave if they got to know the real you
* Constantly expecting grand demonstrations of love and devotion in order to feel the other person is genuine—and blowing up if these unreasonable demands aren't met
* Seeking to control your partner through excessive jealousy and possessiveness
* Believing that a partner's jealousy and possessiveness are signs of love
* Believing that being on an emotional roller coaster all the time is the sign of love (hint: It's not!)
* Being drawn into relationships with users, abusers, and people who treat you as a convenient source of entertainment rather than someone worth devoting their time, attention, and energy to

* Dismissing your own feelings, even when your
  boundaries have been crossed
* People-pleasing, fixing, and caretaking your partner
* Selecting a partner on the basis of their desire for
  you, not on the basis of your desire or the experience
  of having your values align

Thankfully, every pattern can be broken, but we need to give the lover wound time and space for healing if we want to experience transformation. Similar to how a broken bone needs to be set and given a cast to contain it during the healing process, a broken heart needs to be given the same kind of attention. When we take time to come back to ourselves and be with the hurt, as well as the hope, it becomes easier to process everything that happened—and to make decisions that serve us the next time around.

I recall my own experience of finally healing my lover wound with stark clarity. A few years ago, I'd just met a man, and he was perfect. He was a spitting image of the gorgeous Colombian singer Maluma. He was also a multimillionaire with a heart of gold who gave lots of money to charities. Like me, he was sober and oriented toward spiritual matters. We'd read all the same books and had a lot of the same passions. On our first date, he was a perfect gentleman who didn't want to hook up because he wanted to get to know me better. I was bowled over. Had the universe finally sent me Mr. Right?

But just as quickly as the romance had started, the red flags began. His communication was inconsistent, and something in me found it hard to trust him. Despite his obvious charm and all our commonalities, I could sense that he wasn't truly making anything more than the bare minimum of effort. It was confusing, because he would often say things that didn't match the energy I was feeling, such as "Wow, you'd be an amazing wife and mother!" or "Babe, I can't wait to see you again!" There was so much potential in our conversations, but when we weren't together, I could no longer *feel* him. And by this time, I was tapped into my own capacity to feel the energy out pretty damn well! Maybe he was being genuine in everything he shared, but I didn't like the feeling of "out of sight, out of mind" or the fact that we'd sometimes go days without being in communication. It didn't feel like a promising start to any kind of relationship. I doubted his sincerity, because his actions were not matching his words.

At the same time, I was dating other people, including Fernando, who would become my daughter's father. I felt comfortable enough to discuss this other relationship with Fernando, as it was a source of distress and confusion in my life. I wanted it to work, and I wanted very much to understand why it wasn't, so I thought a man's perspective would help.

Fernando wisely said, "If it doesn't feel good, then it probably isn't right."

For whatever reason, something immediately shifted in the way I looked at Fernando. Until this point, he was a friend, a lover, and someone I felt very comfortable around. But as I was sitting there, talking about my life and my other romantic prospects in the most vulnerable and open way I could, I realized something: I felt really, really, really good around Fernando. I felt so safe and held by him. Here I was, talking to him about my drama with some other guy, and there he was, listening and holding nonjudgmental space for me. My body could feel the buzz of heightened energy . . . a sense of immediate resonance and trust that I'll never forget.

I believe I broke a long-standing pattern—of being drawn to guys who looked good on paper but weren't truly emotionally available—when I took the time to simply notice the energy I was experiencing in Fernando's presence. It was the energy I'd always wanted to feel, the energy I'd worked for years to cultivate in my life: an energy of fun, ease, openness, and honest communication.

Sometimes I ask myself whether I would have picked up on the peaceful vibes between me and Fernando if I hadn't done so much of my own Worthy Work already. Would I have even realized that this man would become my co-parent? I don't know the answer to that question, but I do suspect that meeting the other guy was a final test that helped me to recognize that the years of devotion to myself and all my parts had paid off. I'd honed my intuition and developed the clarity to know what I really wanted . . . and to actually move toward it, and away from the old pattern.

The most magical part of this all is that the external love and all the blessings of my life are simply that. My root and my core is my love and deep devotion to myself. The rest is simply a bonus. My inner marriage with me is the root of all the good in my life. I, like every other woman on this planet, am an embodiment of La Diosa. And when we know this truth in our very DNA, the way other people react to or treat us doesn't matter. We can love ourselves deeply and unconditionally, no fucks given. And I promise that when we do that, the world will meet us with similar tenderness and infinite blessings.

For me, it all begins and ends with using the lens of the Great Mother, La Diosa, and tending to ourselves with so much care and love that we feel nourished and stabilized. From this inner stability, from this place of being resourced, it becomes easier to receive messages from our intuition and from the divine—messages that show us so clearly where the red and green flags are. It's harder to cultivate that clarity when our lover wound is still bleeding all over the place.

But we must remember that men, too, have their own

unhealed lover wounds. The systems and structures of the overculture impose limiting models of masculinity and femininity that do not often serve tender, flesh-and-blood men and women. The overculture values passionate sexual love, but not necessarily strong bonds between souls. In some ways, developing a stronger connection with myself is precisely what helped me to develop greater empathy for men and the kinds of pressures they face in love and intimacy. Instead of harboring poisonous thoughts about every jackass who'd ever done me wrong, I learned to forgive them. After all, love was now overflowing from me, and I could afford to be gracious.

I remind myself often that all people are both divine and human. And as divine human beings, we are abundant with endearing imperfections. Even the minor annoyances are opportunities for me to cultivate a greater sense of love and compassion—because, just as I have all these different parts inside me with all their different sets of needs, so does he.

That said, I've learned that while healing the lover wound can move us into mutual, reciprocal love, life is not tit for tat. Every day is different. In any long-term relationship, our capacity for showing up with 100 percent of our energy is going to shift. There are days when we can't give as much, and days when our partner can't give as much. The balance is always shifting, and we do our best to communicate our needs and to find support in other places when we may not be able to offer it to each other.

While all the couples I know are navigating their own personal relationship preferences. I believe it is important to emphasize interdependence over codependency in any relationship. What's the difference? Codependency is an unhealthy reliance on another person such that it can negatively impact both of your lives and create gnarly webs of resentment, helplessness, and attachment. In contrast, interdependence allows us to share and balance out our roles according to our needs, leaning on each other, but never to the extent that we lose ourselves.

Overall, interdependence enables us to overcome the lover wound because it emphasizes a reciprocal attachment between mature adults who commit to loving each other, communicating about each other's needs, exercising grace and forgiveness (as well as accountability), and remaining present and alert when life happens and priorities need to shift. When we work to heal the lover wound, we acknowledge that genuine love is not about escaping our reality and living in la-la land; it occurs amid the twists and turns of daily life, and it requires us to cultivate the faith that, no matter what, we'll always find our way home to each other.

UNWORTHY LIE:

True love is meant to sweep me off my feet, check all my boxes, and save me from a life of boredom, self-doubt, and despair.

WORTHY TRUTH:

True love is meant to amplify the love I already feel within myself—and when I meet me where I am, the right person will match that vibration, and we'll grow together as two equals.

+

Reclaiming Your True Beauty

A huge aspect of self-love is recognizing that our bodies are divine. There is nothing shameful about bodies that bleed, scar, wrinkle, soften, or go through periods of illness. This is part of the life/death cycle we discussed in Chapter 8. Our bodies mark time, as well as the experiences of ebbing and flowing that each of us goes through as we cycle from maiden, to mother, to crone. After our mother's body, our body is our first home—but why do so many of us feel so bad about it?

I still meet plenty of people who are obsessed with looking at themselves in the mirror—not for the sake of self-connection, as in the earlier Worthy Work in this chapter, but for the sake of almost clinical self-evaluation. Others I've met avoid mirrors because they make them feel unworthy or ugly. I've also had clients who obsessively picked at their skin, or literally spent hours brushing their hair and applying makeup. All of these are control mechanisms that actually end up making us feel more out of control.

Sadly, the beauty industry and social media (with all its filters, advertisements, and excessive focus on appearance over substance) have peddled so many false ideas about what beauty is. For me, genuine beauty is a way to connect with my soul and my unique qualities, which include my body. The goddess comes in infinite forms, and this world reflects a stunning diversity of shapes, sizes, and colors. When we honor our own unique expression—which is also a reflection of the innumerable souls it took to make us!—we honor the goddess. When we do not honor our own goddess-given beauty, we dishonor her, as well.

I'm not saying that we can't work on changing certain aspects of our bodies that we aren't content with. Every single one of us is a work in progress, and I believe every woman has a right to make these decisions for herself. But we also have to be very careful and consider the ways in which the overculture and its patriarchal, heteronormative, white-supremacist standards have informed our notions of beauty.

It is possible to decondition ourselves in loving, kind, and proactive ways. I often suggest the following to my clients and community:

* Ask yourself where body shame began. For many women, it was during puberty or after a family member commented on their body. Sometimes we simply mimic the self-defeating attitudes of other adults, especially our parents/caregivers and peers. Recognize that we don't start out feeling ashamed of ourselves. Consider the way a beautiful, bouncy baby meets the world— with eyes wide open and an innate sense of worth and wonder. Have conversations with other women in your life about body shame, as well as its roots. When we can identify the origins, we can dig this shame out of our system. Where there is shame, there is power that's waiting to be catalyzed, which is what the overculture doesn't want women to know. Don't walk away from your shame. Face it, and use what you find to pull out the weeds of the overculture!

* Consider going to a women's bathhouse. I love going to Korean bathhouses, where I can see women of all ages, shapes, and sizes caring for themselves. Historically and across a wide swath of cultures, women spent a lot of time together in such spaces, meaning they were able to normalize the diversity of bodies in their midst—an opportunity few of us have today. Consider gathering in these spaces with other women. If it feels good, lovingly mirror to one another the beauty that you see.

* Often, we see beauty as a means to an end—a way to get someone romantically interested in you, land

a job (sadly, lookism prevails in the workplace), or demonstrate a high status. But when we see beauty as experiential, as something we get to feel and be when we are in our bodies, doing what is pleasurable to us, it changes everything. Refer back to Chapter 10 and your pleasure list. Allow yourself to sink into your sensuality. Beauty isn't about how you look—it's about how you feel.

* Connect with women across the age spectrum. We often erase middle-aged and elderly women from our conversations about beauty, but when we actually interact with more of them, we get a chance to broaden our ideas about who a beautiful woman is. In fact, diversifying your circle in terms of age, socioeconomic status, race, and so forth is a wonderful way to celebrate the beauty of diversity and recognize that there is no one-size-fits-all.

* Notice who you follow on social media. Do these influencers fit a narrow archetype when it comes to beauty? Are they about style over substance? Notice which follows make you feel a sense of expansive love and which ones trigger body insecurity. Consider unfollowing them and expanding your community to include body-positive role models who are proof positive that you can be radiant and gorgeous no matter what you look like!

* Catch yourself in the act if you routinely talk poorly about yourself. Transmute "I'm ugly today" or "I'm having a bad hair day" into "Wow, my eyes are so sparkly!" and "I love how flexible and good I feel after a workout!" Let your reframes be genuine while changing

the focus on aspects of your body and beauty that you love. Flirt with yourself in the mirror. Be playful. Take compliments by saying "Thank you" instead of denying or deflecting. Drop into feeling good rather than looking good.

* Notice if the women in your circle speak poorly about themselves. No need to lecture them to change, but gently draw attention to what you truly admire about them, inside and out. I know that every time I've received a sincere compliment from another woman, especially when I was feeling hard on myself, some part of me that previously felt tight or restricted usually ended up relaxing and breathing a big, deep sigh of relief. Wherever you can, be a beauty activist who takes every opportunity to challenge narrow, colonized ideas about beauty.

It might not always feel like it, diosa, but confidence *is* your true nature. The body is a vessel for the soul—and the more you connect with your soul, the more you connect with your body.

Think of all the times when you've felt the most like *you*. You might not have realized it then, but you were beaming your essence out into the world—and I know that your essence was magnetic, that it was effortlessly beautiful. As you embody the goddess within, let confidence and love radiate from your core and illuminate the path ahead. Embrace your unique qualities, understanding that there is no one on the planet who's quite like you, who knows what you know, who's lived through exactly the same lessons and adventures you've lived through. You have irreplaceable wisdom and medicine, and your true beauty is a powerful source and force for goodness.

Embracing Wholeness

Worthiness encompasses the totality of our being—light and shadow, masculine and feminine, strength and weakness. We must embrace our flaws, our imperfections, and our wounds with compassion and willingness, in order to step into our essence as walking, talking, breathing embodiments of love. For it is through this embrace that we weave the tapestry of our wholeness, where our worthiness shines brightest.

We are each awe-inspiring, multidimensional, and complex tapestries, which is why I don't think it's possible to truly love ourselves despite our flaws; we must love ourselves *because* of them. In antiquity, tapestry makers included "imperfections" that were deliberately placed for the purpose of amplifying the beauty of the masterwork. After all, when everything is "perfect" and uniform, it makes for a boring experience—one that doesn't engage all the wild, feeling aspects of who we are that long for dramatic contrasts, dynamic tension, and opportunities for awe and breakthroughs.

It's fine to strive to be better versions of ourselves, but perfection is a colonial myth that's meant to keep most of us in our place. When we look carefully at ideas of perfection, we often find ourselves coming up against some very dangerous dogma about purity, who is or isn't deserving of love, and who deserves salvation vs. who must be violently eliminated.

So many women in my community have been through the wringer with perfectionism. I usually teach them to gently notice when it rears its head. There's a myth that we have to be radically happy or perfect in order to have the life of our dreams, but this just isn't true. One of the best ways to deepen our experience of life is to recognize that the tiny moments most of us are likely to gloss over in pursuit of perfection are the ones that matter the most. If life is a mystery school, then every single moment becomes a test of our character. It's the kind of test that requires us to bring along *all* of our experiences and unique characteristics if we want to level up. When we bring everything along for the ride—our tender parts, our jagged edges, our eloquence, our potty mouth, the entire bag—we break free from the limits of believing that we have to shoehorn ourselves into one tiny identity.

Like mystics, we must entertain paradox. We must break bread with the angels and demons of our inner sanctum. We must release the grip of perfectionism and welcome ourselves into a more expansive experience of who we are. This is one reason I enjoy activities like ecstatic dance or reading mystical poetry, as both can send me into an altered state of perceiving myself and the world through a more holistic and heart-centered perspective that doesn't operate by the rules of logic.

And why would it? We are the fuckin' universe! We are La Diosa incarnate. We aren't just one thing—we're *everything*.

Worthy Work:
The Holy Union

Archetypal couples representing and reminding us of the importance of sacred union are found around the world, as well as in every major religion. In ancient Sumer, the divine couple of Inanna and Dumuzi helped ensure that cycles of prosperity and fertility would continue (although it's important to note that Inanna was the one who conferred on Dumuzi the "divine right" of rule, as the divine feminine was considered the primordial source of creation). In ancient

Egypt, Isis and Osiris represented the perfect balance of male and female energy. In some traditions, Mary Magdalene and Jesus Christ originally represented the union of male and female energies, although the patriarchal Church kept that out of their canon.

Although these "myths" are epic love stories between gods and goddesses, in truth they're just metaphors for the concept that we find true union within ourselves. In medieval alchemy, the idea of coniunctio posited that a union of opposites leads to a sense of wholeness and inner balance that enables us to manifest our heart's desires. So, diosa, sacred union is not primarily about meeting "the one"—it is about unifying the many parts of you, including the ones that seem to be at polar opposite ends. It is about bringing together your inner feminine and masculine and becoming the lover to your own beloved. You're the one you've been searching for all along, worthy woman!

This exercise will help you come into the holiest union of all—the union between you and all parts of your magnificent self. You'll literally be marrying yourself! The various parts of this exercise will take time to fulfill, so be patient with yourself and go at the pace that suits you.

1. First, come before your altar and light candles or burn incense in honor of your worthy woman within. Give yourself at least an hour to write personal vows for your sacred union/wedding to self. What do you want to say to honor yourself—your inner light and shadow, masculine and feminine, and everything in between? Think of this as an opportunity to pledge the deepest and most sacred love you will ever experience— for your wholeness and your divine essence. This is about bringing together the fragmented parts of you

and swearing allegiance to holding them with tenderness, clarity, and love. Consider anything you've ever wanted to hear from someone else, and let yourself profess those words to yourself. For example, here are some vows I wrote when I did this exercise (feel free to use them or adapt them for yourself): "I vow to continue to walk the path of the worthy woman. I vow to remember that heaven isn't later—it's now. I vow to own that I am the embodiment of La Diosa. I vow to birth visions of peace, of joy, of abundance, of truth, of love. I vow to birth my soul dreams into reality. I vow to commit to living as I truly am—divinely, inherently worthy. I vow to be in the version of me that is most true. I vow to walk on my path instead of the path I think I should walk for everyone else. I vow to own who I am now. I vow to commit to my fullest expression of self, not what others feel comfortable with."

2. Now or during another dedicated time, plan your wedding—the same way you'd plan a wedding with another person!

* Where do you want to exchange vows with yourself? Do you want this to be a destination wedding on your favorite beach? An intimate gathering at home? A sacred site? A place in nature that is a source of refuge and comfort?

* Do you want others to participate in your ceremony as bridesmaids, officiants, guests of honor, or performers? How and why? (After deciding, make an invitation to them, sharing everything you've learned about self-love and your reasons for wanting to undertake this ceremony.)

* Is there a particular "theme" you'd like to center your wedding on? What about archetypes?
* What would you like in terms of things like music, decorations, attire, and props?
* Are there any spiritual traditions or rituals you'd like to ground your experience in?

3. After working through the logistics, set the date. Remember, this can be a truly intimate event (as in: me, myself, and I), or it can be a full-on extravaganza. Feel into what's true for you. Only *you* get to decide. Whatever you do, make this the best and most memorable event you can—after all, it's your wedding day, and you'll be making the most important commitment a diosa can possibly make!

✳ Worthy Affirmations ✳

◎ *I am worthy of loving and being loved, and all parts of me are lovable.*

◎ *Love is my divine human essence.*

◎ *It is safe to open my heart to genuine love.*

◎ *I am worthy of lovers and partners who respect and honor the diosa I am.*

◎ *I own my lovability and wholeheartedly make my life a space for love to flow effortlessly into.*

◎ *I am whole and beautiful.*

◎ *I am my soulmate and my own best friend.*

12

You Are Worthy as You Are

Another world is not only possible, she is on her way.
On a quiet day, I can hear her breathing.

—Arundhati Roy

Reclaiming the one I call and know in my bones as my inner worthy woman saved my life. Knowing who I truly was—a woman who carried in her bones the cries and wishes of her ancestors, and of the Great Mother, La Diosa—allowed me to walk away from things, people, and habits that hurt me and were killing me slowly but surely. Instead, I walked into the greatest love I could ever know: connection to my authentic soul, to the true self within, the one who is never bereft of anything because she is connected to the most powerful forces of nature and to universal benevolence. And I have seen this same process at work in the lives of countless women in my community.

For years, just like the many clients who have come through my doors in search of a clear and radiant mirror to remind them of their true self, I had denied my authentic knowing. I had replaced it with toxic, unworthy habits. I had cast off my own power and beauty. I had starved myself of self-love. I had dishonored the temple of my body and spirit by allowing toxic, abusive men to enter my life, over and over again. I had used alcohol to numb my feelings. I had become caught in a loop of repetitive trauma that pulled me away from the life I knew, deep in my soul, I was worthy of.

And because some part of me knew all of this, I hadn't extended to myself what I actually needed the most: my own softness, my own holy forgiveness. Ironically, my realization that I'd fallen short of the gifts I knew were within reach only caused me to pummel myself into the ground with a renewed vigor. I felt defeated. I was alienated from the one within who might welcome me home like the prodigal daughter. The part of me that was lost kept turning away.

When I began to reclaim my worth—first, by courageously owning all the parts of me and of my life that were loudly denying it—I started to heal. Radical honesty, tempered by compassion, was the first step. And then the others—the sisters and comrades who similarly sought the same thing because they were disenchanted by the status quo—came flooding into my life.

But first I had to understand, on my own terms, the forces that had sent me into a tailspin, and to recognize that while I'd made many choices that had generated more and more of the conditions that kept me stuck, *this wasn't my fault*. What I came to discover, especially through my work with thousands of women across the world, was that unworthiness is an epidemic. Beautiful, strong, intelligent, wise, empathetic women everywhere feel all the same things I did: the gnawing inadequacy; the constant struggle to keep our heads above water and to be a superwoman in our families, careers, and even our spiritual life; the feeling that no matter what we did, we were always going to be caught in a catch-22, given all the contradictory ideas about what it means to be a "good" woman: *Be assertive and empowered, but not too bitchy or strong, otherwise nobody will love you. Dream big and fulfill your potential, but don't step too far outside the boundaries, and make damn sure that everyone loves you.*

All of us had swallowed the poison to some degree, believing it would be a medicine—an antidote to the emptiness within.

I learned something important: In order to truly know ourselves, we have to go into the emptiness and be willing to dig ourselves out. We have to recognize the people-pleasing measures we took on as a coping mechanism that may have helped us get through the day once upon a time, but that no longer serve us. I learned that it is our sacred duty as women to reclaim worthiness, which I have come to see as the key to planetary healing.

Worthiness gave wings to my soul dreams. First, I was able to love myself. Like, *really* love myself. I learned to love myself enough to not drink over my pain. As of writing this, I am seven years sober, one day at a time. I learned to love myself enough to set boundaries in my life—even and especially with family. My worthiness allowed me to nurture myself with a deep and compassionate inner voice that loves and encourages me and is gentle throughout all of life's ups and downs.

And, of course, from this place, magical things emerged in my external world. I believed in myself enough to step onto the stage and speak my soul purpose to the world—and get paid well to do it, too. In the end, reclaiming my worth helped me to feel steady within myself. I always know I have my back, and that La Diosa has my back. I always know I am safe inside *me*. I always know that nothing and no one can take away my worth, because it's woven into my cells. My worthiness saved me.

I also came to realize something I want to shout from the rooftops, over and over again: **Reclaiming our worth is a revolutionary act!**

As I began to share with my clients and community what I was starting to piece together about the Worthy Revolution, I noticed that as women drew together to vulnerably share everything that had held them back from loving and accepting themselves, these conversations were a natural way of restoring all the power we've lost in the process of contorting ourselves to fit someone else's ideas of who we should be. We were reclaiming ourselves, from anything and everything that had ever attempted to shatter our relationship with La Diosa within.

I believe this reclamation of our inner worth—our true worth, which has nothing to do with the money in our bank accounts or the number of followers we have on social media—can save our lives. The missing piece is learning not just to neutralize the poison we took in, but to determine how we can keep embodying the worthy woman who lives inside—no matter what is happening in our lives. The missing piece is the ability to quit comparing ourselves to anyone else, and to honor the unique glow that we radiate, which is there no matter how young or experienced or wealthy or loved by our community we are.

This is why I continue to generate tools that will meet us exactly where we are—because I am committed to women reclaiming our inner worth, our inner divinity. I know without a doubt that when this happens, miracles beyond our wildest dreams take place and create a ripple effect that activates the world inside and around us.

Rooting Out the Voices of Untruth

Beloved one, I know that while the words in this book have likely provided comfort, they have also surfaced the places within you that still ache over the injustices you have faced and continue to face. Perhaps certain memories of times when you were hurt, diminished, or cast aside by the over-culture, by patriarchy, by white supremacy, have become clearer in your mind's eye. And that shit hurts like hell. It isn't easy to look at any of this, but I believe these destructive patterns are being shown to us and amplified by a collective consciousness that is meant to take us into a new evolution-ary stage . . . one where we can finally claim our true power. In the words of Alice Walker, "The most common way people give up their power is by thinking they don't have any."

It's time to quit it with that BS. You are *here*, diosa, which is already proof of your strength, your resilience, your awe-inspiring worthiness.

While I love personal development as much as the next human (hence the work I do), the "inner work" ain't worth a damn if it just ends up making you feel worse or causes you to compare yourself to anyone else. I intended for the ac-tivities and teachings in this book to root you into the deeper voice of your soul, not to be used dogmatically. I don't wish for it to be yet another way to beat yourself up if you don't "perform" well, or a way to pat yourself on the back if you check all the Worthy Work off your to-do list.

This book has been, first and foremost, a reminder that came to me as a channeled message from spirit, that I knew came from the depths of my truth. When it began to take shape in my mind, I had to prioritize its voice, above all the other ones I heard in my head—*You're taking time to write a book when you should be working on making more money*

for your family? What's wrong with you? There are already
so many self-help books out there. What are you doing that's
different from the rest? I had to keep coming back to my own
personal North Star, which is sharing the importance of
learning to fully relax into and inhabit our worthiness, not
to feel that we must constantly prove and improve ourselves
in order to be seen as "good" by anyone else.

When you feel overwhelmed and lost in a flood of voices
that are telling you to be something other than what you are
and what you know to be your truth, it's time to take a beat,
breathe, and slow down. What do you *really, really* want, beyond what you've been told you should want? In that sense,
the primary purpose of this book has never been about giving you an answer, because only *you* can do that. The name
of the game isn't "bettering" yourself, either—it's developing
the confidence and devotion to step into even more of who
you are, by making greater room for your true voice and authentic desires.

Worthy Work:
Your "Fuck No" and Your "Fuck Yes"

When it feels like we're still spinning our wheels, hijacked
by the voices of unworthiness, we have to ask ourselves,
"Whose voice is this?" I've become a lot better at interrupting
unworthiness cycles because I've become more intentional
about identifying the voices that are not mine. I've learned
that if the voice in my head is cruel, demeaning, judgmental,
punitive, comparison-based, fearful, or envious, it's a voice
I've picked up from the overculture that got embedded in my
mental patterns until I mistook it for my authentic voice.

I have my own rituals to get through this. These rituals are
grounded in interrupting the pattern of going down a rab-

bit hole of what-ifs and unhelpful rumination. Sometimes I cry if I need to release emotions, or I literally shake it off (a trauma response that helps so many animals to shake off brushes with death instead of keeping the sensations of fear in their system). Sometimes I talk to a friend or mentor who can be a clear and supportive mirror. Often, I stop to journal about whose voices I'm hearing. Whose voices planted these seeds of unworthiness that continue to spring up as weeds in my consciousness?

For this exercise, please give yourself time—at least an hour—to really sit with the process. You may wish to light a candle on your worthy woman altar or play music that helps you connect with your emotions.

Part 1:
Your "Fuck No"

1. First, identify the voices within that have ever made you feel small or less than. Before connecting them to a person, institution, or larger cultural force, make a list of the things those voices say to you. These may sound like: "You need to lose weight before you're beautiful." "You haven't accomplished anything of note, and you probably never will." "You're not lovable or even likable." You may be surprised at what comes up, as well as the ferocity of the voices that surface. If it feels difficult, be gentle with yourself. Breathe through it, but don't stop until you're done.

2. Now look back through these diminishing statements and recognize where they come from. I have identified these voices as belonging to so many different entities. Society. Patriarchy. Racism. Past relationships. Childhood teachers. Family members. Friends. Strangers. The

beauty industrial complex. Television. Mainstream media. Be specific with your identifications. Maybe your supervisor exploited your talents but didn't value you or give you respect through acknowledgment, a promotion, or equitable pay. Maybe your best friend reinforced the fucked-up belief that you're nothing unless you have a boyfriend. This isn't about blaming or shaming anyone else—because we have to remember that if it's a specific person who passed on the false message, they were indoctrinated by someone or something else, too. Instead, this process is about separating what is true from what is not true, separating your authentic voice from the toxic voices in which we're all swimming.

3. Now it's time to let yourself get angry, for real. You might want to turn up the volume on your music. Dance it out. Scream it out. Shake it out. Rage it out. I often end up shouting, "Fuck no! Who the fuck are you to tell me I'm not worthy? I'm a fuckin' child of the divine! These fucked-up beliefs do not come from the divine, and they are not of me. No one can tell me my worth, or anyone else's worth! Worth is a seed that continues to grow within me!"

4. After you're done raging and expressing, give yourself time to ground. You might wish to lie on the earth with one hand over your heart and the other on your belly. Remind yourself that you're here. You exist. You are worthy. I personally like to tear up the list I've made after reading it aloud. You might wish to burn it. Let it go. This act is your "fuck no"; it is all the voices you will no longer be entertaining or allowing to take up space in your consciousness.

Part 2:
Your "Fuck Yes"

1. Finally, when you feel ready, journal your "fuck yeses" in life (or speak them into a voice recorder if you're exhausted from the previous steps, which is totally understandable). What are your deep-down-in-the-bones desires? What are the words you want to hear? What are the emotions you want to feel? What are the behaviors you want to embody, and the ones you want others to display toward you? It can be very vulnerable to admit to what you truly want. I remember doing this exercise with a client who burst into tears when she admitted, "All my life, I've just wanted a best friend, someone I can totally trust and be myself with, without worrying they'll ultimately end up abandoning the friendship." Be genuine with your desires! Don't downplay them! Take in what you are saying "fuck yes" to. Take it in all the way. You deserve all the goodness.

2. Now think of all the voices in your life that have reflected truth, kindness, compassion, care, love—the voices that wanted you to have everything your heart desires, the voices that supported your alignment with your authentic self. What did those voices say? Speak their messages aloud into your voice recorder or write them down.

3. Finally, take a moment to honor these voices, perhaps by moving your body in a dance to your favorite song, writing a poem or making a piece of art that you place on your worthy woman altar, or doing something that really seals the message that you are saying

"Fuck yes!" to your highest good. If you've written down the messages of "fuck yes," place those on your altar.

4. Close your ritual by sending a prayer to La Diosa, to the Great Mother, to your kind ancestors. Ask them to help you listen to the authentic voice within that wishes to steer you in the direction of your North Star, which is a life well lived. You deserve it!

Seeing Through the Eyes of Spirit

One of the ways I've learned to really know in my body, in my bones, in every cell of my being, that I am worthy is to activate my inner senses, what I like to call my soul senses. In particular, I have come to recognize the power of seeing the world and myself through soul sight.

Soul sight and ordinary sight are very, very different. Ordinary sight is based on a system of judgments and comparisons—of looking in the mirror and deeming myself good enough or not good enough. Ordinary sight is fixated on the surface-level details and is largely disconnected from the deeper truths that may be hidden or out of view. It tends to focus on quantity rather than quality. But when I look at myself through a different kind of vision (which is not about literally "looking," but about perceiving with the entire intelligence of my mind, heart, body, and soul), I know the deepest truth there is to know. I know it in such a way that I am embodying my worth without effort; it is literally pouring out of me like radiant light.

Now, it takes practice, just like anything else. It doesn't happen overnight, but the more we take off the darkly tinted sunglasses that color our vision of who we are and what we're worth, the more something magical begins to happen. Our soul sight gets activated. We really begin to perceive the world in a brand-new way. I know today that activating the eyes of spirit helps us to see that the cup is half full, where others might see it as half empty. It's what restores us to an undying sense of beauty and possibility, because we know these are eternally renewable resources. It's what helps us step into our true power, our true medicine, which is radiant and magnetic. Seeing through the eyes of spirit is like seeing through the eyes of La Diosa herself.

For me, activating spiritual vision to the extent that we are living from and embodying that sense is all about reclaiming the goddess on this planet. We have been trained to remain fixated on what is visible, obvious, perceived to have value in our capitalist, comparison-based world. This is a patriarchal and hierarchical way of seeing ourselves, one another, and our Earth. Activating spiritual vision is about connecting to the feminine, to the unseen realms, to the qualities of the heart that tend to be given short shrift in our everyday world.

Worthy Work: Activating the Worthy Woman Within

This exercise is one you can continually come back to in order to refine the guiding light, the North Star, the ultimate vision of the worthy woman who lives within you. First, I want you to start by sitting in front of your worthy woman altar and thinking about your journey through this book. Place one hand on your heart and the other on your womb space. Take a few moments to breathe and attune to yourself. I want you to say out loud:

- *I am already worthy.*

- *There is nothing I need to do in order to be more worthy.*

- *I am the goddess herself, in human form.*

- *And I am ready to activate this part of me so that she is more alive, more awake, and more present in my daily life.*

Next, journal on the following questions, which will help you create your own soul map for activating your worthy woman within. I want you to really pause and breathe and feel into each question, your hands still on your heart and womb. Connect with the one within you who knows not from an intellectual headspace, but from the heart.

In traditions around the world, from Western hermeticism, to Eastern spirituality, to the pagan practices of Earth-based religion, the heart has been a powerful symbol for psychospiritual transformation and healing. It's the place where we integrate polarities like spirit and matter, above and below, human and divine, dream and reality. This is the place where seeming opposites are resolved in the prevailing truth of love. This is why I always encourage the diosas in my community to connect with their heart. In one of my favorite books, *The Little Prince*, Antoine de Saint-Exupéry writes, "It is only with the heart that one can see rightly; what is essential is invisible to the eye."

As you answer these questions, you'll activate the goddess energy that might be dormant within you, so you can step fully into your worthy power. You may have other questions to add to these, so please feel free. Nothing is too mundane or too far out, and the more questions and answers you have here, the more descriptive your worthy woman soul map will be.

If there was no such thing as shame, guilt, or judgment . . .

1. What would a typical day in your life look like? Be descriptive and plot out every hour of the day!

2. Where would you live (city, country, type of location or environment)?

3. What would your home be like? What kinds of furnishings and soulful objects would fill the space? What would it look, smell, sound, taste, and feel like?

4. What kinds of nourishing foods would you be eating?

5. What would your lifestyle look like (including your social circle, your attitudes, your values, and your worldview)?

6. How would you dress?

7. In what ways would you be supported by your community and by life itself?

8. What would your connection to spirit look and feel like?

9. How much money would you make in order to experience abundance?

10. How would you spend your money?

11. What would your soul-led business, career, or work life be?

12. How would you share your essence with the world around you?

13. What would your rest and rejuvenation times look like?

14. Who would you spend time with (friends, family, community, business colleagues)?

15. What would intimate/romantic partnership look and feel like?

16. What would your family relationships look and feel like?

17. What would your friendships look and feel like?

18. What would your business connections feel like?

19. How would you parent?

20. What would your sex life and sensuality look and feel like?

21. What would you do for fun and pleasure?

22. What would you do for mental stimulation?

23. What would you do to honor your connection to spirit?

24. How would you pamper and honor the sacred feminine temple of your body?

25. What would your inner dialogue sound like?

26. How would you deal with changes and challenges in your life?

27. What would your connection to your creativity be, and how would it manifest?

28. What would you allow yourself to receive?

29. What would you allow yourself to give, especially with respect to your connection to the greater good?

30. What social causes would you champion?

31. What would you let yourself desire?

32. How would you fulfill those desires?

33. In what other ways would you allow your worthy woman self to fully be alive in the world?

Take time to read your responses. Over time, map out specific SMART goals that allow you to tap into your worthy woman self—on a weekly, monthly, quarterly, and yearly basis. Of course, we have only so much time in the day to focus our attention, so you might want to choose to work with one to three aspects of this soul map at a time. I also encourage you to come back to this activity annually to see if anything has shifted. Remember, the worthy woman inside you is not limited by rigid definitions for what her goals should look like. Flowing and growing with her, and giving voice to new desires over the seasons, is a wonderful way to tap into her infinite nature and bring her essence to life.

✳ Worthy Affirmations ✳

◉ *I am worthy of all the goodness and beauty that life has to offer.*

◉ *I am worthy of speaking to myself with kindness and grace.*

◉ *I am worthy of having my "fuck no" and my "fuck yes" respected and honored.*

◉ *I am worthy of following the voice of my true north and heart's desires.*

◉ *I am worthy, just because!*

Conclusion

Be on guard so that no one deceives you by saying,
"Look over here!" or "Look over there!"
For the child of true Humanity exists within you.
Follow it! Those who search for it will find it.

—Gospel of Mary 3:1–3

I am so fucking proud of you, diosa! I pray that, more important, *you* are so fucking proud of you. That you revel in the miracle that you are: a walking divine human magical being. I hope that by now you feel equipped with the tools to truly own your extra-ness. Give yourself permission to know you are worthy exactly as you are, and that you deserve to really dream and ask for and claim the life your soul self, your worthy self, absolutely wants for you.

You've made it to the end of this book. You have slain with your golden sword the ways in which social conditioning has gotten in the way of your true worthy self. Every initiation you have walked through is meant to help you live as the diosa you are meant to be. Although most of us have forgotten our true beauty and divinity, each of us is worthy of being our full, authentic self. Each of us is worthy of wanting more and getting what we actually desire. Each of us is worthy of taking the space to rest, dream, and unpack the things that are no longer our burdens to carry.

Reclaiming our worth as women is an act of remembrance—a remembrance of our divine essence, our inherent beauty, and our sacred connection to all of creation. Remember, your worth is not contingent on external validation. Embrace your uniqueness, celebrate your strengths, and let go of judgments. By reclaiming your worthiness, you inspire others to do the same, creating a ripple effect of empowerment and self-acceptance. While we may feel we walk the path alone, it is only in a community of worthy women that we can unravel the threads of societal conditioning.

In the depths of every woman's soul lies a dormant power, waiting to be awakened—a power that transcends social constructs and patriarchal conditioning. This power is the essence of the divine feminine, La Diosa, an archetype deeply rooted in our collective unconscious. In reclaiming our worth, we remember our intrinsic connection to La Diosa, the creatrix of all that is. We embrace the truth that we always are and always have been deserving of love, respect, and fulfillment.

But, of course, beyond the words on this page, each of us exists as a beautiful component of the divine mystery. Within each woman is a dance of duality—a harmonious interplay of light and shadow. As we embark on the path of reclaiming our worth, we must embrace both of these primordial aspects of our being. It is easy enough to claim the "love and light" aspects of who we are, which tend to align with our good-girl conditioning. The shadow, oftentimes suppressed and disowned, also holds profound wisdom and transformative potential. By courageously embracing our pain, our tears, our badass warrior selves, we illuminate the path toward self-acceptance and integration.

We refuse to die with unworthiness in our bones. We recognize that our warrior spirit is fueled by righteous indignation, by sacred rage. Women are trained to suppress our anger, but it is the blazing fire that burns inside us, the screams that erupt from our very souls when we know something is wrong, that will serve us on our journey. We innately know that we can do better, and that another way is possible. When we rise from the flames of our anger, we no longer burn ourselves out within it. We no longer stifle our dreams under a blanket of resentment. Instead, we allow ourselves to be like the phoenix, rising up and out of our suffering and creating new possibilities for the entire planet.

We allow all facets of ourselves to shine like a diamond.

Most of us have not been raised to celebrate our own worth, which might have provoked responses like "Stop tooting your own horn" or "¿Quién se cree ella?" ("Who does she think she is?") Like so many of you, I come from strong, beautiful women who still felt unworthy, who allowed less-than-adequate partners into their lives, who persistently felt "not good enough," who believed they needed to burn out in order to burn bright. I honor them; I understand that they were busy breaking other cycles, meaning they didn't get the privilege to spend that much time healing their feelings of unworthiness. I love them for all the ways in which they did manage to break the cycles, for I stand on their shoulders and on the foundation of their hard work. I also acknowledge the parts and places—especially in the emotional domains of worthiness—where they never got the opportunity to claim the full extent of their authentic selves.

Recognizing that the Worthy Revolution is not an individual endeavor, I have written this book and devoted my life to

uplifting women. I do this for you, and for my female ancestors. I do this for the past and future generations. Because
when it comes down to it, Worthy Work is liberation work.

Am I angry that the world I live in doesn't see our interconnectedness or honor our sacred legacies? Hell yeah! And I
think every single one of us must use our anger strategically,
as a tool that can help us disrupt the conditions that don't
do our happiness and well-being any favors. Because if we
don't, we will never reclaim our worth. We will die a spiritual death—*it's that serious.*

So let's break the cycle of unworthiness. Let's push back
until we can distinctly hear our soul singing its truth to us.
This is a call to undo the lies of unworthiness, to reclaim your
holy inherent power, and to live the soulful life you are meant
to live. My deepest prayer is that you have found something
in these pages that inspires and unlocks a deep remembering
and a bold awakening within you.

Our worthiness is all about remembering who we truly
are, what we really desire, what we want, what we need,
what makes us come alive and sing from our souls. It's about
remembering that first, we must own that our worth is inherent. From that rooted knowing that we are inherently
and divinely worthy, we will reclaim the rest.

You did that in this book, on this journey. You reclaimed
so many pieces of what makes you *you*. I want you to celebrate what makes you yourself. I want you to own and dance
in the unique rhythm of your soul. To live in alignment with
our worthy woman within heals us and the world. It's that
potent. Life wants all of you. The world needs all of you. So
come be free, and bring it all.

When you remove all the external voices and systems and
you get to the core of your human holy self—that self that
preceded patriarchy, capitalism, white supremacy, and a

widespread culture of degrading the feminine—you will come back to the timeless, essential truth that has the power to change your world and everything in it.

You are worthy.

You are divine.

Now the only remaining question is: What will you do with that truth?

Closing Worthiness Ritual

In this closing ritual, we are going to seal the soul skin into your bones so that you remember she is there with you. You can always call on her. We are meant to remember the voice of steady, clear knowing that is our birthright. This is the temple we must make our way back to over and over again.

You are the worthy temple, my love.

Light the candle at the seat of your heart, lay the flowers at the throne of your soul, and dance with every curve of your graceful being.

Come to your worthy woman altar and speak the following words, feeling free to improvise where you wish:

Dear Diosa, Mother:

- *I ask that you continue to remind me of my worthiness.*

- *Help me to walk in deep devotion, courage, and bravery every step of my path.*

- *I ask that you help me to lay down my armor and any of the places where I am stuck in inauthenticity, so that I am always in my soul's truest truth.*

- *Help me to feel my softness as my strength.*

◎ *Allow me to know that my body, my voice, my passion, my very being, is medicine that is meant to be known and shared.*

◎ *Help me to remember that when I heed my soul as my compass in this life, all becomes aligned in the way it should.*

◎ *Gran Diosa, hear my prayer and my proclamation!*

◎ *I offer all of me to you.*

◎ *Help me to continue to return, over and over again, to the worthy temple within me.*

◎ *In times of joy and sorrow, help me to break open to my infinite essence.*

◎ *Guide me to live as my worthy self, and to choose thoughts, words, actions, and rituals that align with the worthy woman within.*

◎ *May it be so!*

Next, breathe three deep, cleansing, and nourishing breaths in through your nose and out through your mouth. Close your eyes and imagine yourself in a beautiful forest full of gorgeous tropical flowers and plants. It's almost sunset, and the sky is filled with all the colors of the rainbow, while the earth is moist and fertile. The flowers, plants, and trees all around you bow and dance with the wind, singing their knowing into your breath. You sit on a stone by a very special tree, whose roots emerge from the earth and cradle your bare feet. You ask the spirit of the tree to nurture you with their wisdom and love. This is the love of Mama Earth, of La Diosa, of the divine feminine spirit of eternal creation. Sit for as long as you wish, feeling the light of the Earth and the light of the cosmos enter your body until it becomes a single pillar of light, a radiant star that beams throughout the galaxy and universe.

When you're ready, open your eyes, knowing that you are always held in the embrace of the Great Goddess . . . for you are her, and she is you. You have never been separate.

Although you have concluded your ritual, life itself is the greatest ritual of all. Live it in honor of your essential worthiness. If you ever find yourself lost, or if your inner wounds snake around your spirit and make you feel trapped or small, come back to this ceremony. Allow the light of your true self to burn the lies away. Let the space of the divine alight your soul self, your worthy self, so that you can come back to her in every season and remember who you really are.

You are not meant to tiptoe through life.

You get to be who you really are.

You get to be sacred, wild, authentic, and wholly holy you.

You are worthy.

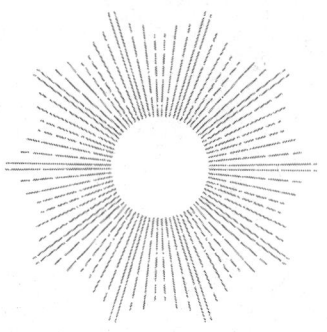

Resources

BetterHelp: If you're in need of therapeutic support, Better-Help offers online therapists from all over the world. Join at betterhelp.com.

The Diosa app: This app is personal growth meets soul sister-hood. I created it as your one stop for cultivating deep friend-ships and joining monthly online women's circles and select in-person pop-up events. Join at diosaapp.com.

My website: For all the courses, mentorships, resources, re-treats, and everything else I do, feel free to head to my web-site, where you can sign up for my free newsletter and get a free meditation and free fifty-four-page digital soul journal. Check it out at christineg.tv, and be sure to follow me on In-stagram at @cosmicchristine. Feel free to tag me and use the hashtag #iamworthy so that I can cheer you on!

Acknowledgments

In any soul project like this, it takes a weaving of so much personal and professional support to bring it to life. First I would like to thank the soul of this book for allowing me to birth this into reality. Thank you to the Divine Father and Mother for holding me through it all. To Fernando, the father of our beautiful daughter, for believing in all of my dreams and encouraging me to be a badass mama and author. To my book agent, Steve, I believe we are a divine fit. Thank you for believing in all my ideas and helping me get the best deals. You are soul family to me. To my first editor, Sara, thank you—your YES gave me the possibility of this all being a reality. To my second editor, Lauren, your skillful editing and tears of resonance allowed this book to be clean and the exact expression I wanted it to be. Nirmala, words don't do justice to my gratitude for being my book doula through this process and giving wings to each of my words. Thank you to the entire team at TarcherPerigee for working with me on now two books—it's a true dream for me. To my entire puta parade for always giving me feedback on all the things when I ask. My soul sisters Beatriz Bonnin, Carolina, Anneli, Nata, and so many more. My entire Diosa community, you are the reason, my deep why. We are so powerful together. To my mentors Terri, Mali, Alexis, Natalia Price, my late teacher Psalm, and so many more. Thank you. To my daughter, for giving me a fuel within and a power I didn't know was possible—all the unworthiness wounds I heal I do in honor of the lineages before and the lineages to come. You're the biggest gift of all.

About the Author

Christine Gutierrez, MA, LMHC, is a Latina licensed psycho-therapist, self-worth expert, and spiritual thought leader. Through her work, she offers group coaching, transformational retreats like her annual Diosa Retreat in Puerto Rico, and soul-based business mentorship via the Madre Legacy Council. She is the author of the book *I Am Diosa* and the affirmation deck *Wisdom del Alma*, as well as the founder of the forthcoming app Diosa, a global community where like-hearted women gather to meet soul sisters. Sign up for the waitlist at diosaapp.com. Gutierrez's work has been featured on *The Kelly Clarkson Show* and in *Latina* magazine and *O, The Oprah Magazine*, among many others. Subscribe to her free newsletter at christineg.tv and follow her on Instagram at @cosmicchristine.